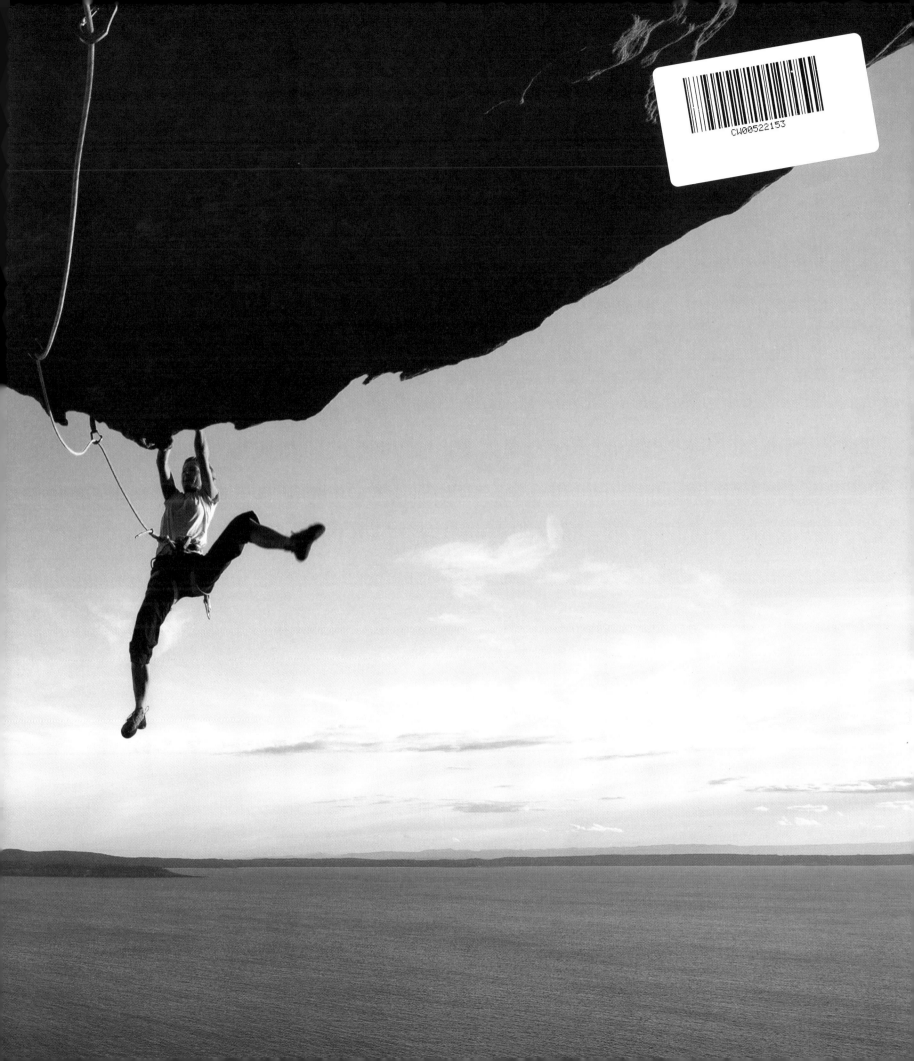

WORLD
CLIMBING

ROCK ODYSSEY

Photography SIMON CARTER
Area introductions MONIQUE FORESTIER

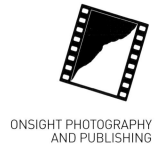

ONSIGHT PHOTOGRAPHY
AND PUBLISHING

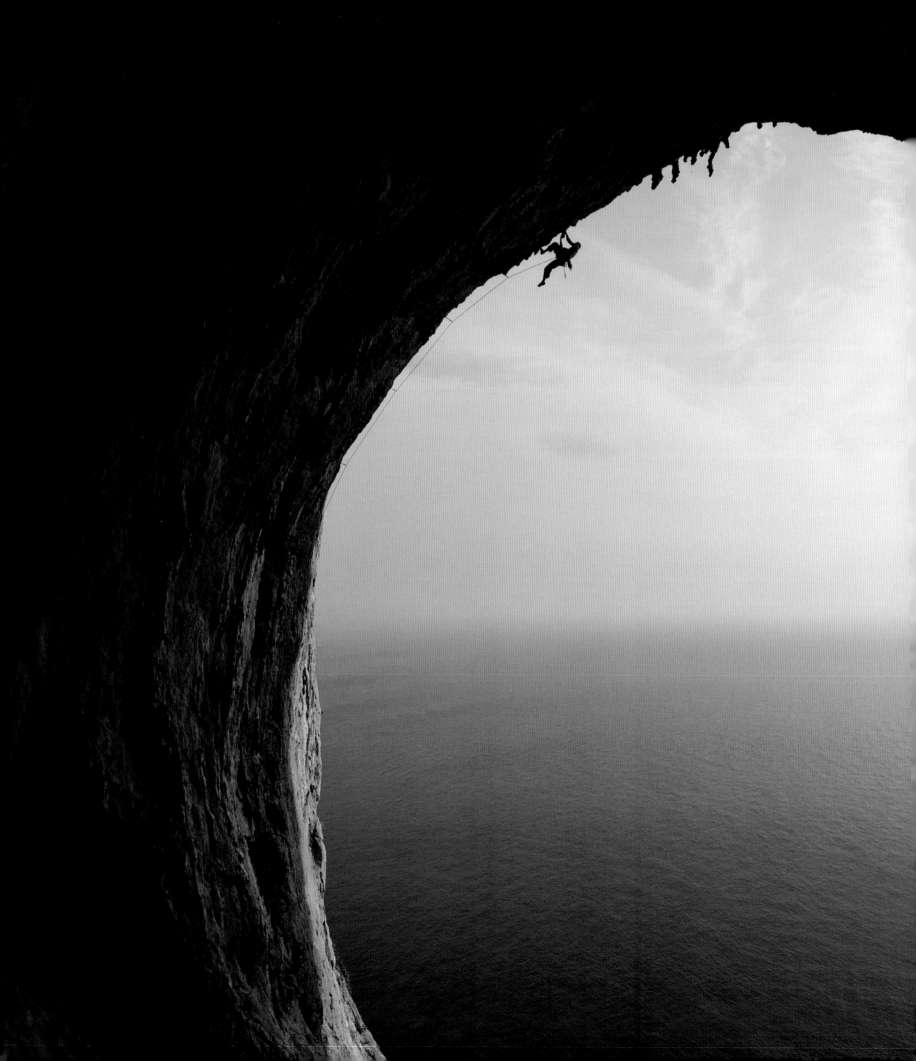

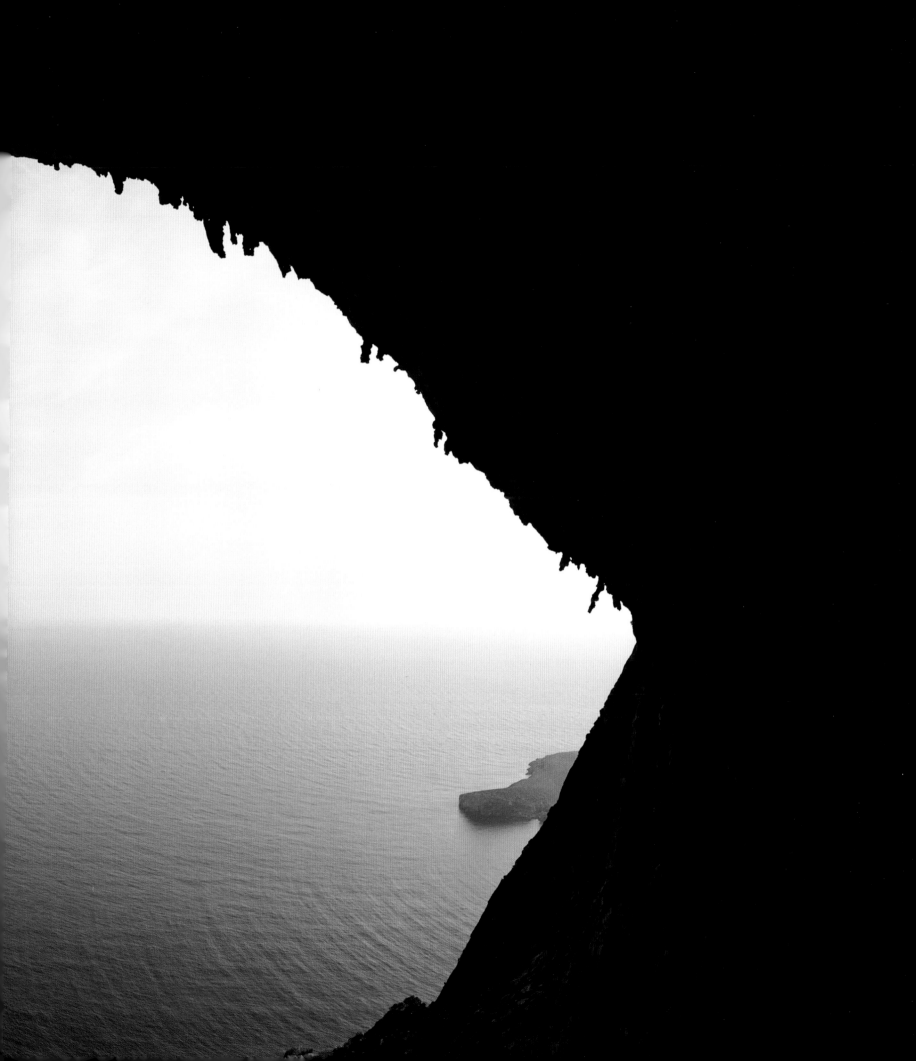

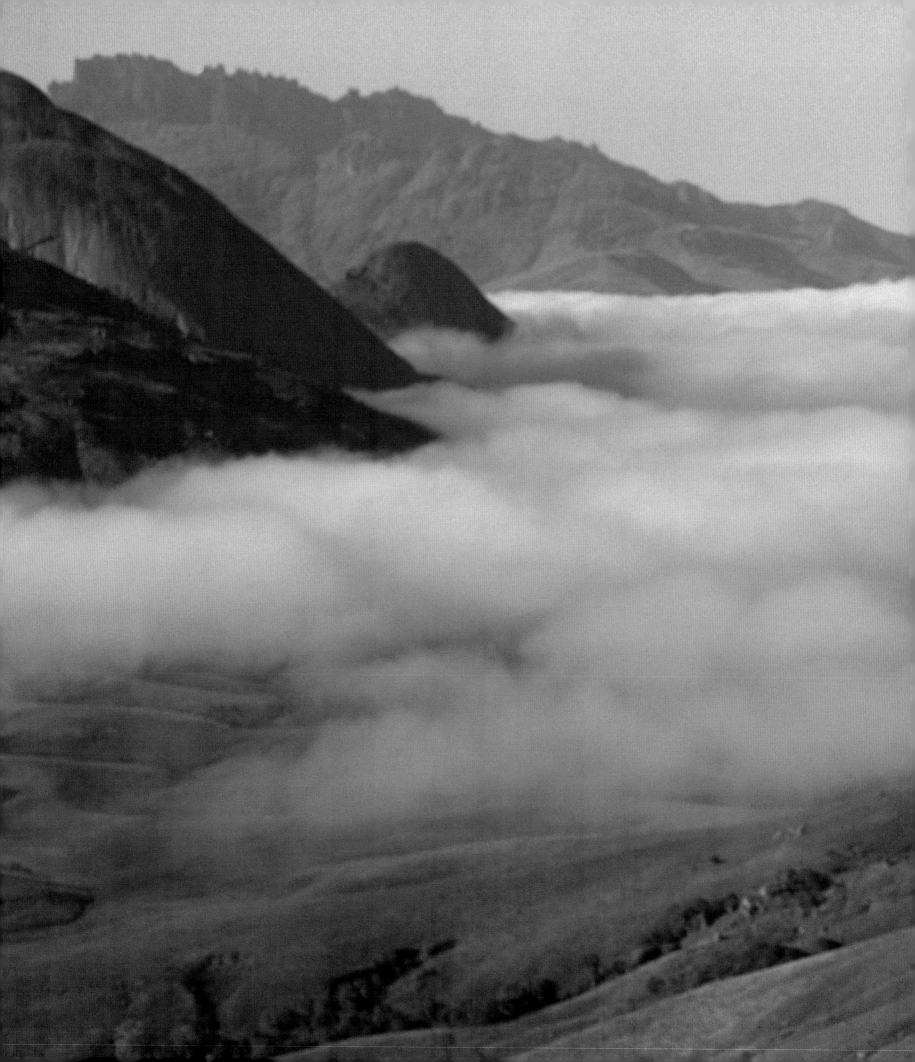

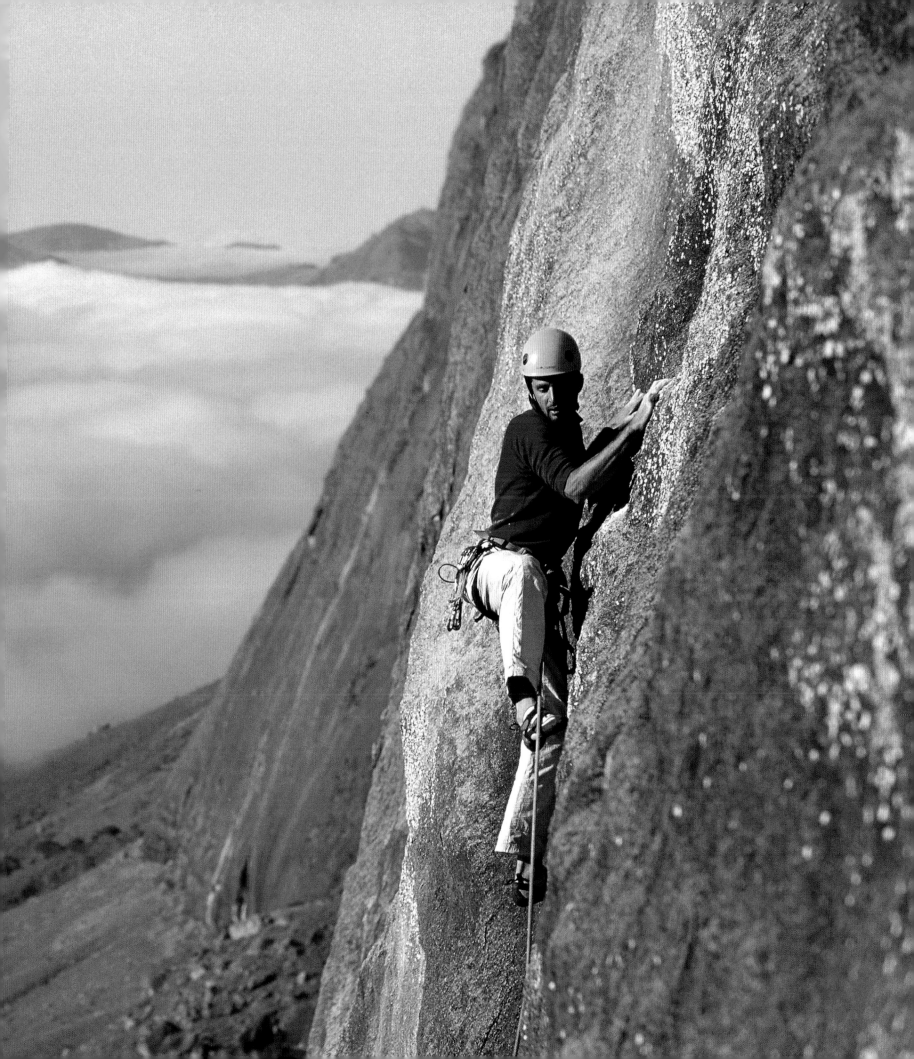

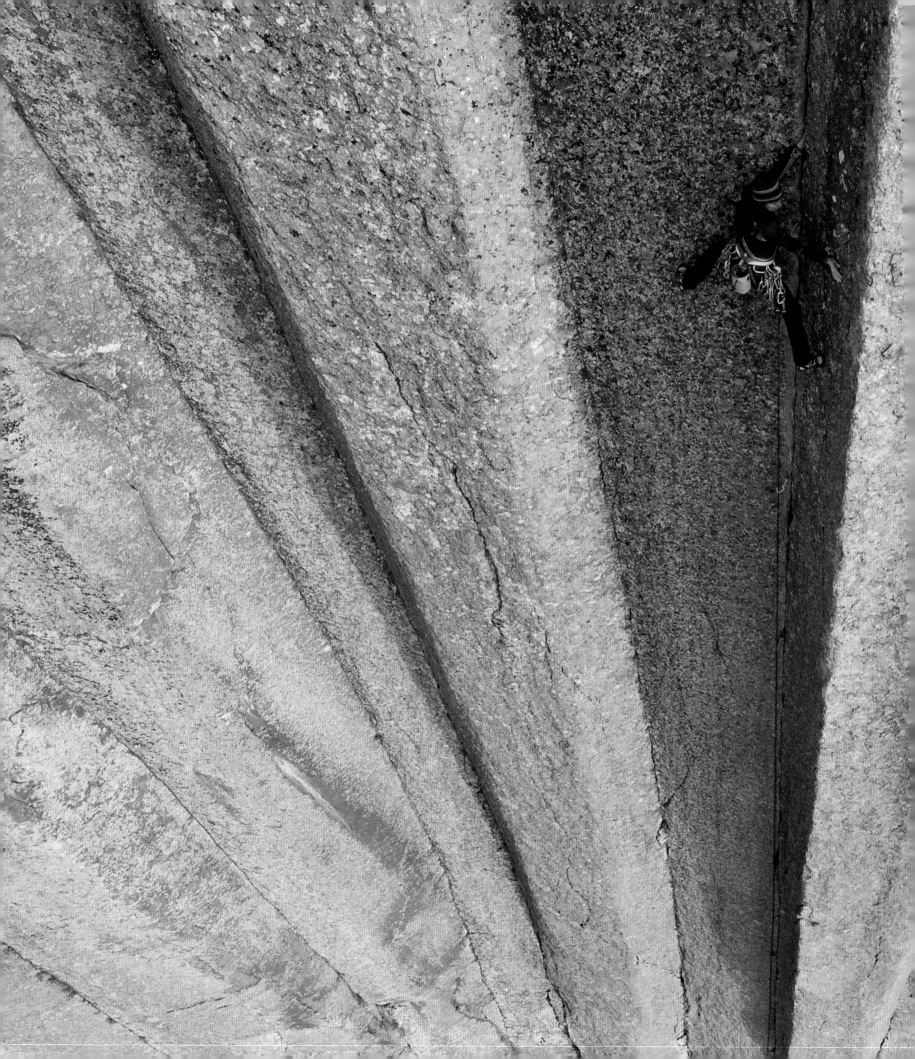

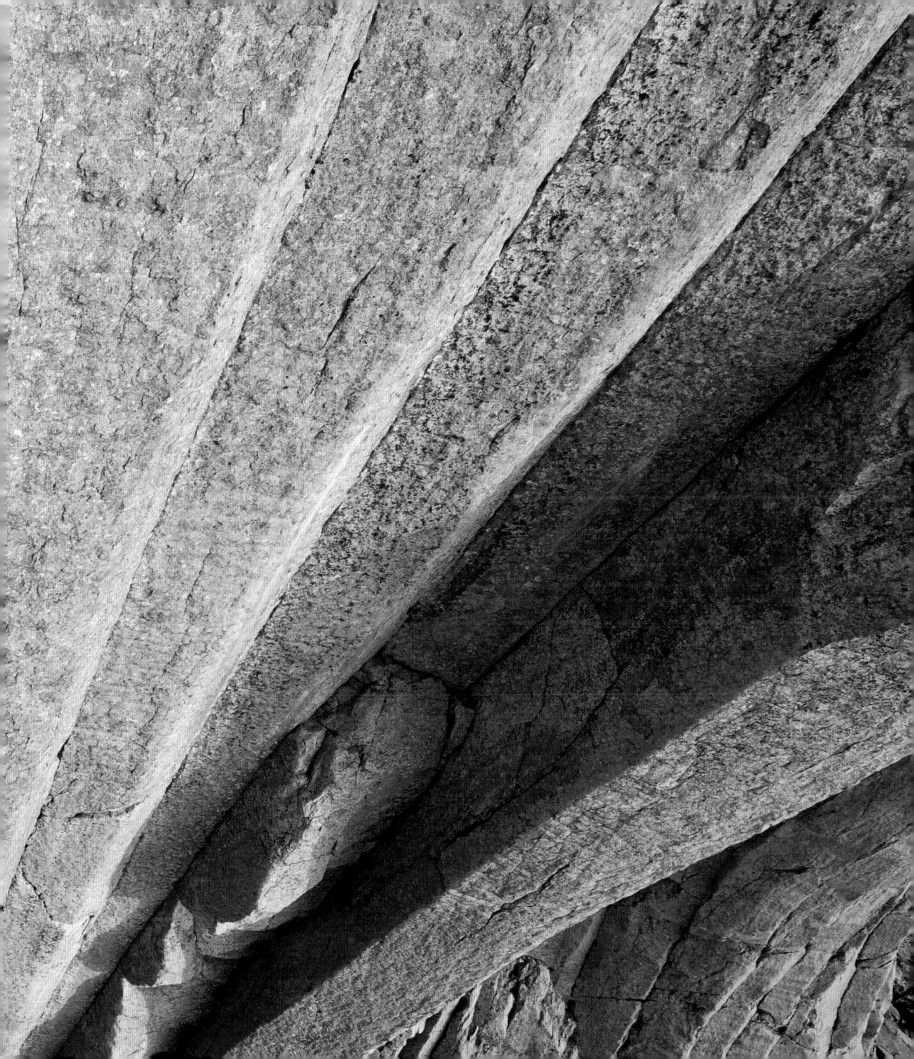

WARNING CLIMBING IS AN INHERENTLY DANGEROUS ACTIVITY THAT MAY RESULT IN SERIOUS INJURY OR DEATH. PLEASE READ THE FOLLOWING:

To enjoy a long life, free of the risk of grievous injury or untimely death, we recommend that you do not climb anything! However if you do decide to ignore our advice and climb, then you do so entirely at your own risk!

You may not rely on the information presented in this book, and the authors and publishers accept no responsibility whatsoever for any death, injury, loss or inconvenience sustained by any person as a result of or related to the use of this book.

This is neither a guidebook nor an instructional book; it is a picture book designed for your viewing pleasure.

Onsight Photography, the authors, and publishers make no warranties or representations, express or implied, of any kind and expressly disclaim any warranty or representation regarding the accuracy or reliability of the information contained in this book or its fitness for a particular purpose.

This book is not a substitute for professional climbing instruction. If you have questions regarding the information presented in the book, hire a competent, formally trained climbing guide to help you understand the information.

World Climbing: Rock Odyssey

Published by
Onsight Photography and Publishing
PO Box 49, Blackheath NSW 2785, Australia
www.onsight.com.au

Copyright © Simon Carter 2011
Copyright © Onsight Photography and Publishing 2011

First published 2011

All rights reserved. No part of this publication may be reproduced, stored in a retrieval system or transmitted, in any form or by any means without the prior written permission of the publisher.

Design by Onsight Photography and Publishing

National Library of Australia Cataloguing-in-Publication Data:

Author:	Carter, Simon, 1966—
Title:	World climbing : rock odyssey photographs by Simon Carter; area introductions by Monique Forestier.
ISBN:	978 0 9870874 1 6 (hbk.)
Subjects:	Rock climbing - Pictorial works.
Other Authors/Contributors:	Forestier, Monique.
Dewey Number:	796.5223

◁ Olivier Michellod on *Typhoon* (7c), Crystal Cave, Telendos Island near Kalymnos, Greece.
◁◁ Felix Frieder on pitch nine of *Manara-Potsiny* (8a), 600m (18 pitches) on Tsaranoro Be, Tsaranoro, Madagascar.
◁ Brittany Griffith on *Mr Clean* (5.11a), Devils Tower, Wyoming, USA.
▷ Mathieu Geoffray on pitch one of *Arête de Marseille* (5c), on La Grande Candelle, Les Calanques, France.

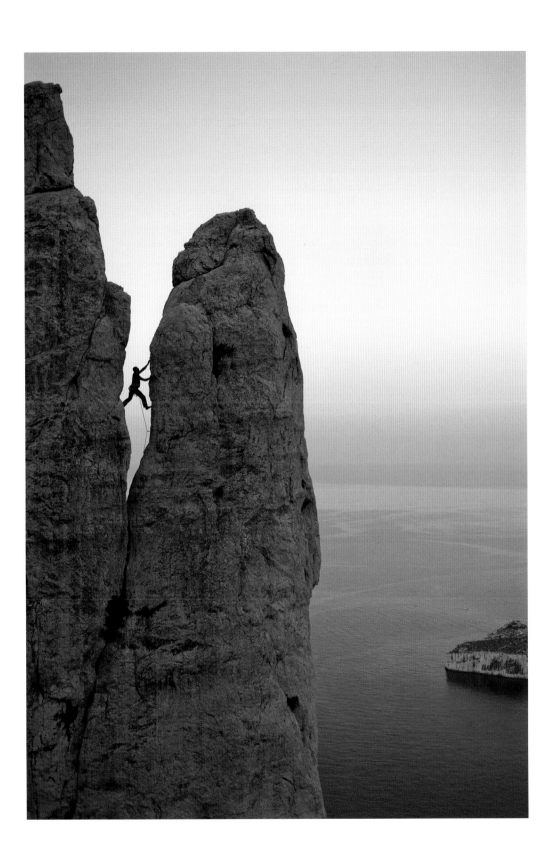

CONTENTS

FOREWORD

Climbers have always been vagabonds, restless spirits traveling the world to discover new summits, new crags, new boulders. The mere mention of a road trip sets our heads swimming with notions of freedom, new cuisine, new cultures and, of course, of climbing the unknown. It's safe to say that of all sports enthusiasts, climbers are the most prolific travelers — there's hardly a point on the globe that hasn't been trod by sticky boot rubber.

I've been climbing for over 40 years, and in the climbing publishing business for much of that time. I like to think that I've been out and about — to the frightening sandstone towers of the Elbsandstein, to the soaring granite buttresses of Chamonix, to bitter Canadian ice, to warm Mexican rock and other parts beyond, but my ventures are humble relative to the gallivanting of Simon Carter. He seems to have been everywhere!

We are lucky that Carter is bitten by wanderlust, and luckier still to have his talented photographic eye documenting our world of climbing. The book you hold, **World Climbing: Rock Odyssey**, is the fruit of Carter's gift and hard work. Within the pages we are treated to the best climbing photography ever taken, and all distinctly Simon Carter, who artfully merges landscape with action, and sets off the works with untrumpable natural light, often waiting hours if not days on a rope or in the rain for that fleeting moment when everything comes together.

It has been my pleasure, as the Editor in Chief of **Rock and Ice** magazine, to have worked with Carter and been privy to be among the first to see his photos. It is my pleasure to present his new book, a visual feast for us vagabonds that is certain to get us all scheming for our next great road trip.

Duane Raleigh
Publisher and Editor in Chief
Rock and Ice

➡ Olivia Hsu devouring **Breakfast Burrito** (5.10d), Drive-By Crag, Red River Gorge, Kentucky, USA.

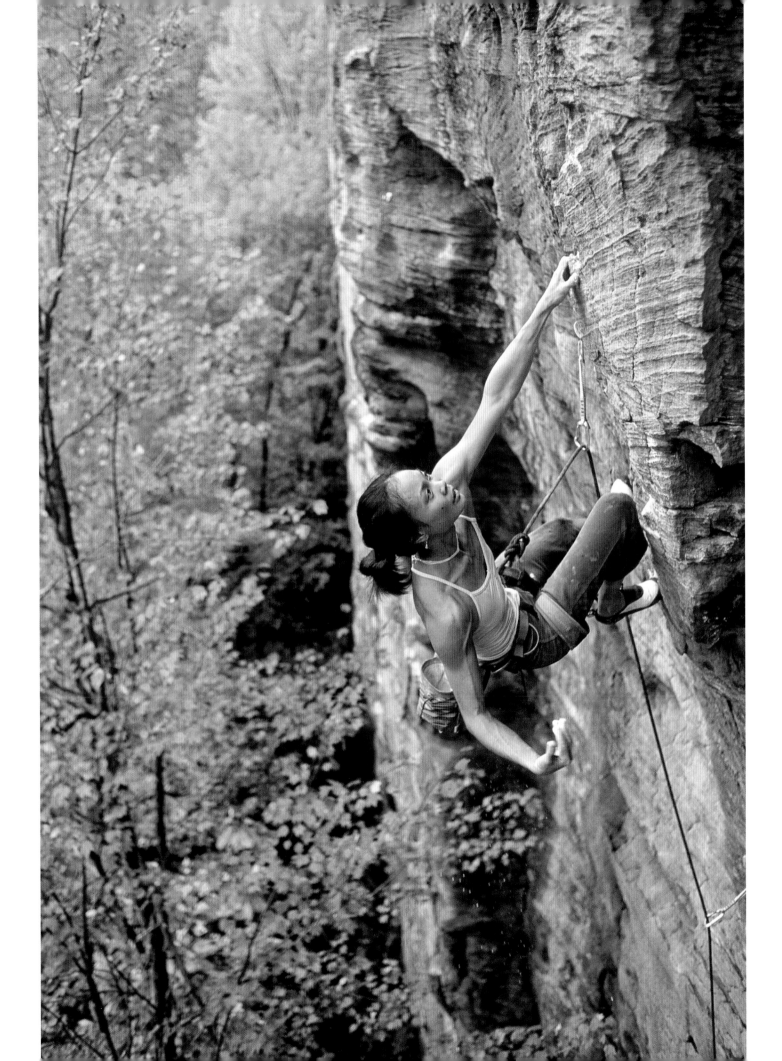

INTRODUCTION

I can still remember that first trip to Mount Arapiles. It was eons ago — I was still in my teens. Oh, the anticipation! I had read and heard so much about that place. After twelve bum-numbing hours our cramped van finally crawled into the dark campground. We stumbled out of the van and I stared into the black night sky until my eyes finally adjusted and I managed to make out the faint outline of the towering Bluffs, frustrated that I couldn't see more. I spread out my sleeping bag under the pines and tried to catch a few hours sleep — if my racing brain would allow it. Finally the dawn light started to work its way down the cliff, slowly exposing the giant golden buttress. It was a spectacular sight. As if a curtain had opened, a new world was revealed to me. I was excited by the possibilities that lay ahead.

New destinations have always been an essential part of my climbing addiction. Not only for the incredible routes, or because it's fun, or for what you learn, but also for the life experiences. The precious memories, such as the five days spent off the coast of northern Madagascar, looking across the misty depths of the Dolomites, or living near the steep walls and infinite blue of Kalymnos.

Nature's art is my inspiration. I dream of colossal caves, beautiful buttresses, proud prows, airy arêtes, wonderful walls and slender sea-stacks. The first time I saw the Totem Pole, I thought, "Wow, I've got to get a photo of that". My photographer's mind is filled with images and questions. How to capture that? How to do it justice? What is unique here? Finding those elusive moments when the rock architecture, the natural elements and the climbing action come together in harmony is my challenge as a photographer.

As a climber, I find the most satisfying routes are those that push the limits of my skill, mental strength, and fitness — whatever my level is at the time. And when it comes to memorable routes, there's nothing better than getting strung out on an incredible hunk of rock. The shape of a cliff is what captivates me most as a climber — and also as a photographer.

When *World Climbing: Images from the Edge* was published in 2005, I knew there was still so much out there to explore. So I decided to set myself a personal challenge: to focus on new climbing destinations and routes which tackle amazing cliffs. Having already visited some of the world's great crags like Ceuse, Yosemite, Pembroke and the Grampians, it was a delight to look at a whole new set of classic crags.

This rock odyssey stems from my personal quest but in fact it has been a marvellous journey that I've been able to share with my wife, Monique Forestier. Recently we've been blessed by the presence of our baby daughter, Coco. For this my life and my memories are much richer.

Monique is a true climbing fanatic. We still laugh about the time when we were climbing at Siurana in Spain and she was pregnant. Normally on trips she'd prefer to climb many routes rather than get involved in one hard project, but this time she became psyched. They say morning sickness is a bitch and I believe it. It was only five minutes hike to the crag, but by the time we got there, she'd often be exhausted and need to lie in the dirt and take a little nap before even thinking about roping up and trying her project (a beautiful 35-metre face climb called *Zona 0*). I can admit now that I thought trying such a hard climb in her condition was a waste of time, but tactfully I kept my opinion to myself. She tried the route every few days, but as she got it more wired she was also becoming more pregnant, and success was becoming more elusive.

All too soon we were down to our last day in Spain, no changing flights, and anyway by now Monique was fourteen weeks pregnant. Last shot, near the top of the route, she snagged a finger pocket the wrong way, strained her finger and fell. I lowered her back down to the ground. It was all over, no more climbing for perhaps a year. A tear trickled down her face. We sat there in silence for twenty minutes. The sun hit the cliff and started frying the rock — conditions now were bad. But then, as if a light came on, Monique looked at me, smiled, and said,

"Well, the finger doesn't matter, it will have plenty of time to heal, and I have to get the gear off this route anyway..." She pulled the rope down and tied in again... And then, with conviction and flawless precision, she pulled off the most impressive climbing I'd seen from her yet.

With Monique's support for my work and her endless energy for climbing, it's fitting that she has voiced her perspective by writing the area introductions for this book. After all, this has been Monique's rock odyssey too.

Six years and sixteen climbing areas later, it's clear that the game remains far from over, there is still so much out there to explore. And I am incredibly happy about that! I'm still dreaming of new adventures, new challenges, and anticipating the next time a curtain is opened and a new world is revealed. The search for the new still keeps me excited even after so many years.

This *Rock Odyssey* has only been possible because of the inspiration, hard work and generosity of many, many others. I'm forever indebted to all the climbers and kind individuals who've encouraged and helped us out along the way. Also, I'm grateful for all of the inspiration and opportunities provided by others. By those who've been inspired by nature's art and also treated it with respect. Those who've had vision, put in the hard work to establish great routes and to help make cool playgrounds. Those who bring their passion and positivity to crags, share the love, and help make the climbing community something so special. Thank you all!

Simon Carter

➡ Steve "Moss" Moon on **Pole Dancer** (22), Cape Raoul, Tasman Peninsula, Tasmania, Australia.

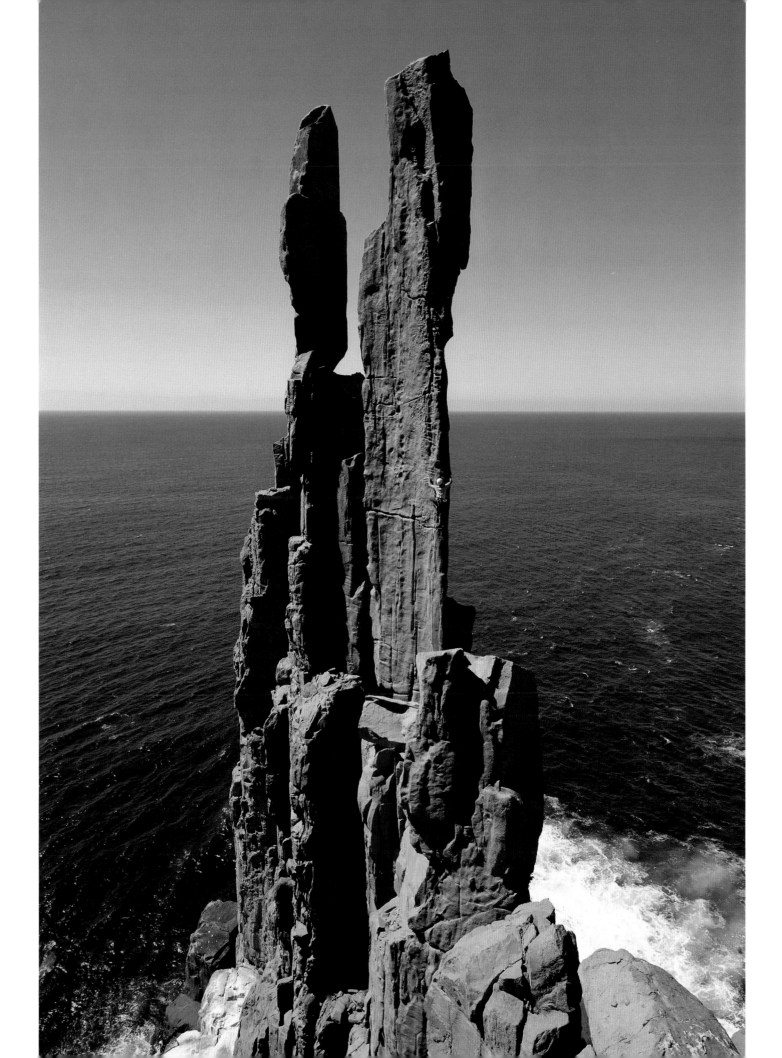

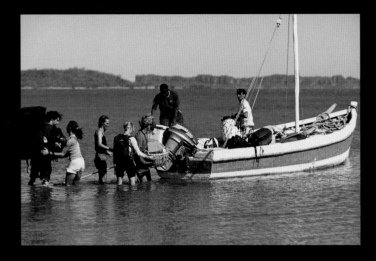 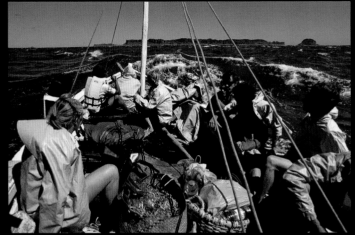

↑ ↗ Loading supplies, and then riding the choppy seas out to the islands.

→ Fred Moix getting into the swing of things on *Vatorange* (6c), Sector Mozambique, Nosy Anjombalova.

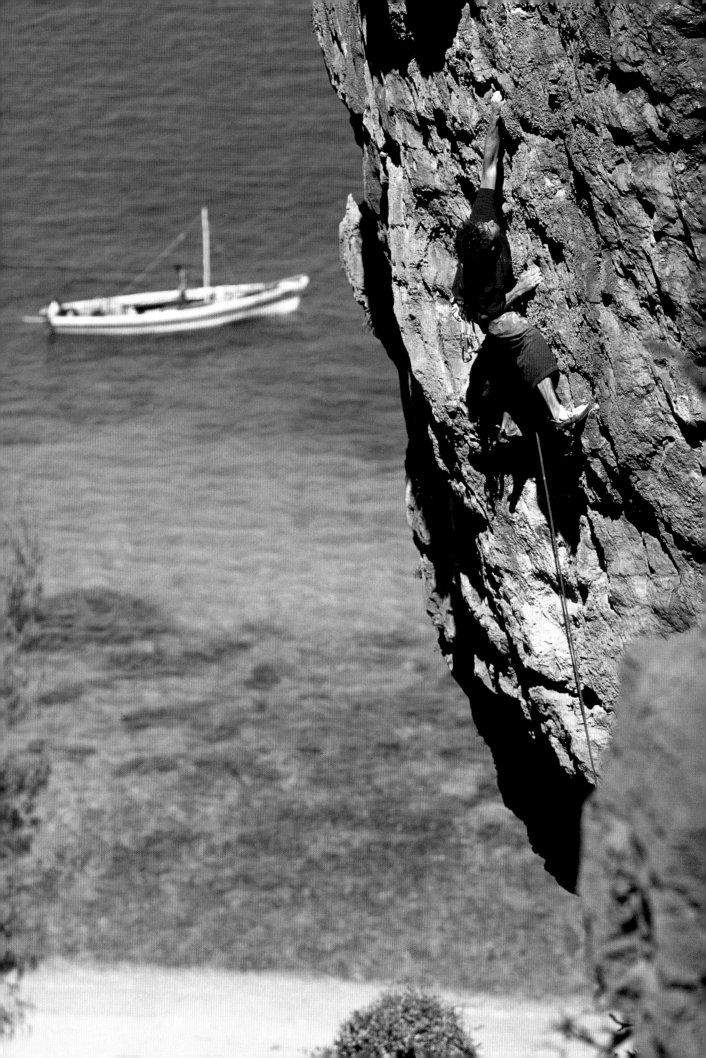

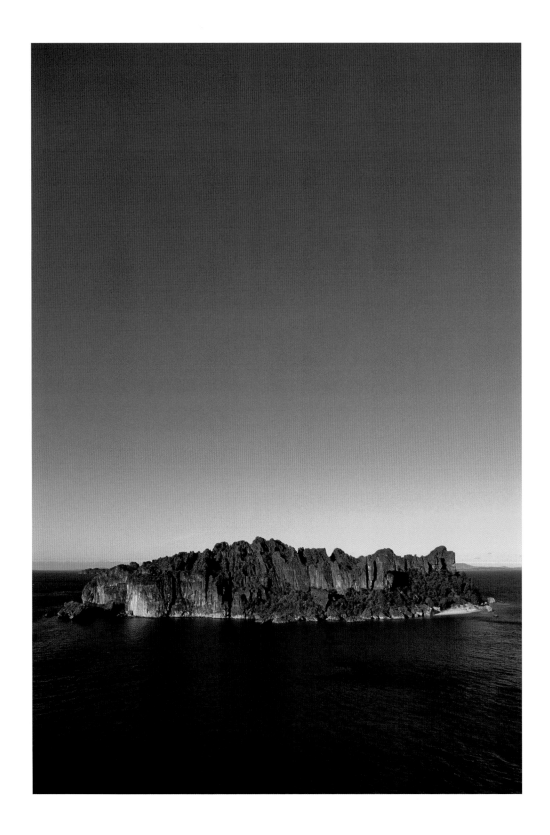

⬆ A view of Nosy Anjombalova (which has some of the best climbing) from Nosy Andantsara (our island home).

➡ Jean-Francios Reffet sampling one of the gems from this treasure island, **L'île aux Trésors** (6b+), Nosy Anjombalova.

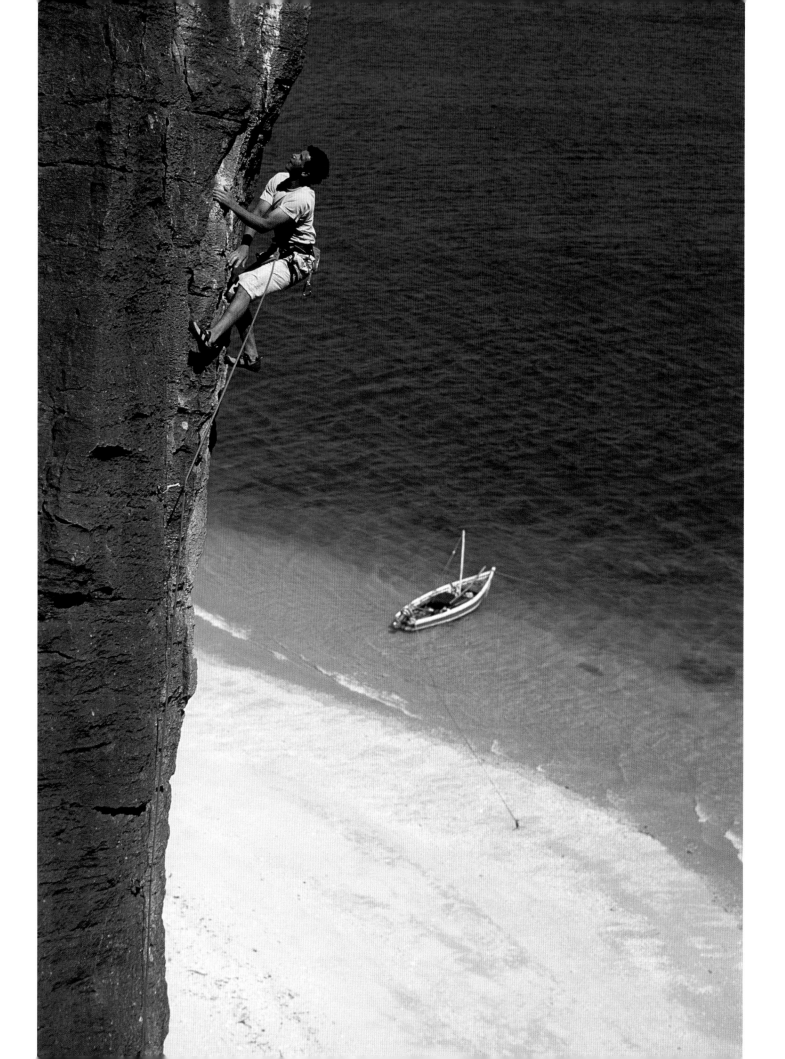

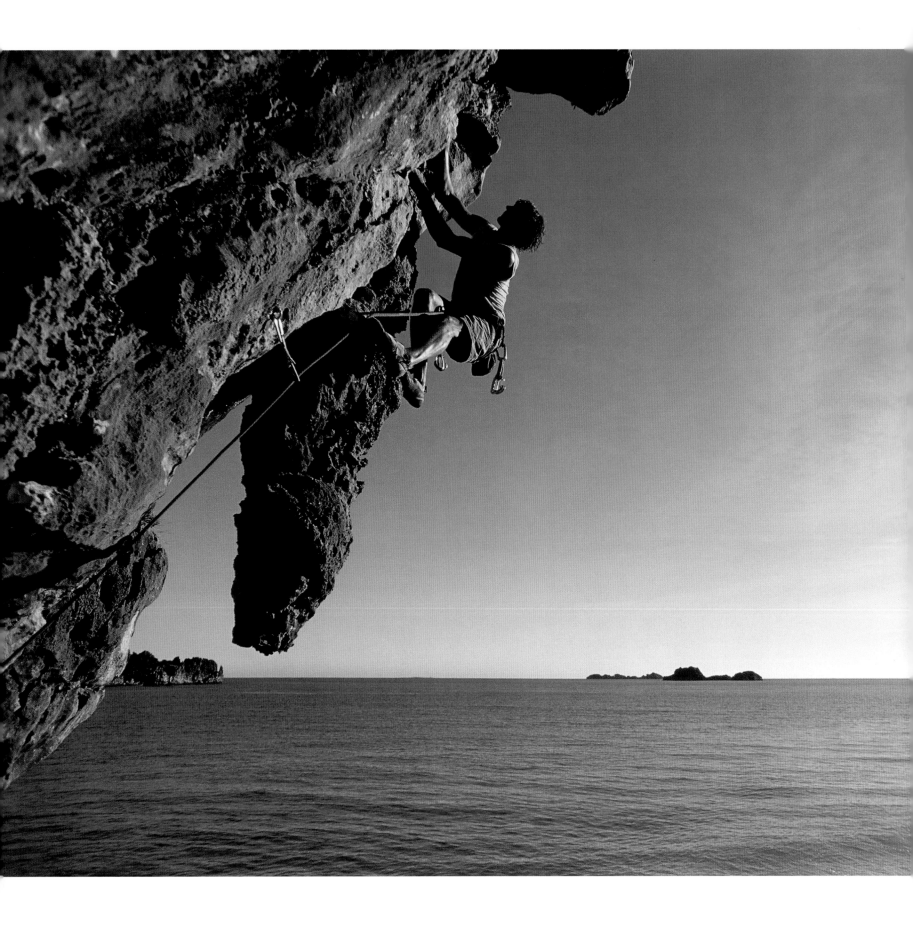

Mathieu Delacroix grabbing a quick bite before breakfast on
Les Dents de la Mer (6b), just 30 metres from the dining room.

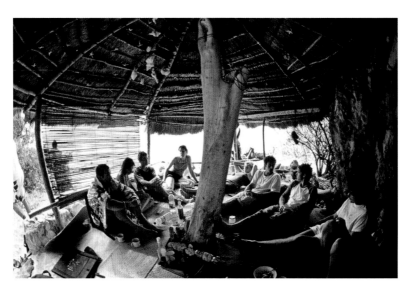

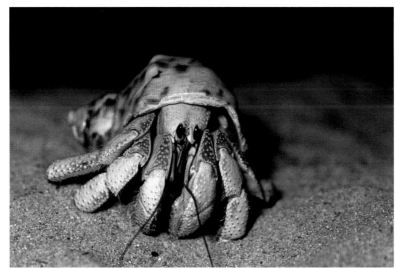

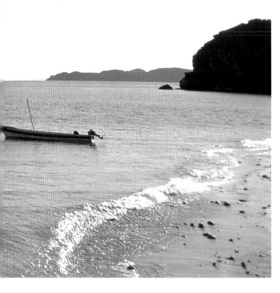

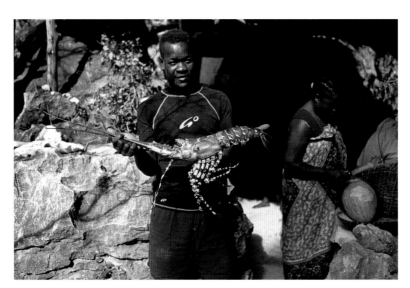

Chilling out in the dining room at the New Sea Roc camp.

An after dinner guest, a hermit crab, visiting our camp.

Catch of the day! While climbers climbed, the camp boatmen spearfished for dinner.

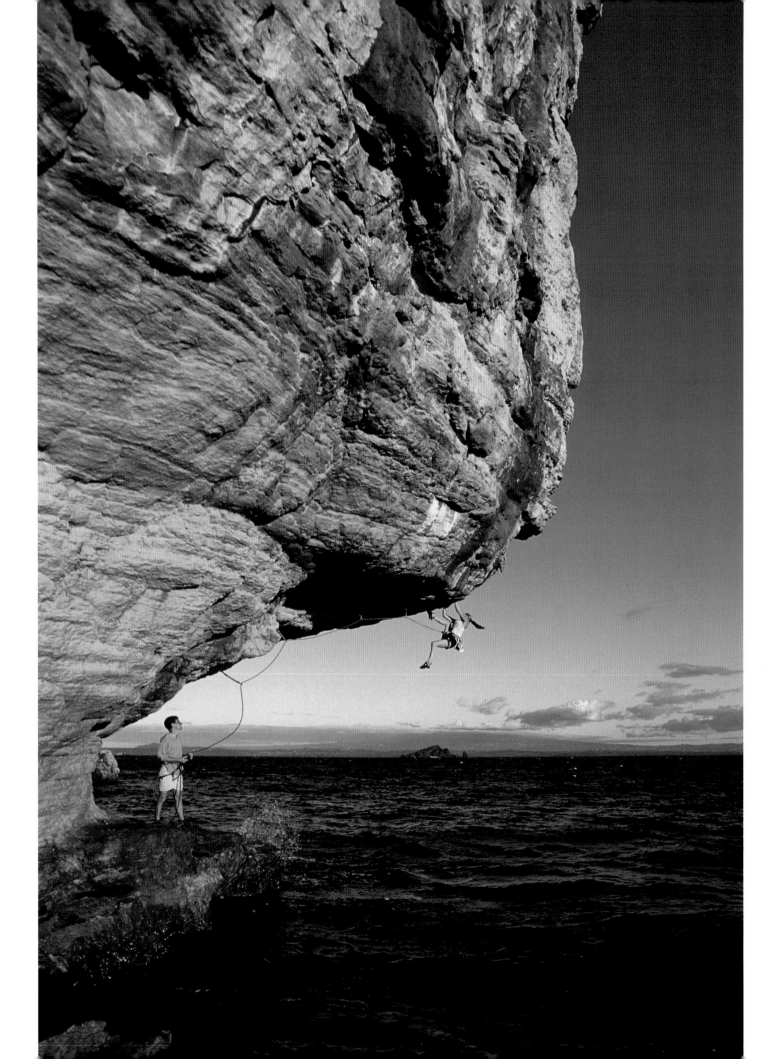

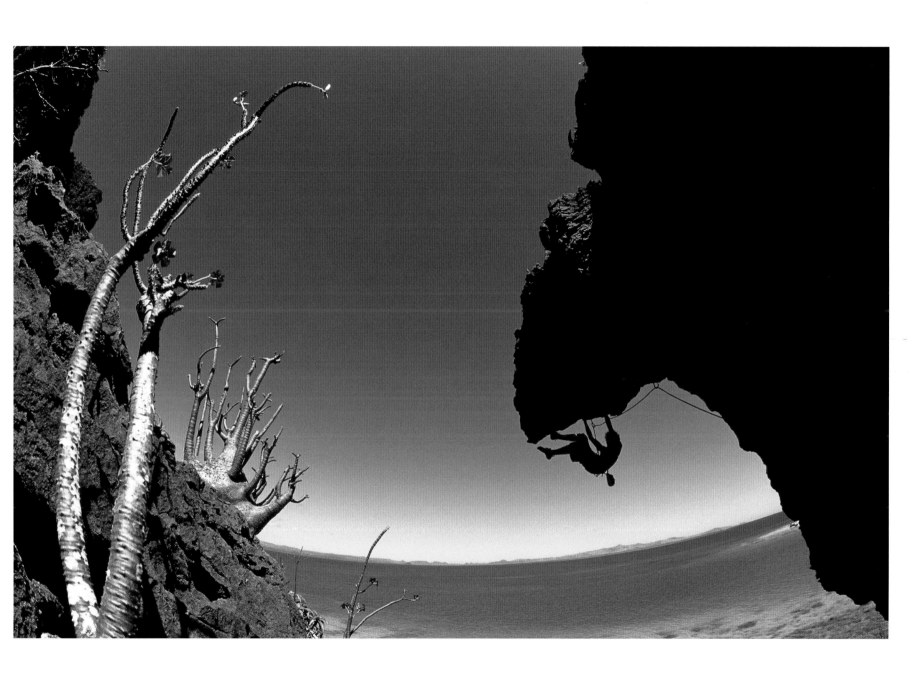

Monique Forestier attempting **Les Naufragés du Rhum** (8b), on Nosy Andantsara.

Fred Moix surfing the barrel of **Tafo Masina** (8a), Sector Mozambique, Nosy Anjombalova.

Tsaranoro Massif's black and orange streaked cliffs, with distinctive sparkling green highlights, forms an imposing crown towering up to 800 metres above the surrounding plains. The first route, *Rain Boto* (7b+) was climbed by big wall veterans Kurt Albert and Bernd Arnold in 1995. Today there are over fifty free climbs between 6a and 8c+. For climbers the true beauty of this place is found on the multi-pitch moderate (and hard) classics tackling the gigantic walls.

Squatting demurely in the shadow of the Massif, the privately operated Camp Catta is a base camp with an oasis-type feel. Every evening the dining room is abuzz with an international cast of climbers telling tall tales and exchanging route beta. Abba's "Dancing Queen" plugs any unlikely gaps in the conversations as climbers copy topos for the next day's escapade.

On another flank, the east face of the Karambony, Team France (Francois Legrand and Greg Sobczak) attempt to free climb the 380-metre *Tough Enough* (8c+). It's certainly the hardest big wall in the southern hemisphere, having ten pitches of highly technical and finger intensive moves up an almost featureless granite face. It was later free climbed by Adam Ondra in 2010.

On our way out we say goodbye to the endangered Lemur Catta, a pint-sized nutmeg-coloured monkey dwarfed by its zebra-patterned squirrel tail which inhabits the forest near our camp. You'd think these critters were invented by pre-schoolers using books of misplaced animal parts. They are a delight to watch, one of the joys of visiting this crazy place.

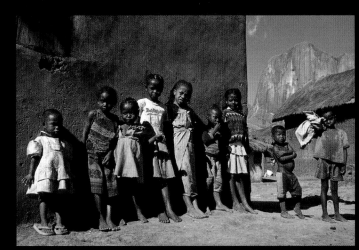

↑ Children in Andonaka village, just below Camp Catta and the Tsaranoro Massif.
↗ Toni Lamprecht carrying the "pig".
→ Monique Forestier and Fred Moix on the sixth pitch of *Pectorine* (6b), 350m (seven pitches), Secteur Lemur Wall.

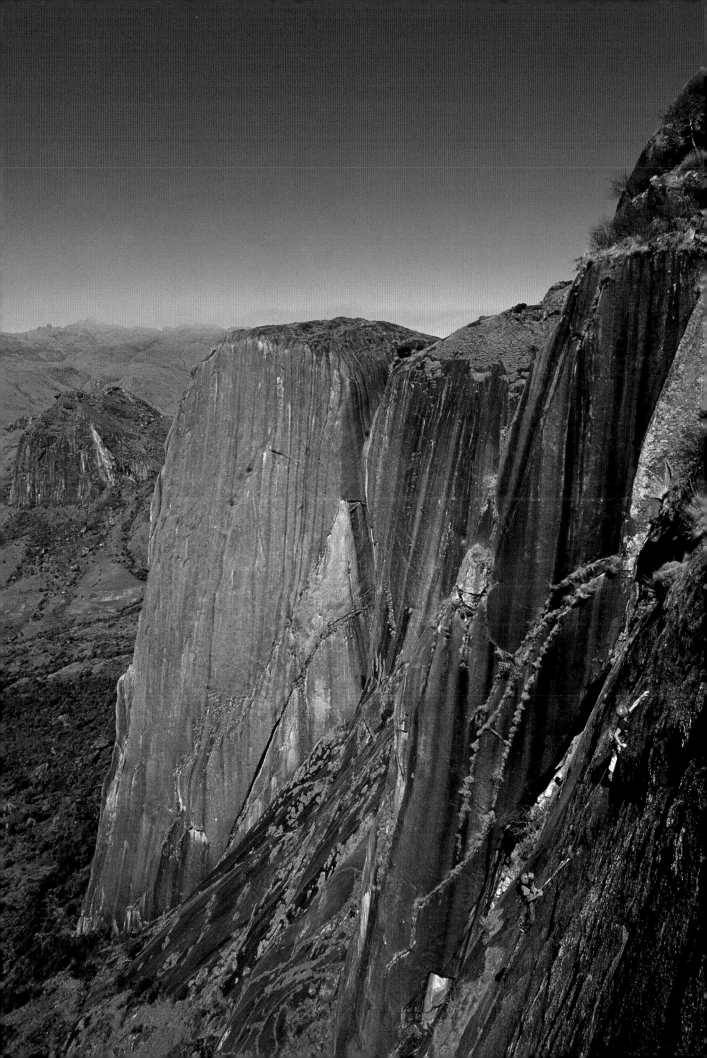

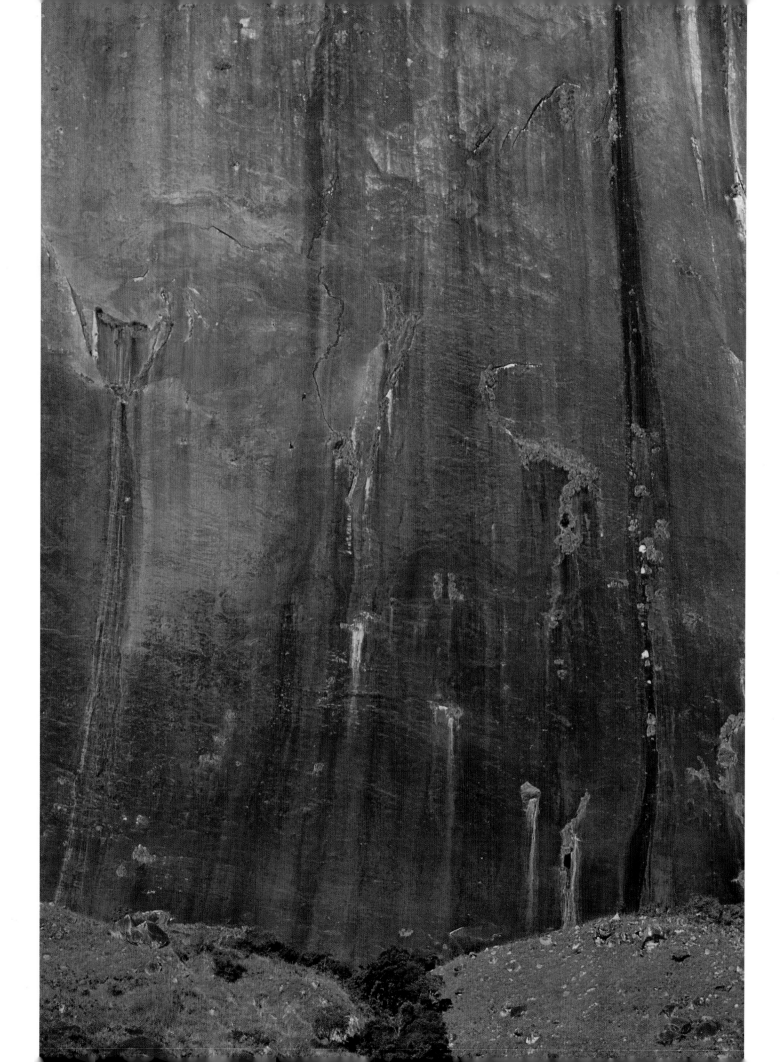

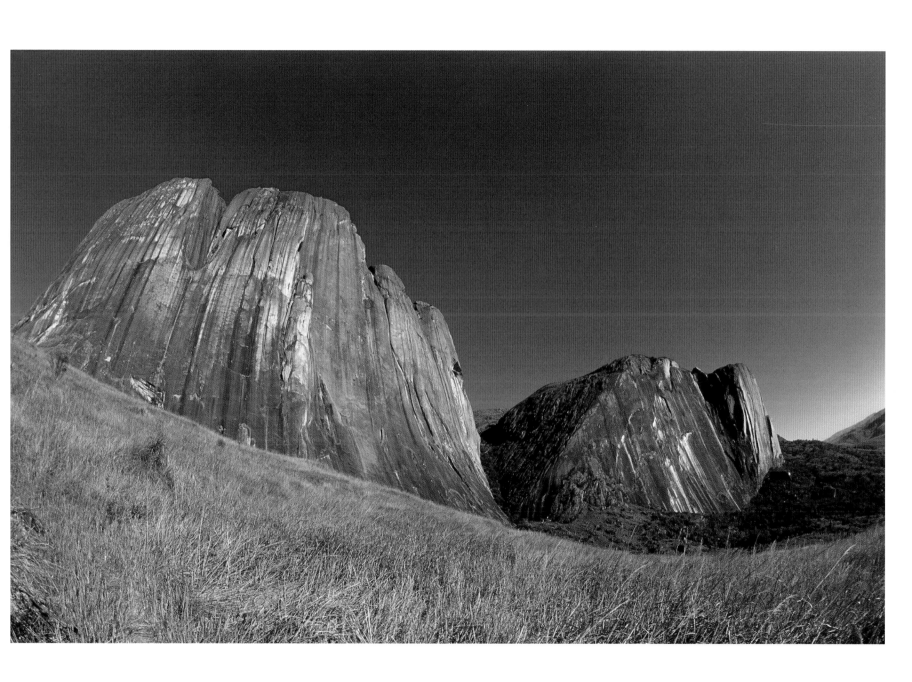

Niels van Duyn and Ilja Bangma several pitches up **Gondwanaland**, 800m, on Tsaranoro Be.
Pitches are 6c, 6b, 6b+, 6c, 7a, 7a, 6c+, 6b, 6c, 7a, 7a+, 7a+, 7a, 6c, 7a, 7a, 6c, 6b, 7c and 3. Phew!

Tsaranoro (with sectors Atsimo, Be, Hely and Nord) to the left and the Karambony to the right.

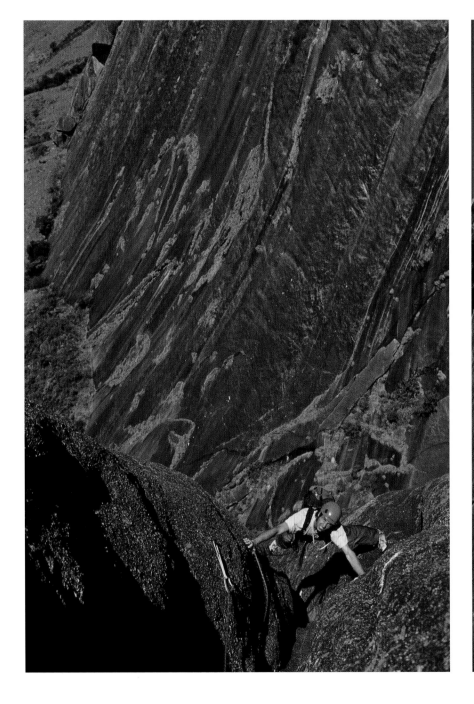

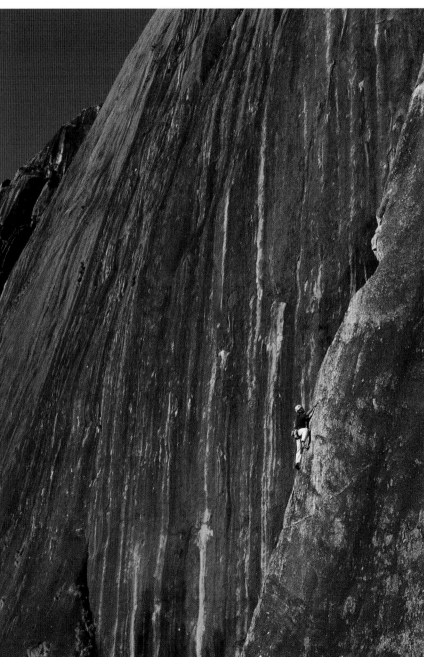

⬆ Fred Moix bridging up pitch six of **Cas Nullard** (6a) which follows massive water runnels for most if its 450m (10 pitches), Secteur Karambony.

↗ Felix Frieder savouring the high quality climbing on the third pitch of **The Swiss Guides Route** (6b+), 100m (four pitches), Secteur Lemur Wall.

➡ Benno Wagner on the neat **Manza** (8a), one of few single pitch routes in the area. Secteur Lemur Wall.

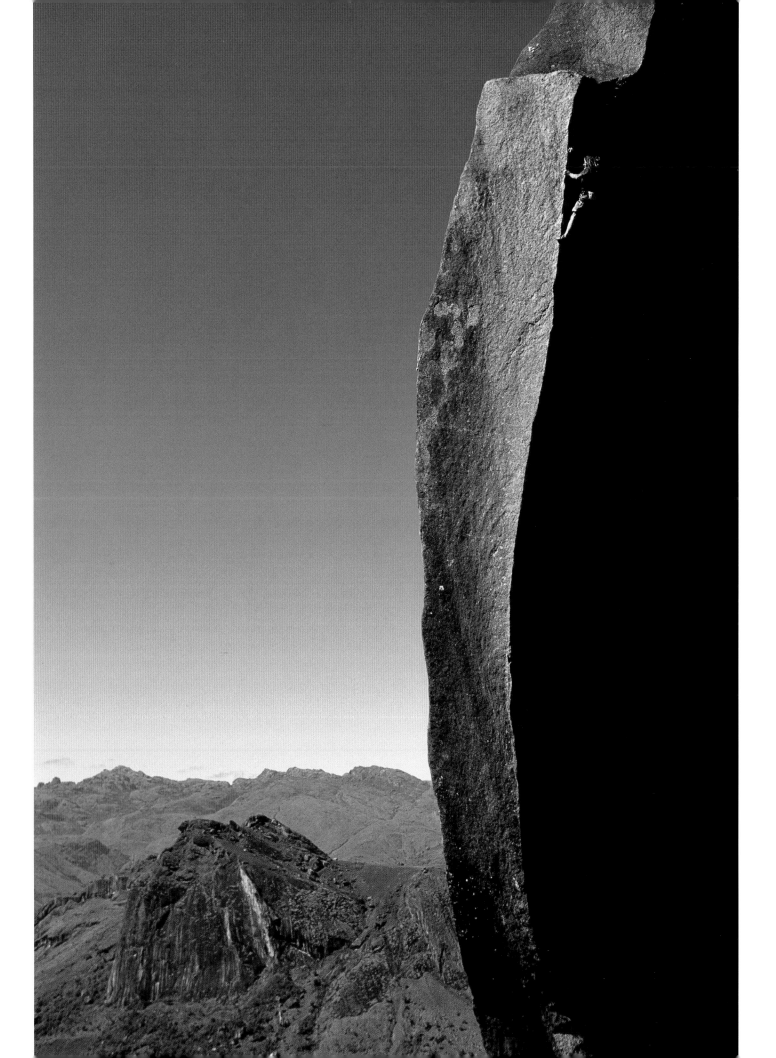

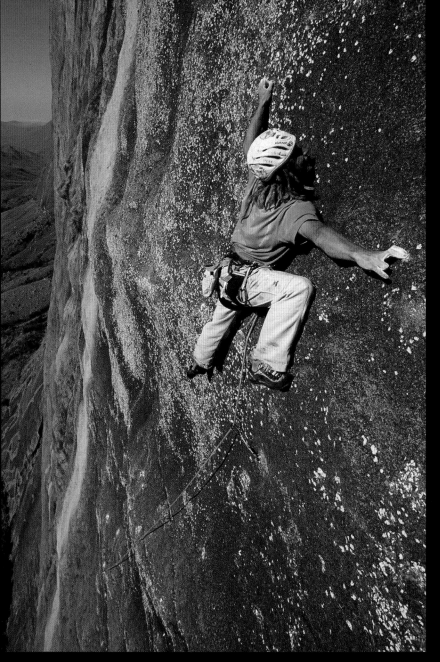
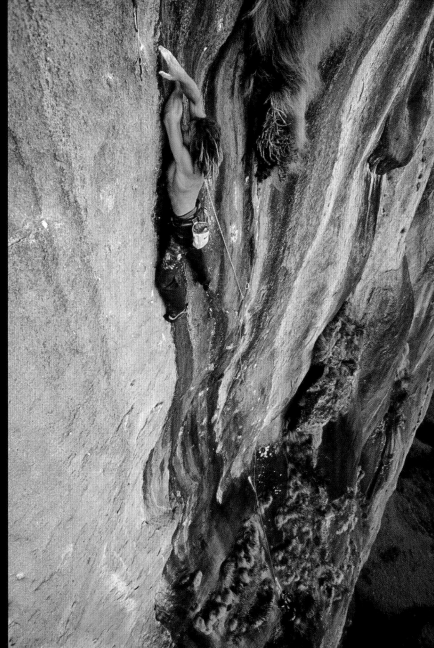

⬆ Benno Wagner suction cupping up pitch nine (7b) of **Manara-Potsiny**, 600m (18 pitches), on Tsaranoro Be.

↗ Benno Wagner leading pitch 13 (8a, crux) of **Manara-Potsiny**. It took some figuring out to unlock the way through this steep headwall.

⟩ More hard climbing. Toni Lamprecht on pitch 15 (7a) of **Manara-Potsiny**.

⟫ Toni Lamprecht and Benno Wagner on top, having just free climbed their new route **Manara-Potsiny**.

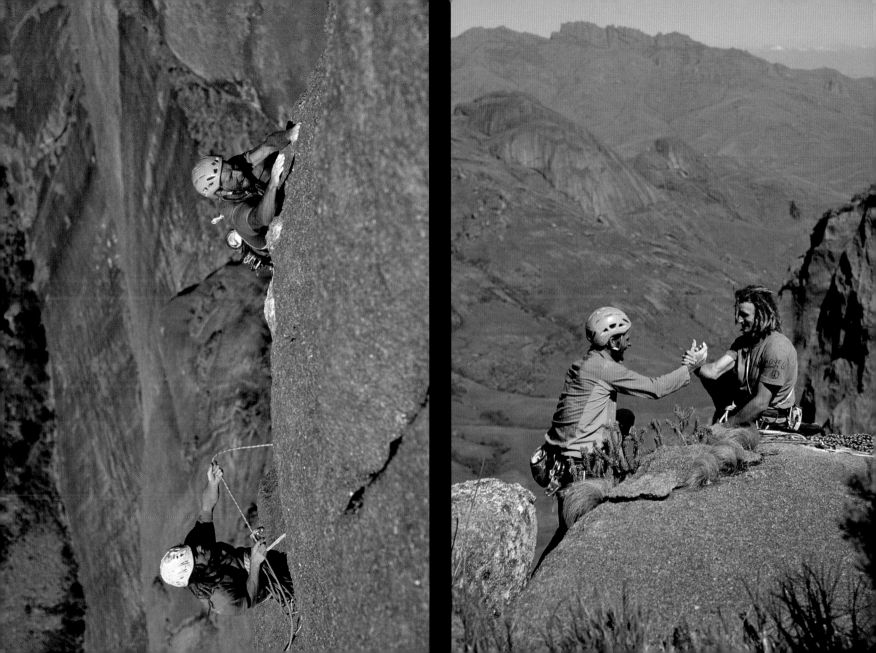

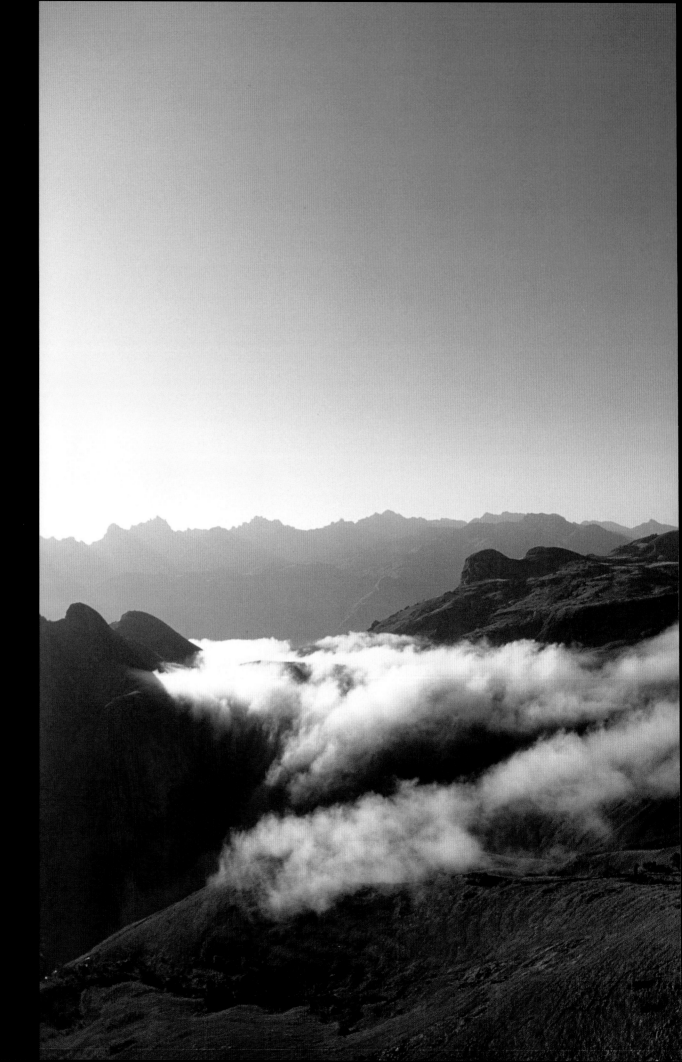

Toni Lamprecht on pitch eight of **Manara-Potsiny**. A few days after freeing all the individual pitches, they returned and made a free ascent of the entire route in a day.

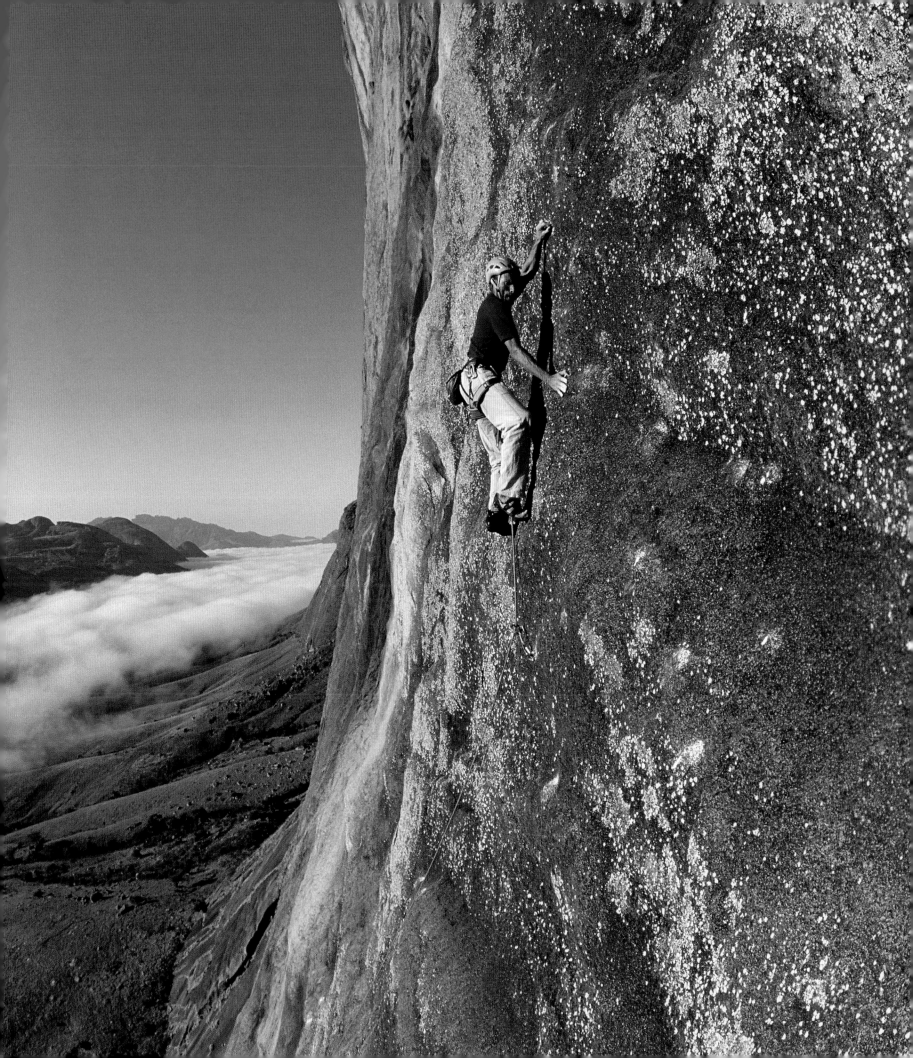

Monstant and Siurana are almost situated in the same grid square; separated only by a wide valley and the cutesy village of Cornudella de Montsant. Despite their proximity the crags are totally different in style. From the valley below, above the vibrant vineyards and fields of scarlet poppies, Serra de Montsant's conglomerate cliffs stand prominently. It is renowned for resistance routes of ridiculous rope stretching proportions. Alternatively, Siurana's limestone crags face every direction and offer a steeper bouldery selection of test pieces. Because they are so close together, you might as well consider them as one area; depending on the conditions or your inclination, you can switch between the two. Barely two hours from Barcelona, and with Margalef only up the road, the Tarragona region is truly one of Spain's great sport climbing destinations.

For years I had been yearning to climb the delectable lines up the compact bullet-holed walls of Montsant. I'm not a pocket-puller, back home I never get the chance. I found these pockets to be surprisingly 'friendly', not sharp tendon busters and not a lot of insecure pebble squeezing either. Similar to the Red River Gorge in some respects, the walls are littered with holds, perhaps having less 'stopper' cruxes — depending on what intermediate rubbish you can hang whilst frantically slapping around to find the 'right' hold.

The left side of Racó de Missa has smooth vertical football field sized walls. There are so many classics here that many don't even have a name, but what's in a name when you'll never forget the sound of your forearms screaming blue murder after 42 metres of relentless stamina climbing? The central amphitheatre has some routes which are just as long, but the angle kicks over and adds a new dimension of pump — and grade — to the equation. It is here that you'll find the famous *Hydrofobia* (8b+) and *L-mens* (8b+). The right side gives some options with afternoon shade.

Across the way, a mere 20 kilometres as the crow flies, a twisted road leads up to the teeny ancient settlement of Siurana, sitting proudly at the end of an escarpment. The seamless views are enjoyed not just by the twenty villagers who live here, but also by climbers scaling the endless cliff lines that skirt the plateau. Near the village, local climber Toni Arbonés and his family run a comfortable camp ground and bar; a popular hang for climbers. Toni, an uber enthusiastic activist who has established countless routes, has also driven the charge to make this one of the premier sport climbing areas in Spain.

Siurana has over 600 routes spread over 40 sectors, most grades, angles and lengths are represented here. Its bizarre mish-mash of moves; balancey to bouldery, crusty crimps to unforgiving under-clings, are dealt out by chance, so what's trumps is anyone's guess and therein lies its appeal. Siurana is home to the famous *La Rambla* (9a+) and many other hard sport routes and historic classics. It is an ideal place for those wanting to throw themselves into the fire and see what charred remains are left at the end of the day.

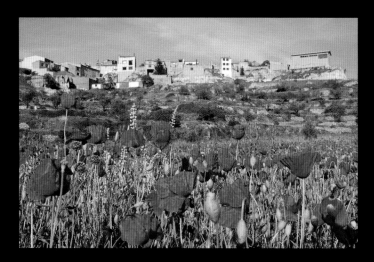

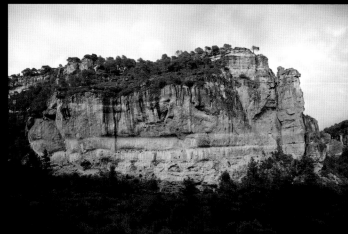

⬆ Tulip time for the village of La Morera de Montsant.
↗ Sector El Pati, home to some of the most famous routes at Siurana.
➡ Dario Zanon on one of those sustained but unnamed classics (6b+) at Sector Racó de Missa, Montsant.

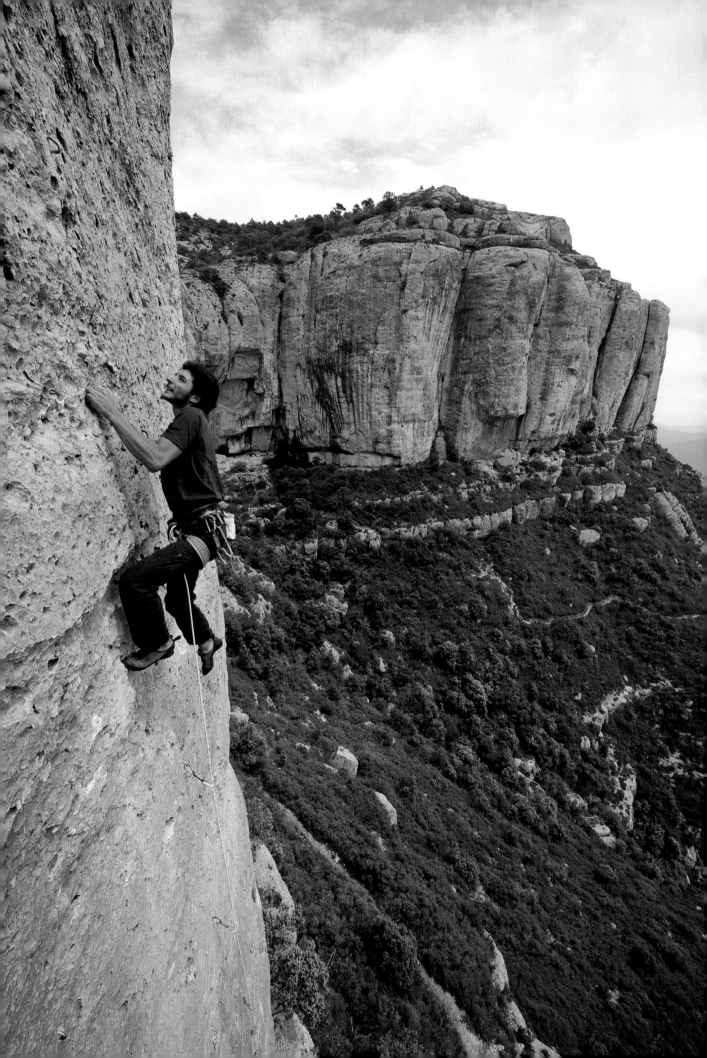

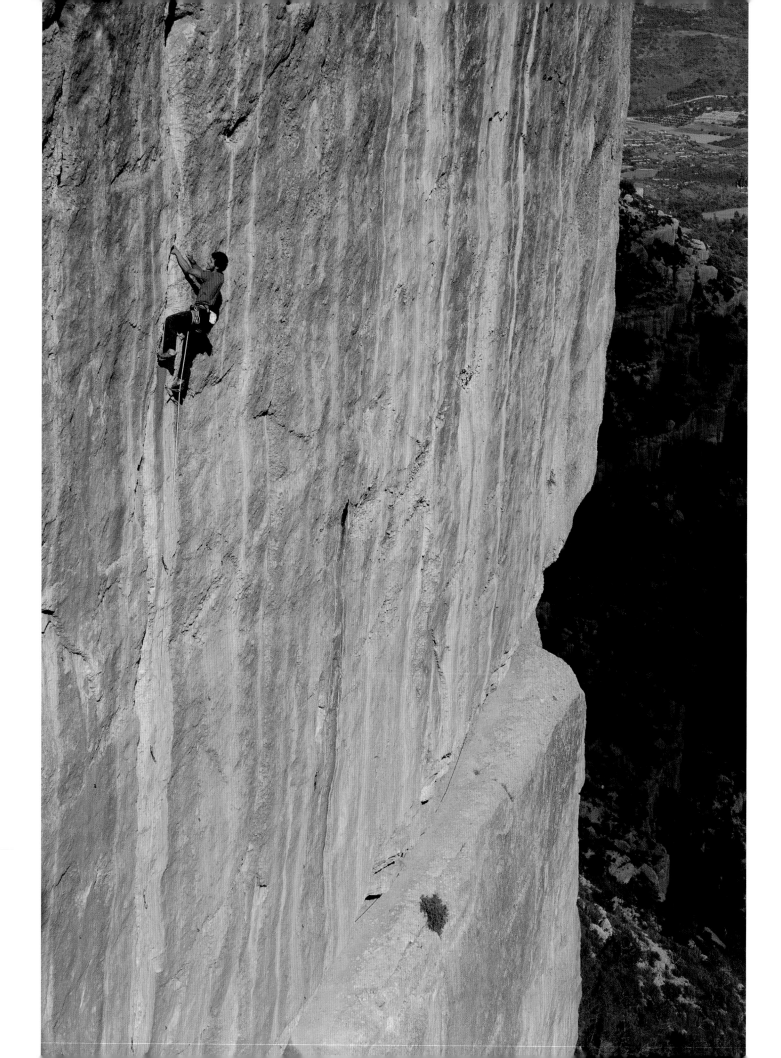

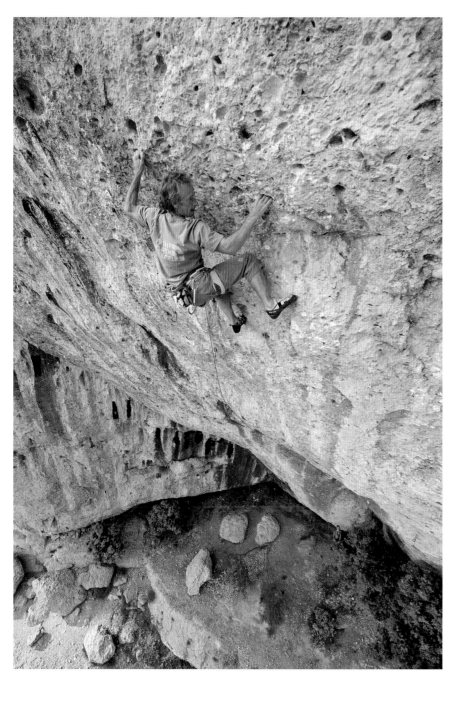

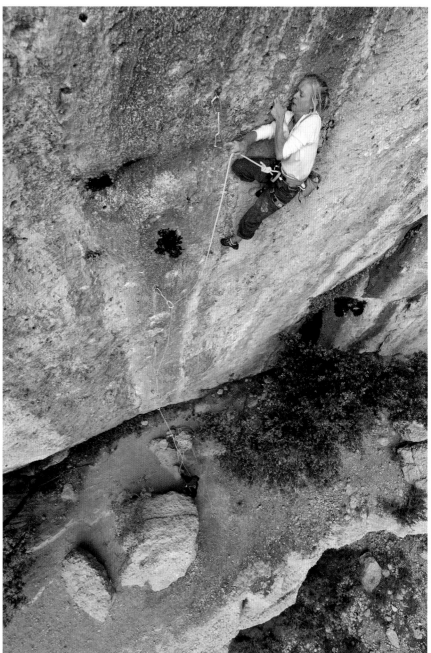

◄ Dario Zanon on **El Gordinflon** (7a+), a crack line at Sector Cingle del Rodes, Montsant.

⬆ Toni Arbones on his **Oxigen** (8b), Sector Racó de Missa, Montsant.

↗ It's black or white: clip or whip. Monique Forestier on **Monochroma** (7c+), Sector Racó de Missa, Montsant.

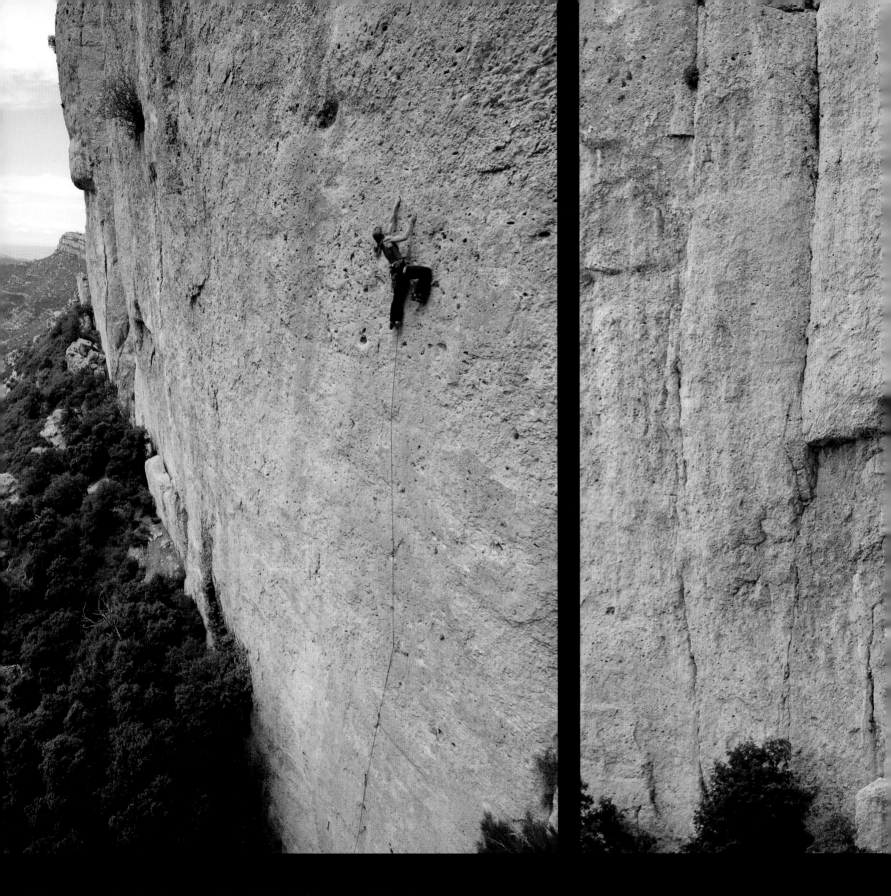

↑ Mariona Marti pulling the perfect pockets of **Purolitic Variant** (7a), Sector Raco de Missa, Montsant.

→ And two routes to the left... Monique Forestier adrift on **Rata Arraconada** (7a).

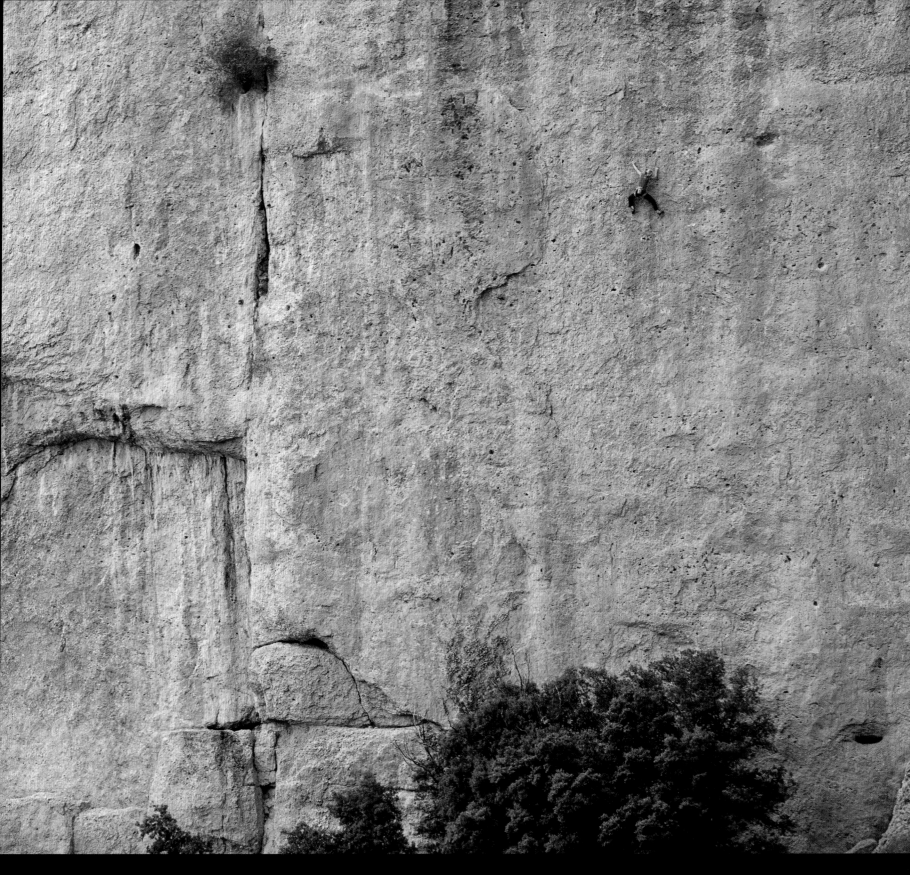

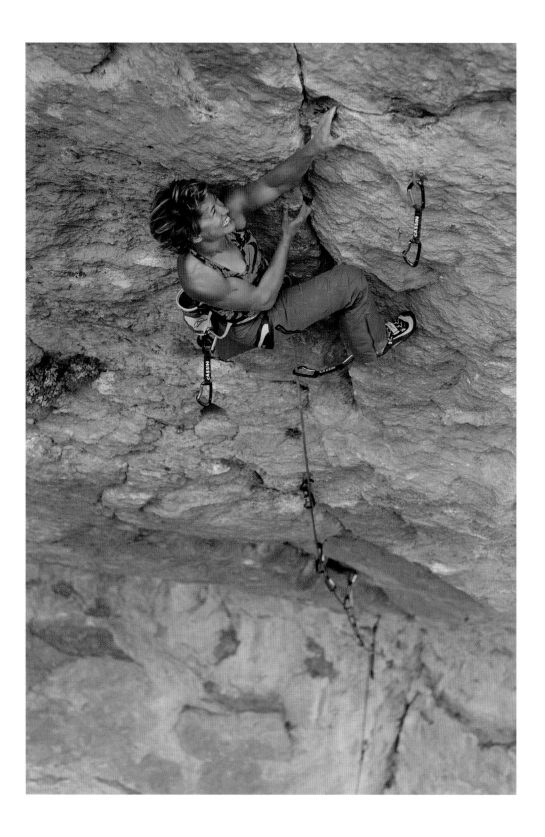

Muriel Sarkany having a good hard crack at quelling **Kalea Borroka** (8b+), Siurana.

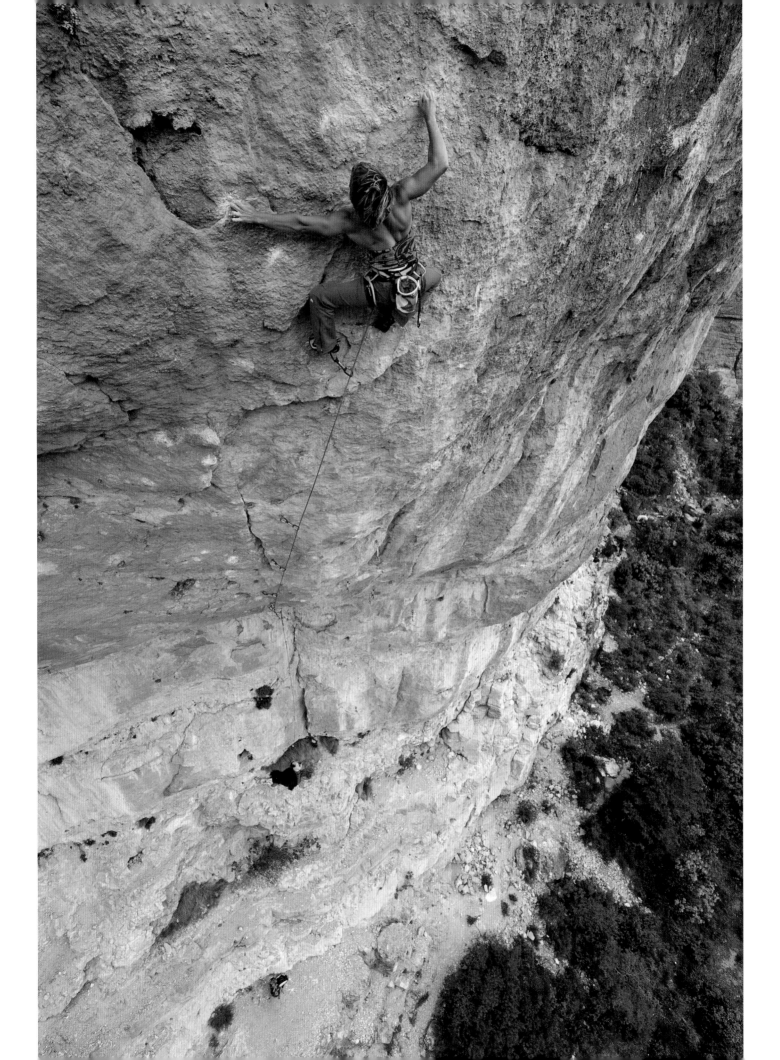

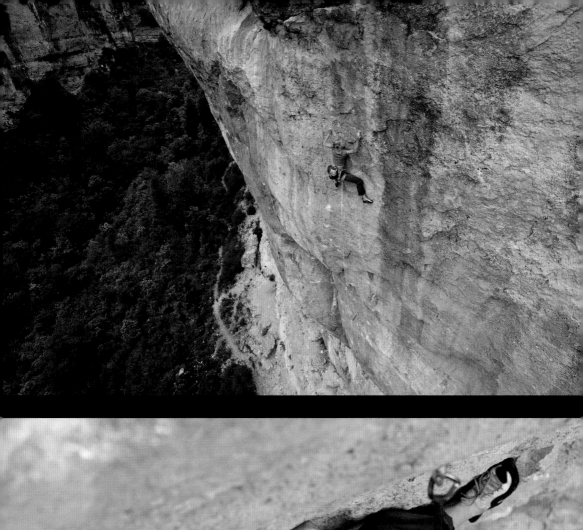
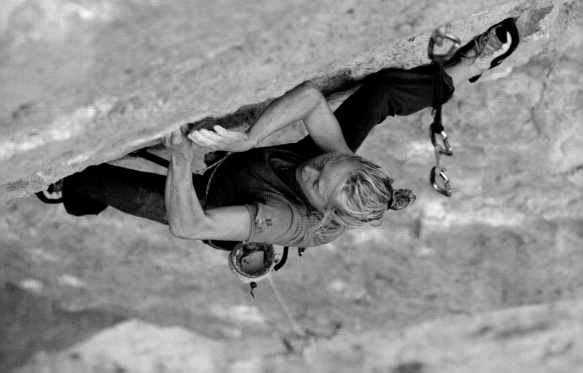

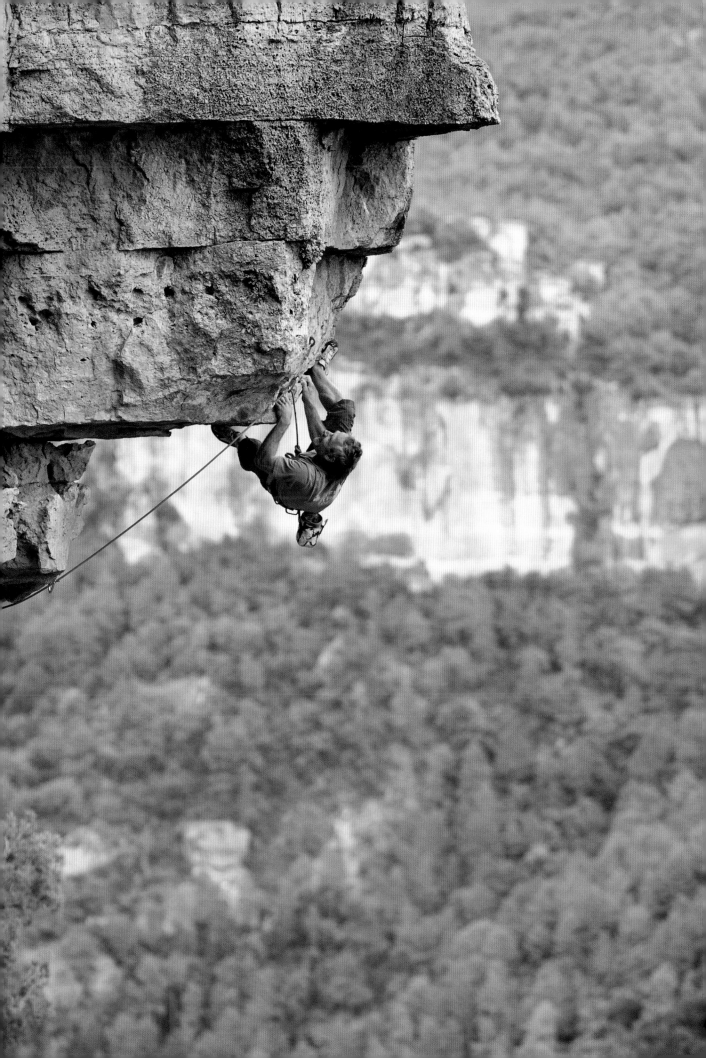

MONTSERRAT

High on the skyline over Catalunya, the saw-tooth profile of Montserrat slashes open the underbelly of the clouds like shark's teeth. But instead of oozing blood, the sky casts a glorious pale crimson light over the unmistakable peaks and surrounding plains.

Located just a stone's throw from Barcelona, tourists flock here to visit the Benedictine Monastery tucked in amongst the cliffs. But the climbers come to fondle and conquer Montserrat's finest cobblestones. From a distance Montserrat looks like a seamless plateau, but on closer inspection the mountain is a haphazard assemblage of hundreds of spires, bulging buttresses and colossal cliffs. Navigating in and around the labyrinth of towers and cliffs makes for long approaches, intricate trail hopping, dead-ends and back-tracking. Getting lost is frustrating and almost expected considering the sheer complexity and enormity of the place. This is not a place that you can rush.

The conglomerate rock may be a phenomenon of nature, but for my first time it was simultaneously a wondrous and terrifying experience. Cobblestone craziness means that while you are marvelling at how your left fingers perfectly fit that unexpected pocket, your right hand is crushing a poor pebble to death because you are adamant that it's about to explode from its cement housing,

not to mention the alarming run-out and potential ground fall occurring below your waist. But keeping a cool head and having some faith in the cobbles can go a long way towards a successful ascent.

Montserrat was a cradle of Spanish climbing, this is reflected in its bold, old school nature. But like many of the world's notable areas, more recent developments reflect how 'the times they are a changing' and these days scores of well protected sport climbs are scattered throughout. In fact, the area offers a huge range of climbing styles. For lower angles and airy views the Gorros slabs and the blunted domes of Sant Benet are popular for their ease of access and relatively easy climbing. "Peak-baggers" search out the stand alone towers such as the immediately recognisable and sportingly bolted Cavall Bernat. And the purists may be found on the atmospheric big-walls of the Paret de l'Aeri, where many routes are over 300 metres long.

Montserrat may not be for everyone. It isn't the flavour of the month, it doesn't hog the spotlight like its trendy Catalunyan counterparts. But it is an old world classic offering superb climbing up amazing features on the demanding conglomerate. There are over 600 individual domes and several thousand routes here, so you could easily enjoy a lifetime exploring its every nook, pebble, and cranny.

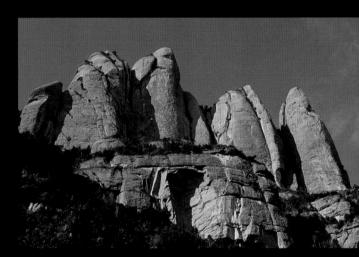

⬆ The Benedictine Monastery gives access to areas like Sant Benet and Gorros at the north east end of Montserrat.

⬆ The north wall of the Frares Encantas with (from left to right) the Novici, Frare Amadeu, Frare Gros, Asiatica and Miranda Del Lloro towers.

➡ Anders Lantz having faith in the pebbles of **Ni Teva Ni Meva** (6c+), on La Momia, Sant Benet.

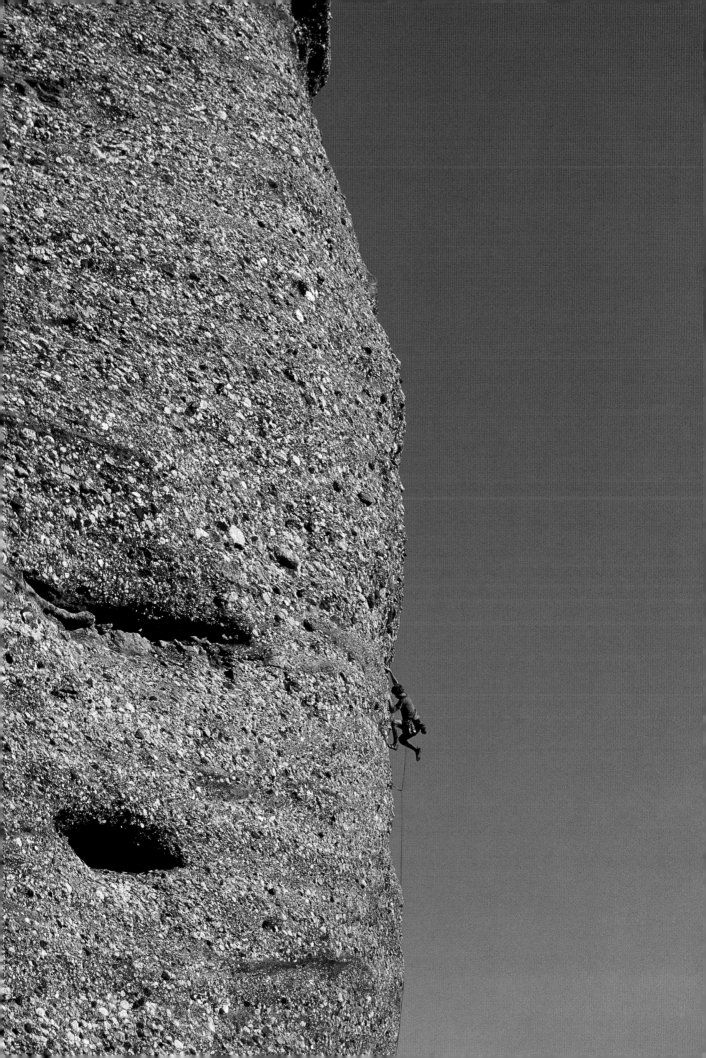

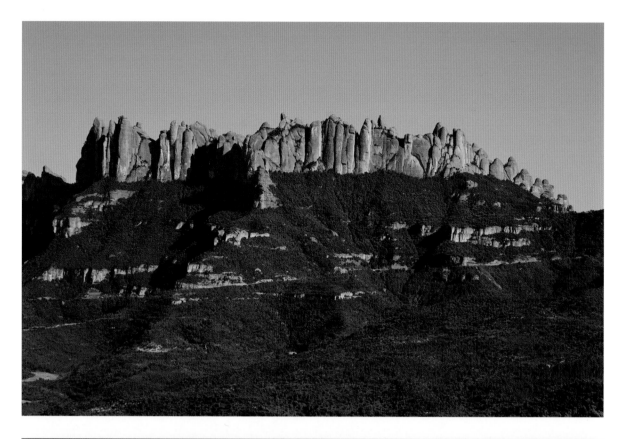

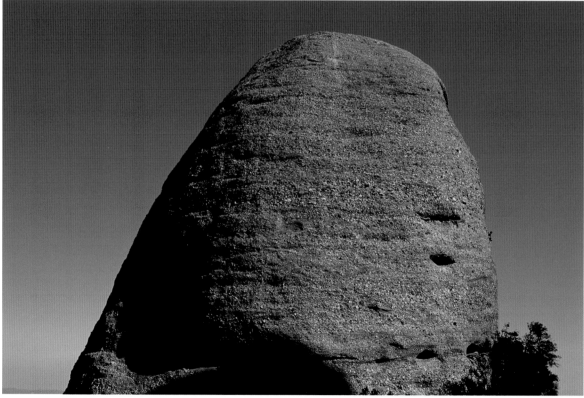

▲ The north face of the Agulles at the north west end of the plateau.

▲ Anders Lantz still believing and a bit higher up *Ni Teva Ni Meva* (6c+), on La Momia (The Mummy), Sant Benet.

→ Michiel Nieuwenhuijsen and Philipp Kessler on pitch four of *Perez-Verges* (7b+), 160m. The first few pitches are hidden behind the ridge.
   The formation is the "Cavall Bernat": Cavall means horse and we don't know what Bernat means but you can guess.

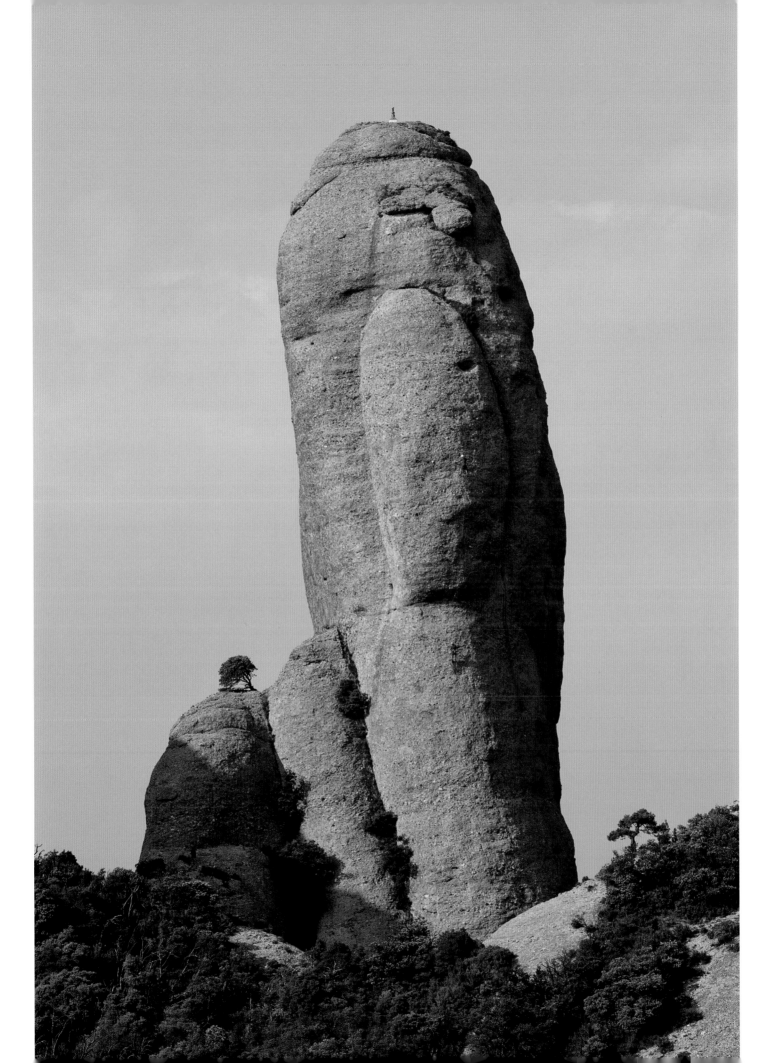

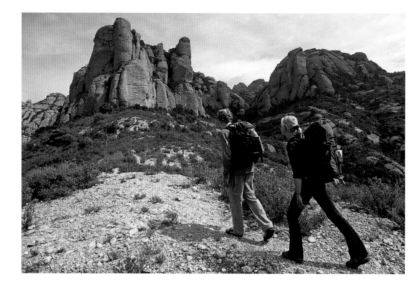

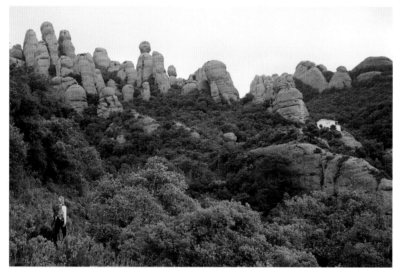

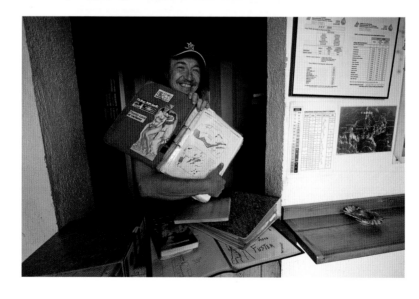

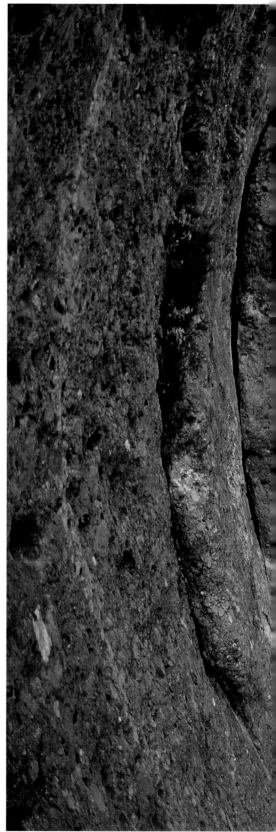

Hiking up to L'agulla del Senglar on Montserrat's south side.

And more hiking, this time up to Refugi Vicenç Barbé in La Agulles.

Hut warden Xavier "Harri" García presenting the topos at Refugi Vicenç Barbé.

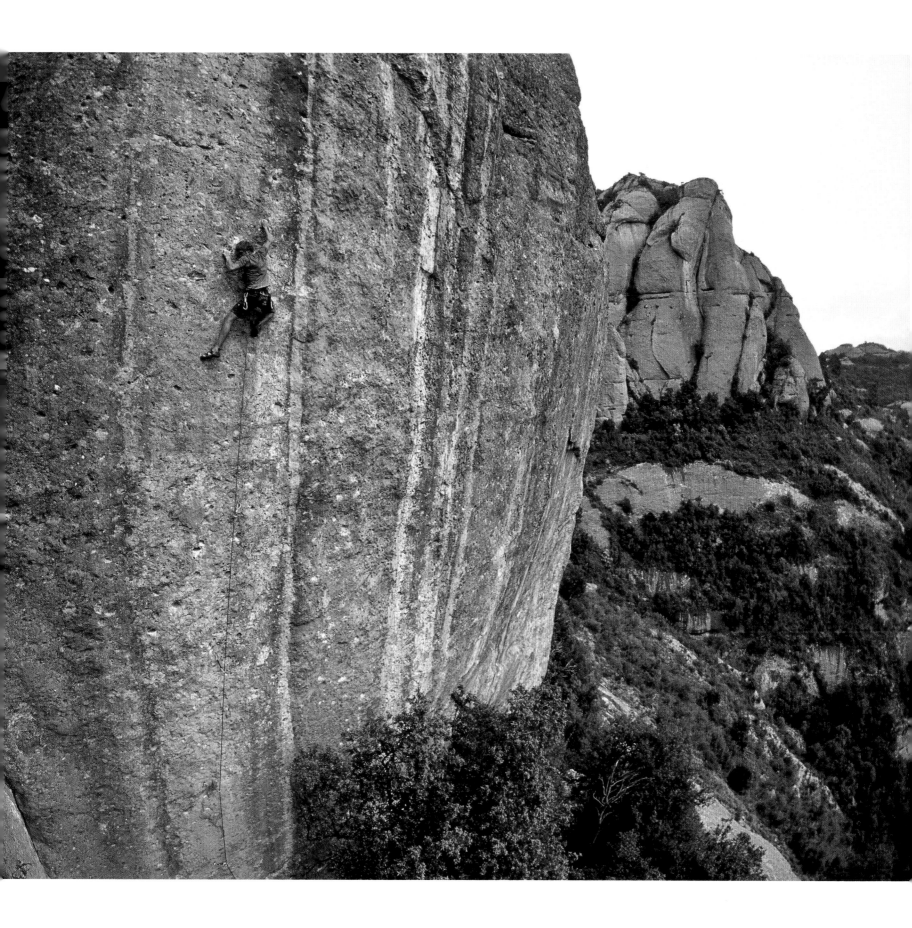

Anders Lantz on **Rush** (7c), at the popular sport sector L'agulla del Senglar.

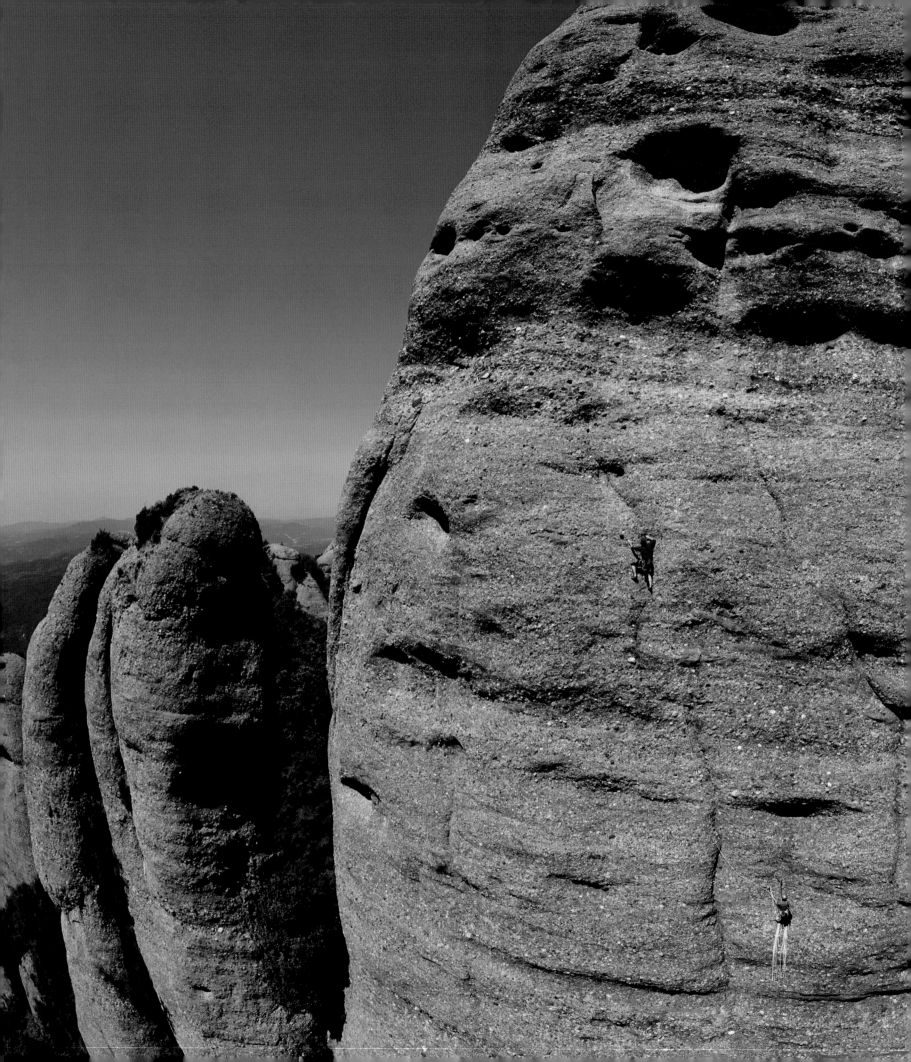

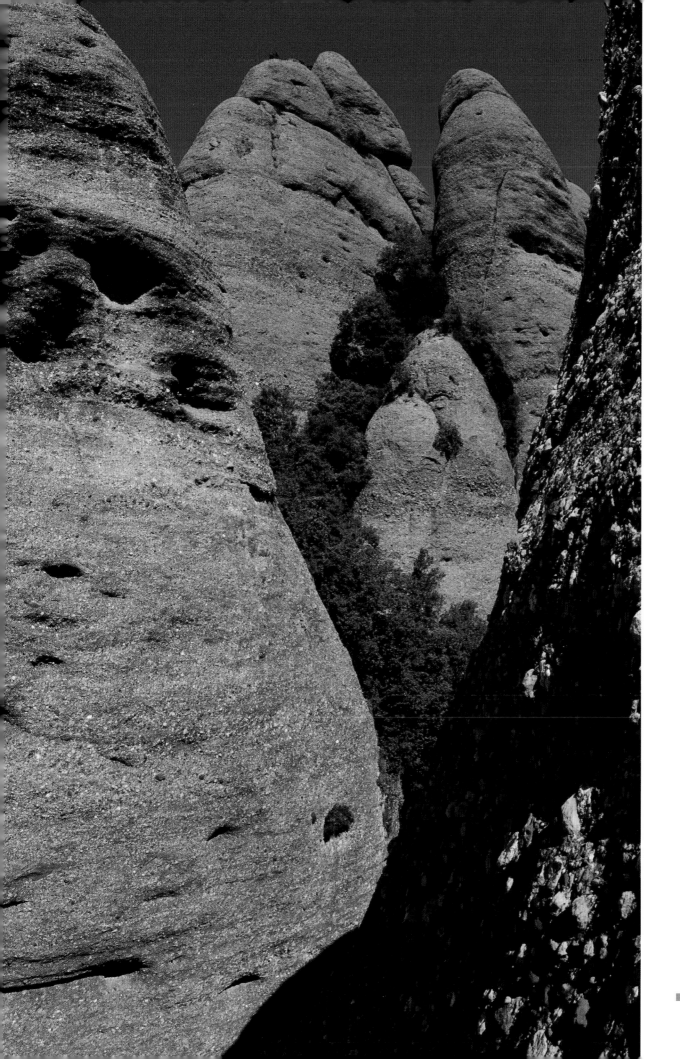

Xavier "Harri" García and Monique Forestier rocking a demanding **Baby** (7a+), four pitches, on Bessona Inferior, the Agulles.

A naked bather nearby is unaware of us until we start giggling like schoolgirls. My dear friend, Nadine Rousselot and I have been traversing, crab-like, just above the supralittoral zone on perfect albino limestone for four lovely pitches. It's hot as you would expect in mid June. I'm being cooked; my eyeballs are like fried eggs, and my feet, like sausages on a BBQ, are about to split and explode. Thankfully, we soon enter the shade, suspended under a roof, where the cool rock soothes my pains. I'd really like to hang around but the bombarding waves herald some urgency to complete the neat little adventure we'd started, *La Commune*.

Les Calanques is a 20 kilometre stretch of ragged rocky coastline extending east from Marseilles to Cassis. This sweep of white cliffs is riddled with deep bays called calanques, where those seeking secluded beaches can tether their yachts and marvel at the turquoise waters tickling the pebbly shores. Above is open parkland, with well trodden paths along cliff-tops or out to promontories, both offering flamboyant views over the Mediterranean Sea.

Les Calanques has seen its heyday and perhaps it's not as trendy or chic as its younger relations now enjoying the limelight: Céüse, Gorges du Tarn or St Leger. But keep in mind it's an area where French modern climbing evolved and countless routes have stood the test of time to become à la mode classics. Consider the old school romp *Arête de Marseille* (5c) on La Grande Candelle. While you bridge between the spire and the main peak with nothing but giddying nothingness all around, remember that this perfect passage was established way back in 1927.

To really squeeze the most out of Les Calanques you can combine its natural beauty with its climbing delights. At En Vau, enjoy the pleasures of multi-pitching knowing that a tantalising swim awaits nearby. At Goudes, take a wild ride along the lip of its cave and be marinated in the sun as it slips toward the horizon. La Triperie's vanilla white cliffs lining the inside of a horseshoe showcase super-technical climbing high above the shimmering sea. And there's no better way to get wet than with some deep-water soloing, being swallowed up by the soothing aquamarine depths is mild punishment for a failed attempt.

The area harbours thousands, not hundreds, of climbs. All aspects of the compass are covered, offering climbing either in or out of the sun. There is a cosmopolitan blend of climbing options, grades and styles on offer. Old routes, and new. So whatever your climbing fascination, enjoy the opulent menu on offer at Les Calanques.

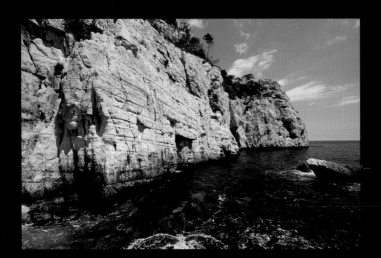

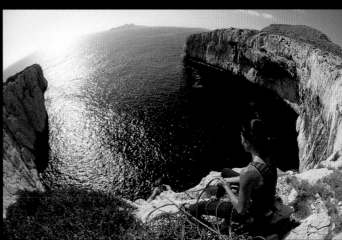

The nine pitch traverse *La Commune* (6b) starts here and finishes up the buttress in the background.

The horseshoe cliffs of La Triperie with Chloé Minoret belaying atop *Chipsy King*.

Chloé Minoret on *Chipsy King* (7a), at La Triperie, near the end of Cape Morgiou.

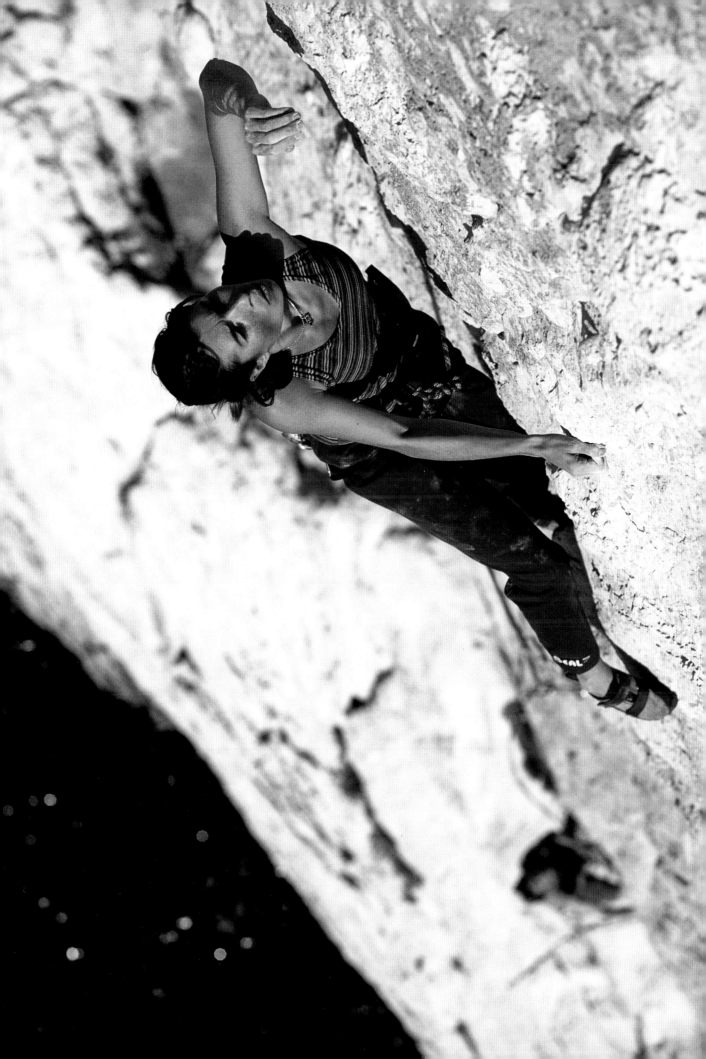

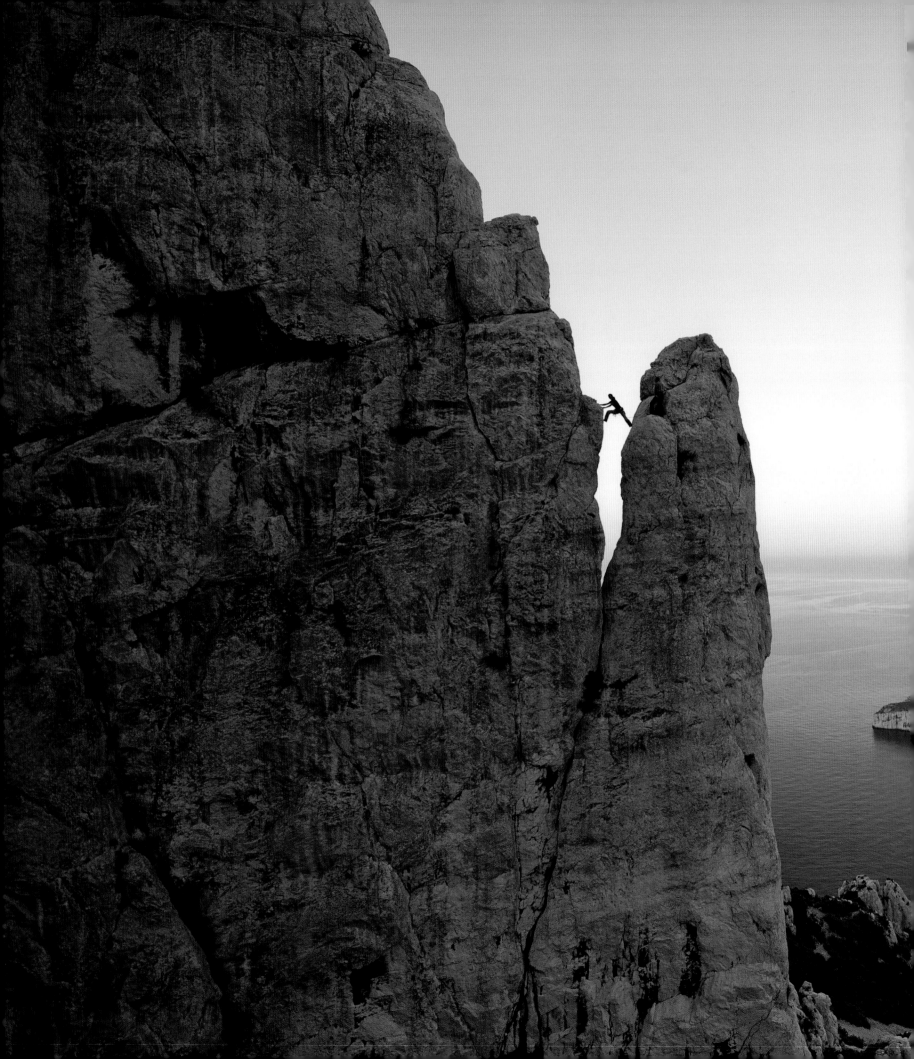

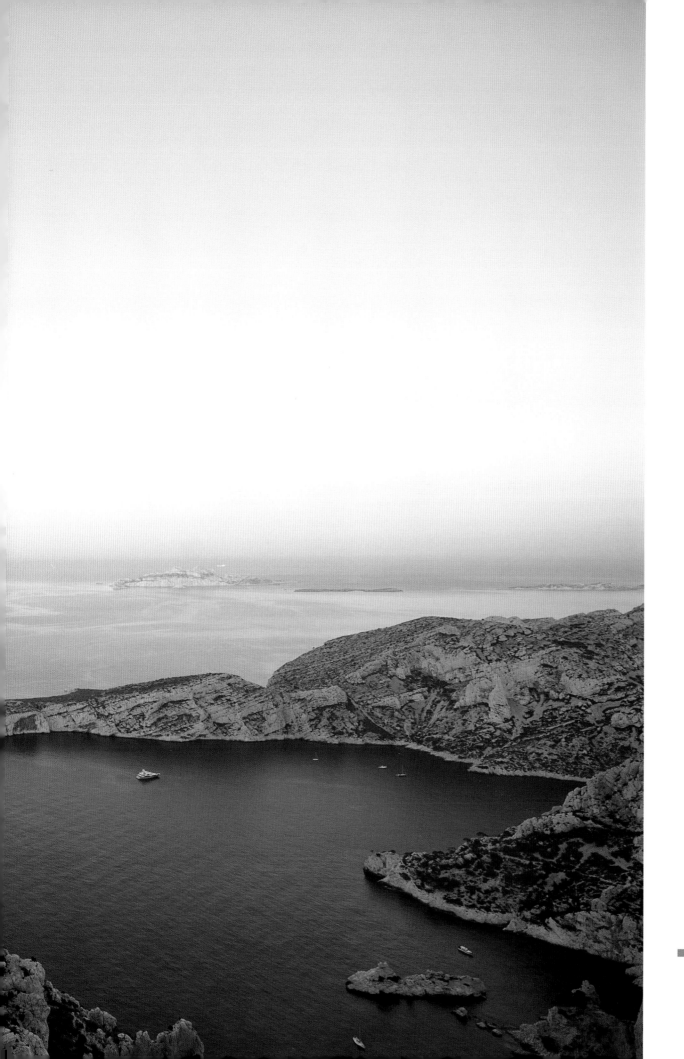

What a great way to start the day. As first light hits the islands Nadine Rousselot and Mathieu Geoffray have already dispensed with the one hour approach and the first pitch of the timeless classic **Arête de Marseille** (5c), five pitches, on La Grande Candelle. Cape Morgiou in the background.

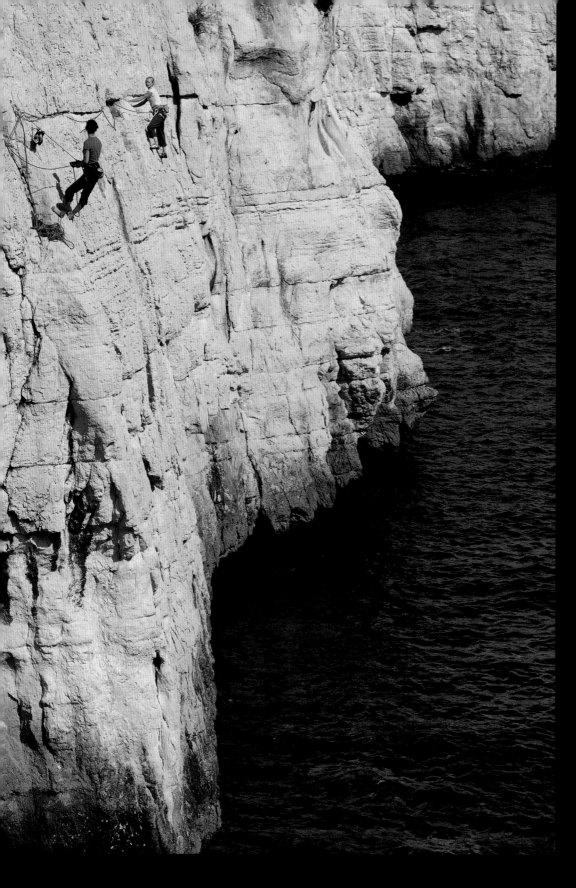
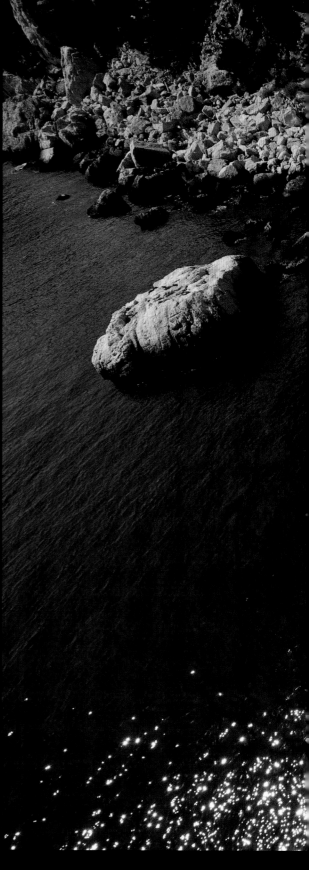

⬆ Monique Forestier and Nadine Rousselot scurrying across the second pitch of **La Commune** (6b).

➡ Nadine Rousselot exiting on the ninth (and final) pitch of **La Commune**. The route starts from the rocky "beach" in the background.

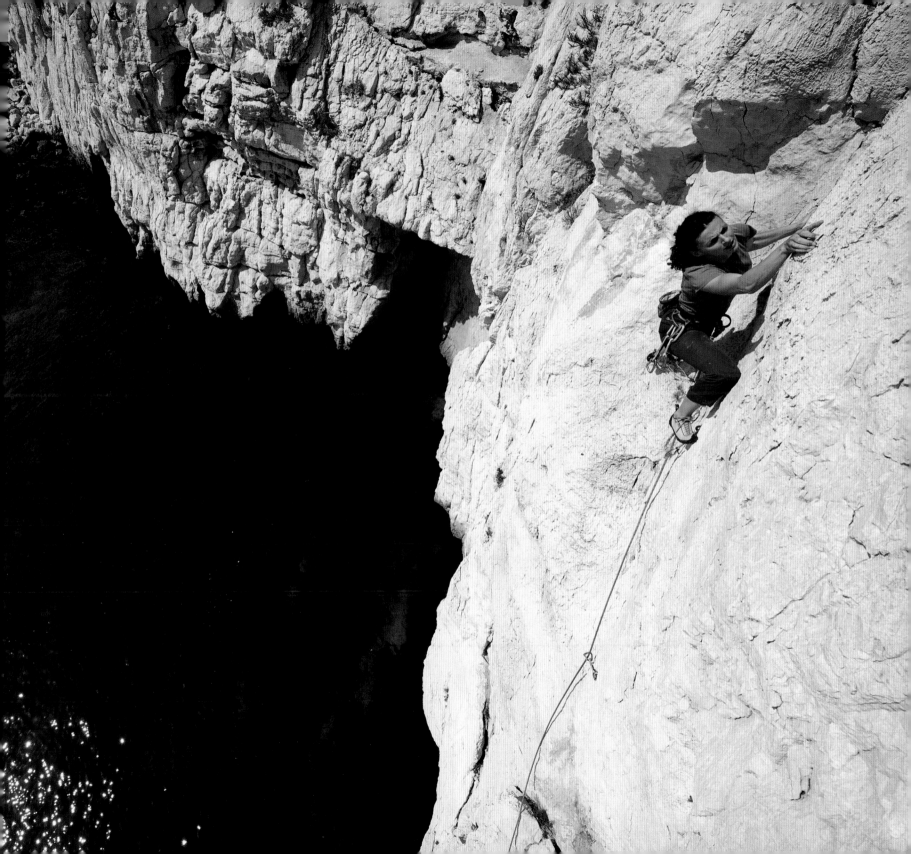

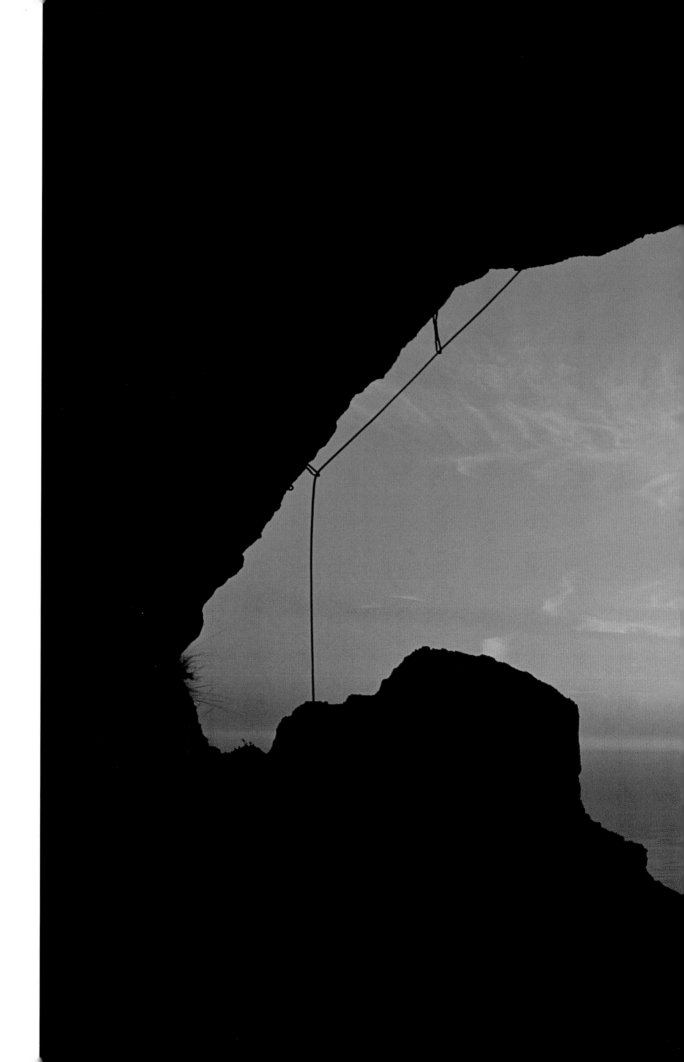

Chloé Minoret sneaking in one last burn for the day on *Le Denti* (7c+), Goudes.

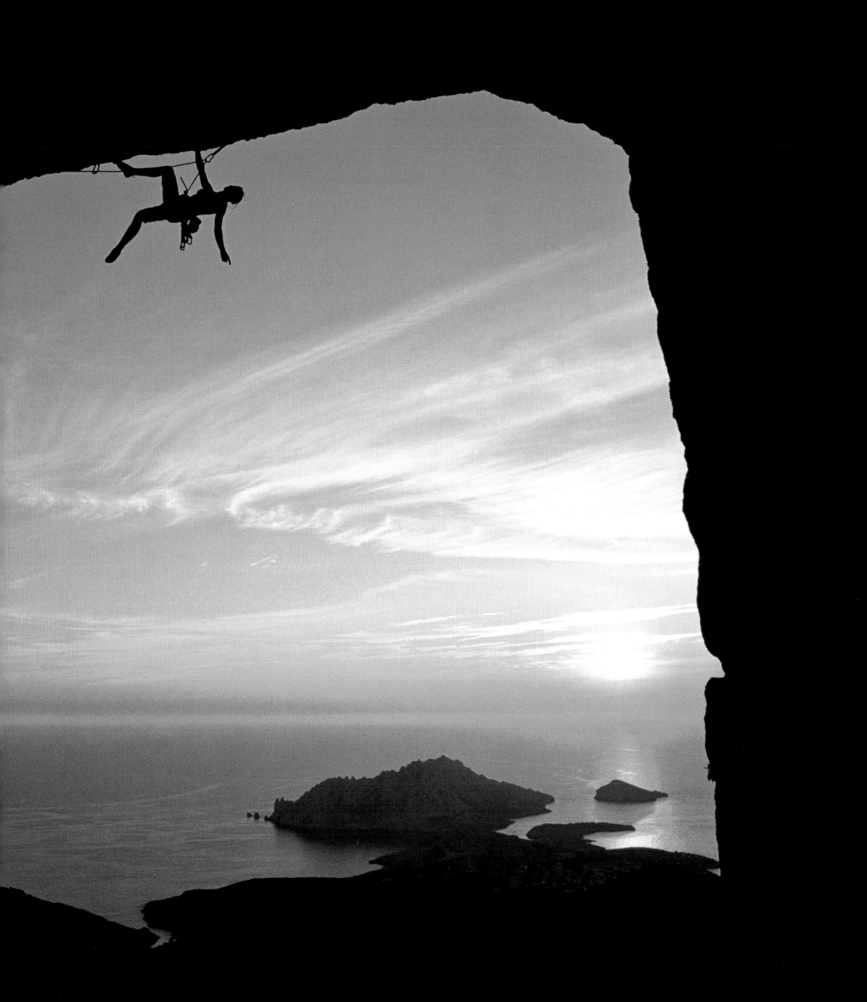

DOLOMITES

The almighty Dolomites are as intimidating as they are enticing, yet surprisingly they accommodate a broad spectrum of climbers. With dizzying peaks, some over 3000 metres, it's notorious for gutsy big-wall adventures on stammering cliffs. Alternatively, rising from alpine meadows, rocky outcrops support less committing multi-pitch escapades, some acrobatic sport routes, and even a bit of bouldering. As if in a vast orchard, you can be choosey and only select the juiciest plums — the five star mega classics on a three star scale. Be whimsical or, if pressed for time, simply pick what's within reach.

Situated in northern Italy, the mighty 'pale' mountains are split into 'groups' of peaks stitched together by a network of zig-zag roads. Centrally located, the Sella Pass can be described as the aorta of the Dolomites, pumping thousands of cars through its trajectory each day. From the Sella Pass, take your pick from the Sella Group for dicey multi-pitching where the clang of your trad rack and rockfall harmonises with the sound of cowbells from the pastures below. Or across the way, the Sassolungo Group offers some wilder excursions including the memorable 580-metre traverse of the *Il Punta della Cinque Dita*. And down in the valley lie the modern sport climbing areas of Cansla and Pian de Schiavaneis and the steep bouldering of Città dei Sassi. But remember, Sella Pass is just a fraction of the area, offering only some of the delights that make the Dolomites one of Europe's superlative alpine rock climbing areas.

On the longer routes the rock, gear, route finding, weather and complicated descents make the Dolomites a serious place to climb.

If you find yourself feeling strung out here, then it's perhaps little consolation that you'll not be the first — or last — to feel that way. Perhaps in an effort to delay the white-knuckled terror that inevitably awaits, we chose the Cinque Torri as our warm up to the area. Its short multi-pitch routes and quick access makes this a relatively low commitment option. A standout here is *Finlandia* with its five stylish pitches slashing the prominent face of the Torre Grande, the gear is good and the air is sweet with alpenrose.

Now a serene playing field hosting numerable activities like skiing, hiking, cycling, and climbing, the Dolomites was once the contrary, a place where fierce battles took place between the Austria-Hungary and Italian armies in the Great War. The extensive web of trenches and embattlements that can still be seen today are evidence of this horrific and ultimately futile war of attrition. The Dolomites is also saturated in climbing history; rock climbing has been practiced here for over one hundred years. You can almost hear the stories whispering from the cracks and crevices as you climb past.

After two weeks we had garnered a tasty sampler — with delicious apples from Cinque Torri, apricots from the Tofana, plums from the Sella Towers, a succulent peach from Sassolungo and voluptuous blueberries from the Vajolet Towers. We had whet our appetite to try the main feast because, of course, no Dolomite compote would be complete without the long ultra-classics from the South Face of the Marmolada and the Tre Cime di Lavaredo. However, it wasn't to be this trip, but we have got plenty to return for.

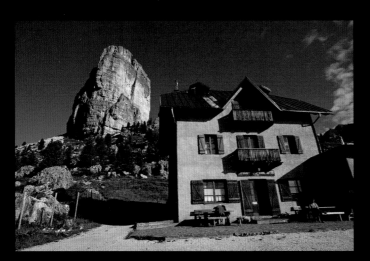

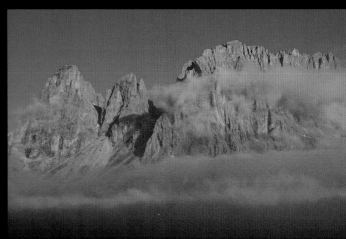

⬆ Cinque Torri Rifugio with Torre Grande behind.

↗ A view of the Sassolungo Group with the Punta delle Cinque Dita (Five Finger Towers) left of centre.

➡ Klemen Keižar on *Per Elisa* (6b+), one of the accessible sport routes at Cinque Torri.

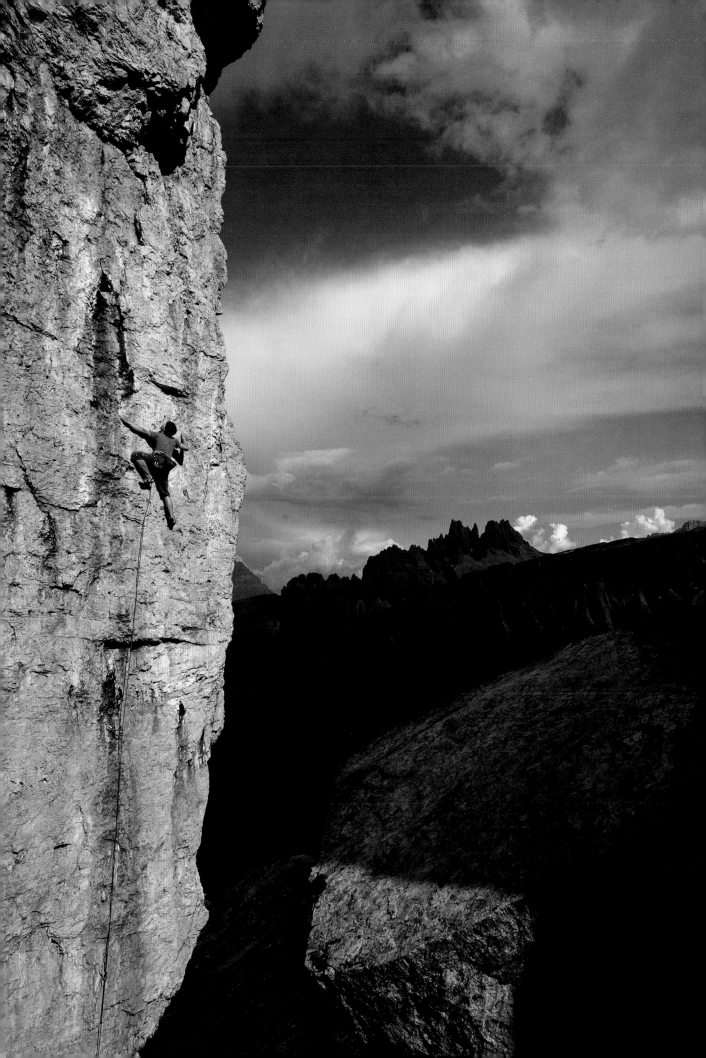

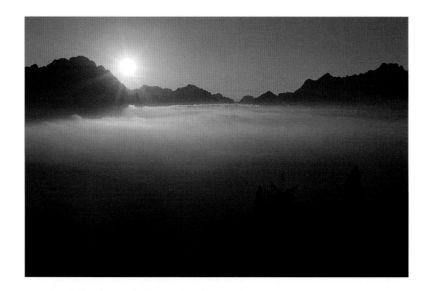

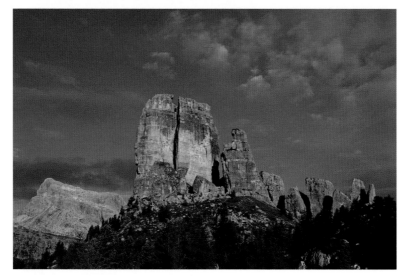

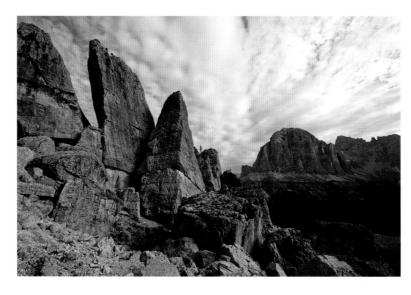

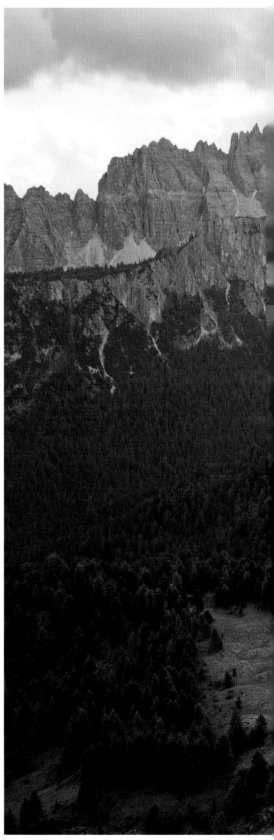

Dawn from Cinque Torri (Five Towers).

The Cinque Torri Group. There are more than five towers in the group despite one collapsing in 2004.

A view from the Cinque Torri to Tofana di Rozes.

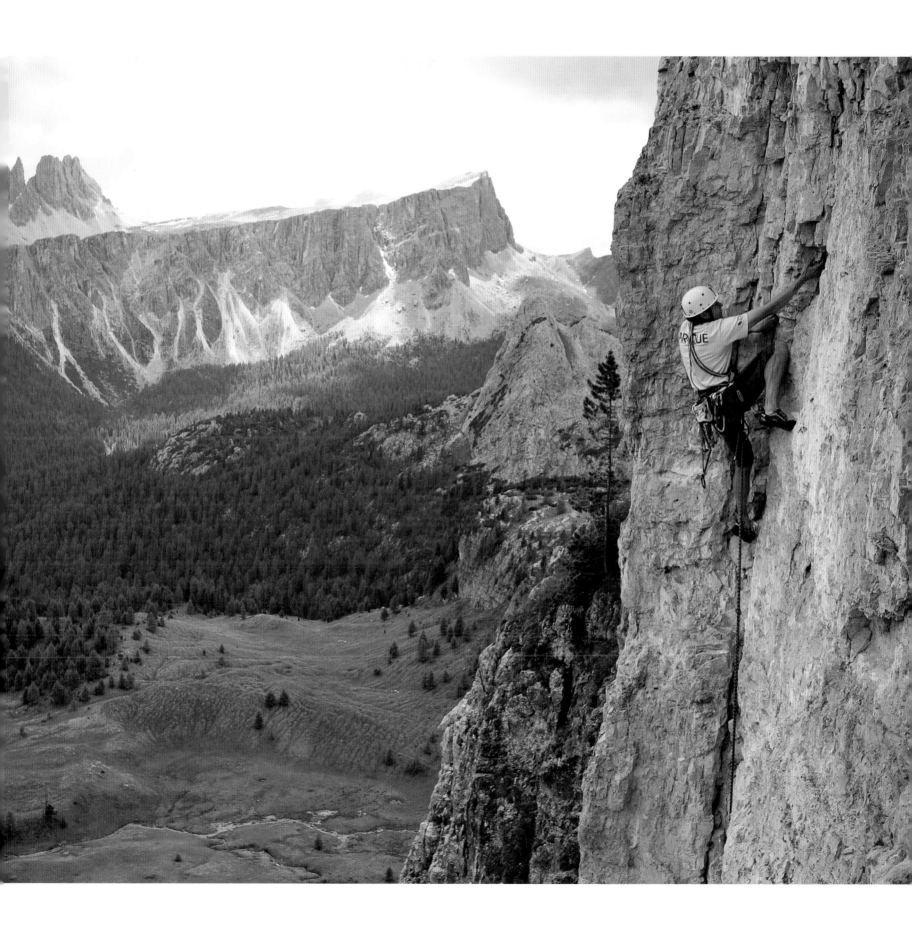

⬆ Michael Schön picking his way up pitch two of the delicious **Via Finlandia** (6b), four pitches, on Torre Grande, Cinque Torri Group (with the Croda da Lago mountains in the background).

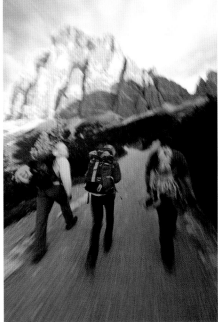

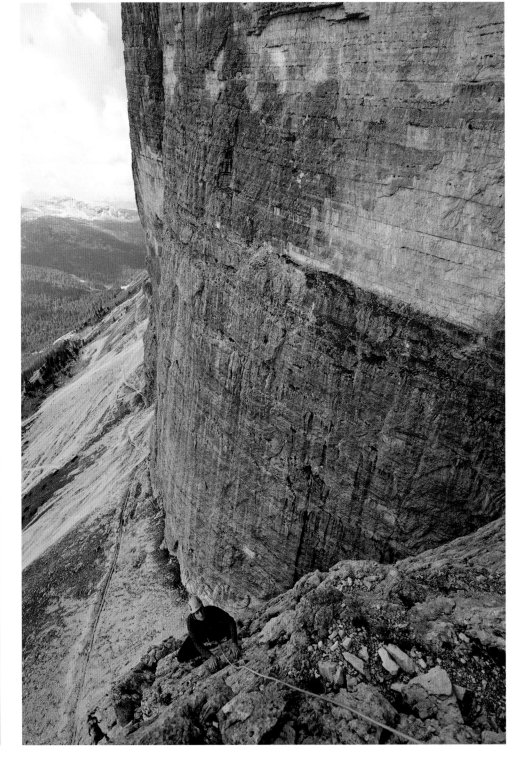

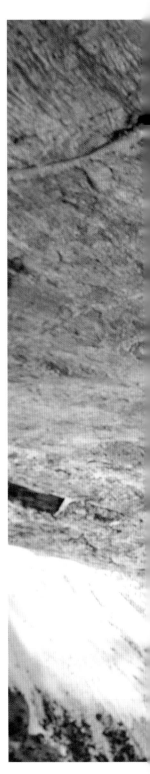

⬆ Early morning dash to get pole position on the **South Arête Route** (UIAA grade V+),
380 metres (14 pitches), on the South Face Buttress of Tofana di Rozes, Tofana Group.

↗ Dave Russell selecting holds on pitch five of the **South Arête Route**.

➡ Rico Miledi topping the terrific tenth pitch of the **South Arête Route**.

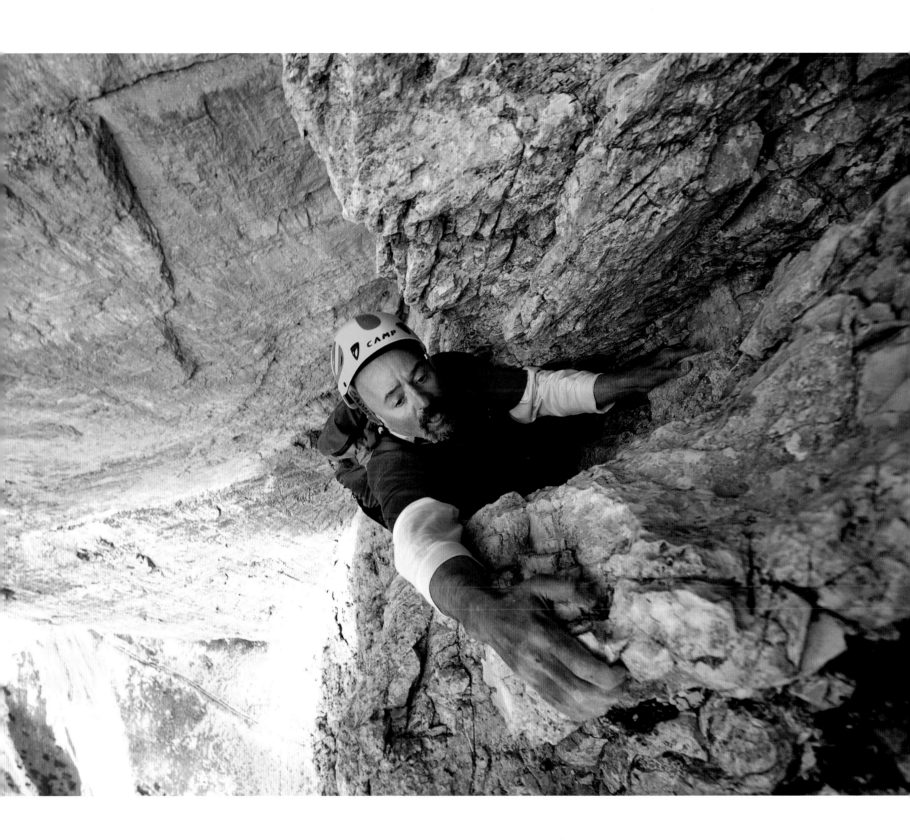

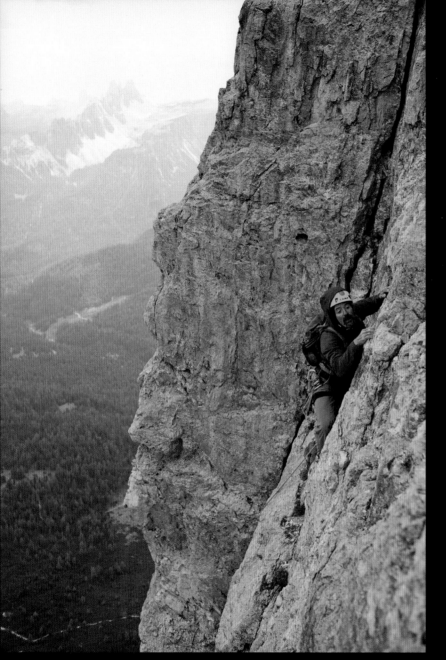

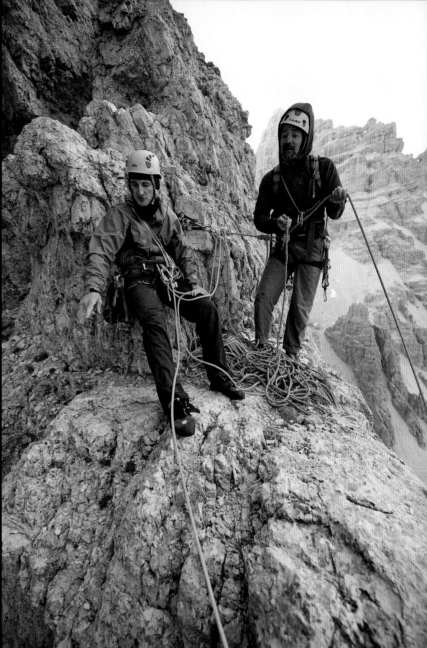

⬆ A couple of pitches higher. Rico Miledi on pitch twelve of the **South Arête Route**.

↗ We climbed in two parties of two. Atop the twelth pitch of the **South Arête Route,** Dave and Rico scope out their next adventure.

▶ As storm clouds brew at 2pm, Monique Forestier and Micky Mouse top out on the **South Arête Route**.

▶ The hike off is no time to let your guard down.

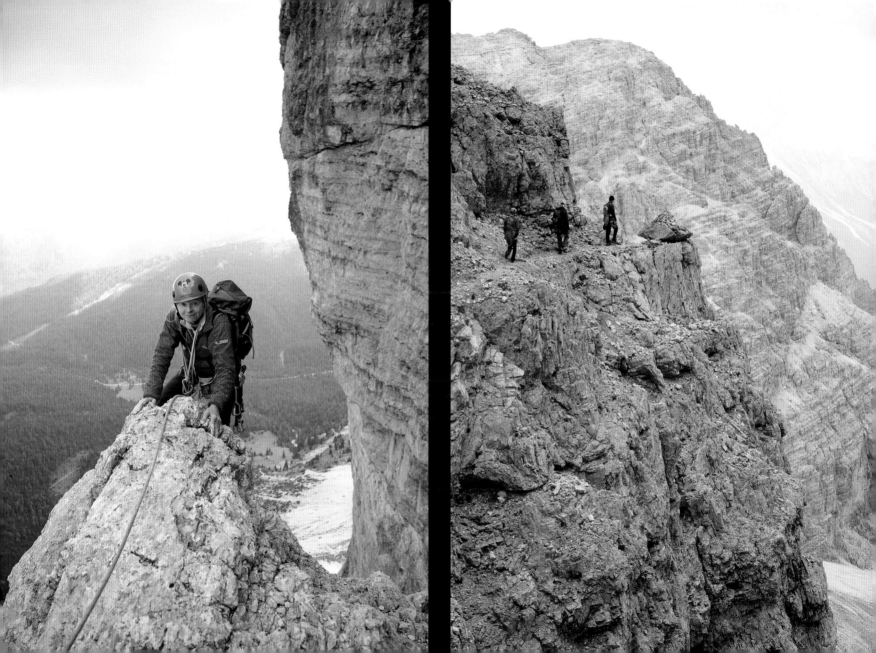

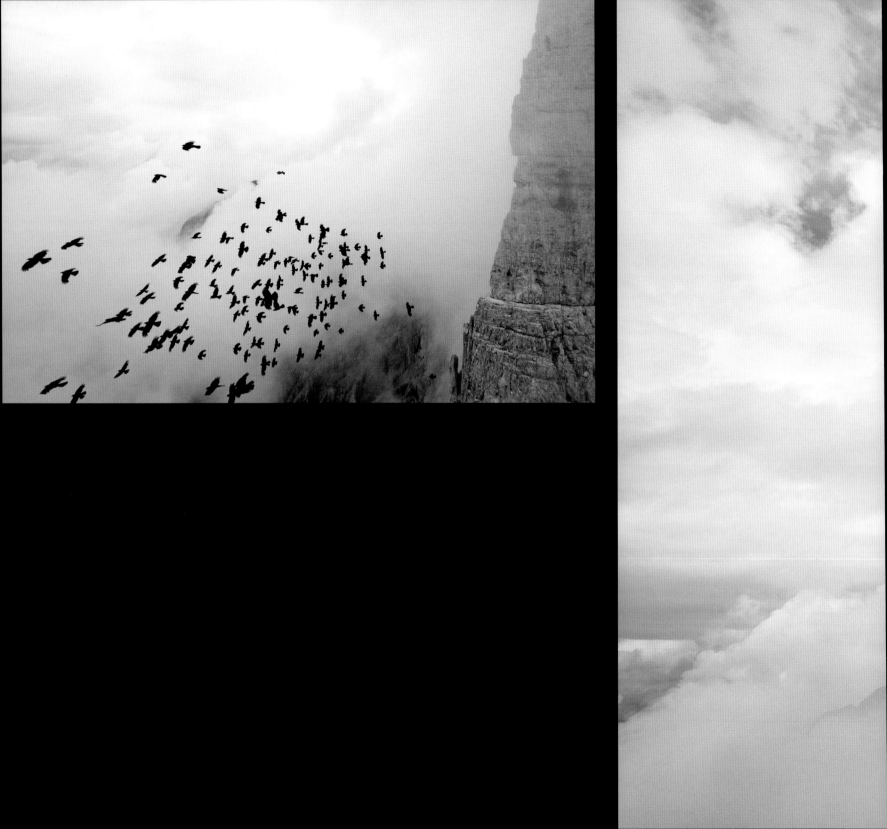

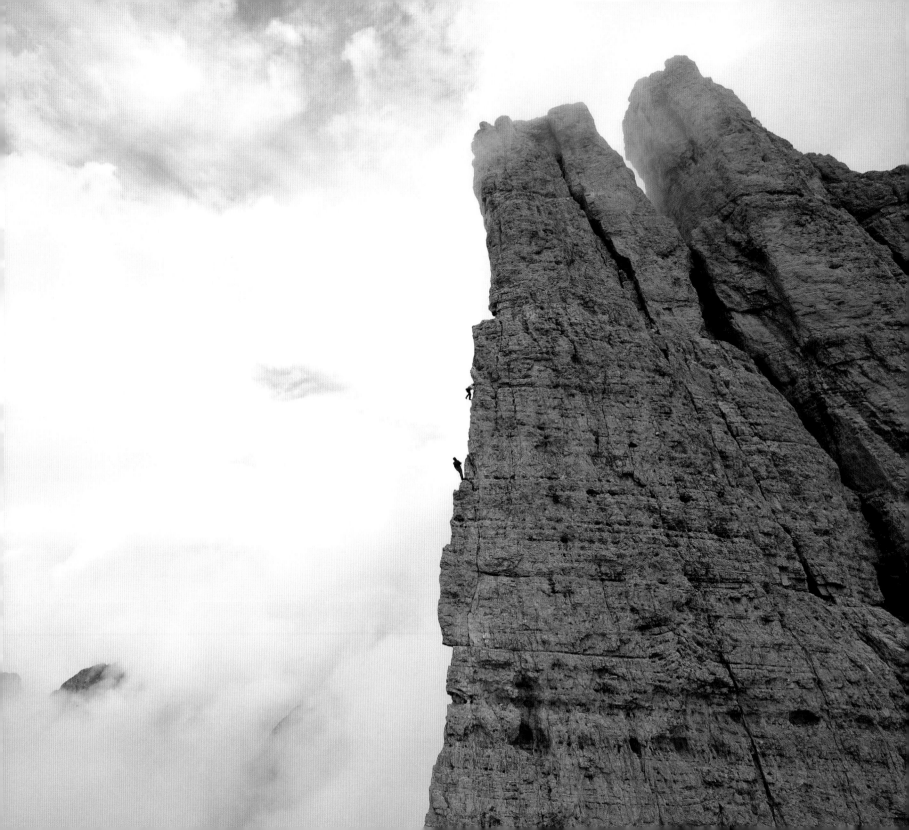

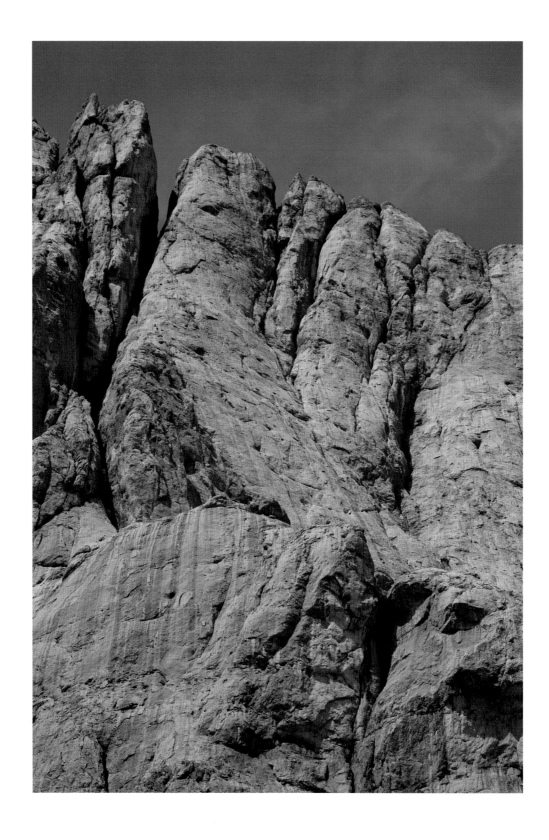

⬆ Hard to see but there are three teams of climbers on **Don Quixote** (VI), 750m (21 pitches), on the south
face of the Marmolada. The route tackles the rounded left prow of the large (second highest) buttess.

➡ Monique Forestier on pitch nine of the **Il Punta delle Cinque Dita Traverse** (IV), in the Sassolungo
Group. The route is 205m to the "Thumb" and the entire traverse of all five fingers is 580m.

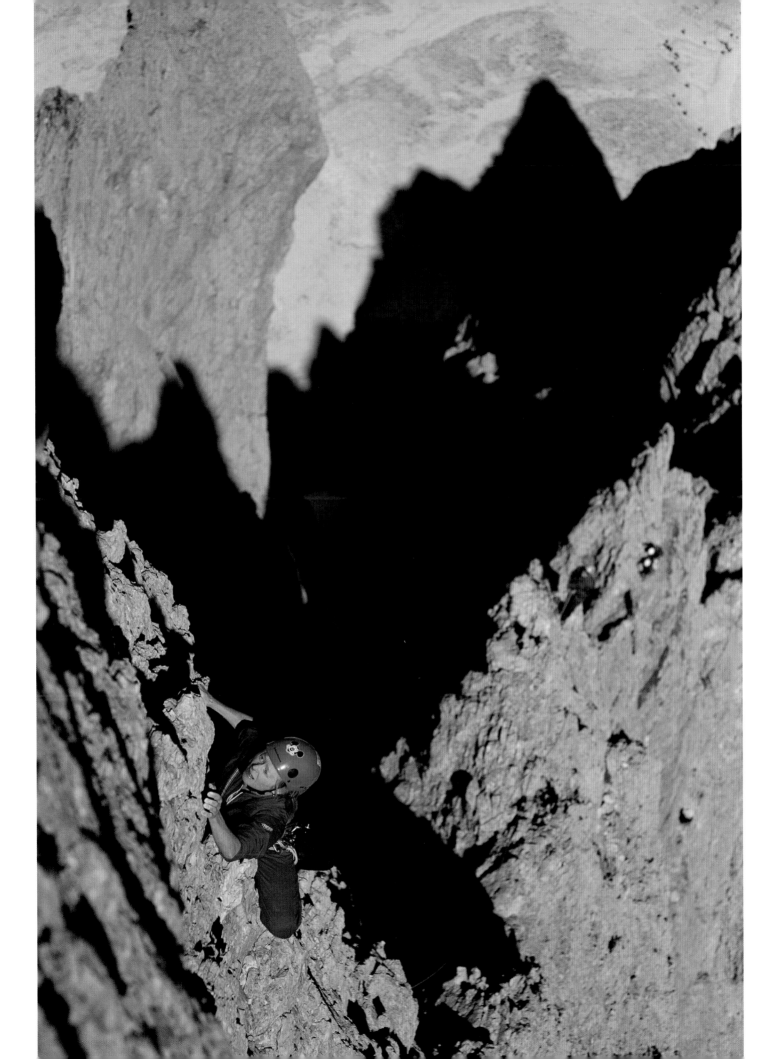

quality limestone, spread over 64 unique sectors each with its own breathtaking view over the Aegean. To complete the package are the short approaches, delectable restaurants, swish studios, idyllic (well, rocky) beaches and an international melting-pot of climbers. The only thing missing is having more time, that is for sure.

For one of the world's great climbing hot spots, Kalymnos is relatively a new kid on the block. The first routes were developed by Italian climber Andrea di Bari and friends in 1997 when they opened 43 routes. A couple of magazine articles later, word was out and the ensuing frenzied development quickly put this place on the climbing world map.

the soft morning light, you watch the shadows lengthen, and the end of your climbing day is marked by the glowing orange sun melting into the sea behind it. Telendos has incredible new route potential on big cliffs but, with so much to do on Kalymnos, the ten-minute ferry ride has been enough to slow development until recently. Now Telendos has several sectors ready and rearing to go along with some moderate multi-pitch sport routes — which complement the range of other worldly experiences.

Inevitably our time in the promised land was up. We checked our bags and walked back through the airport doors. When those pearly gates shut behind me, I realised I had just returned to earth.

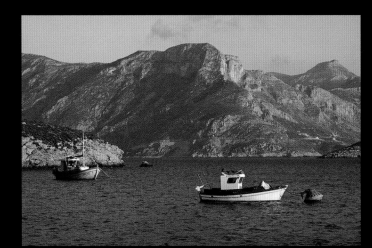

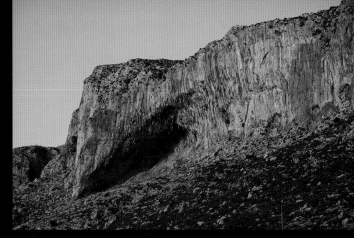

⬆ A view from the town of Emporios.

↗ The uber steep stalactite ridden Grande Grotta.

➡ Simon Montmory starting up **Typhoon** (7c), Crystal Cave, Telendos Island.

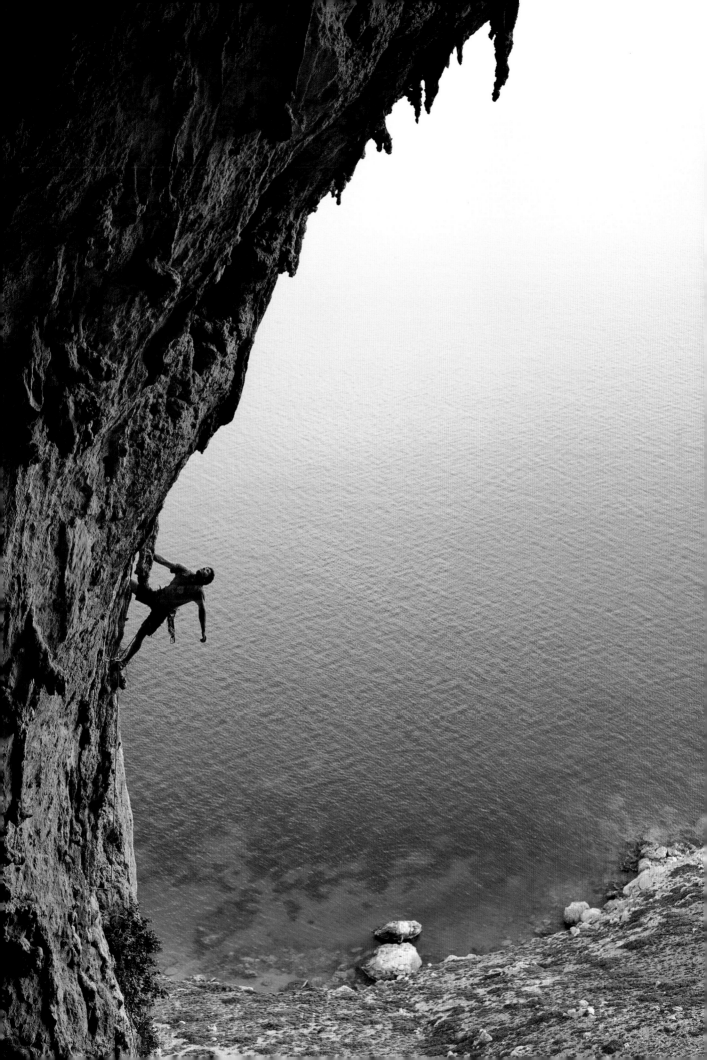

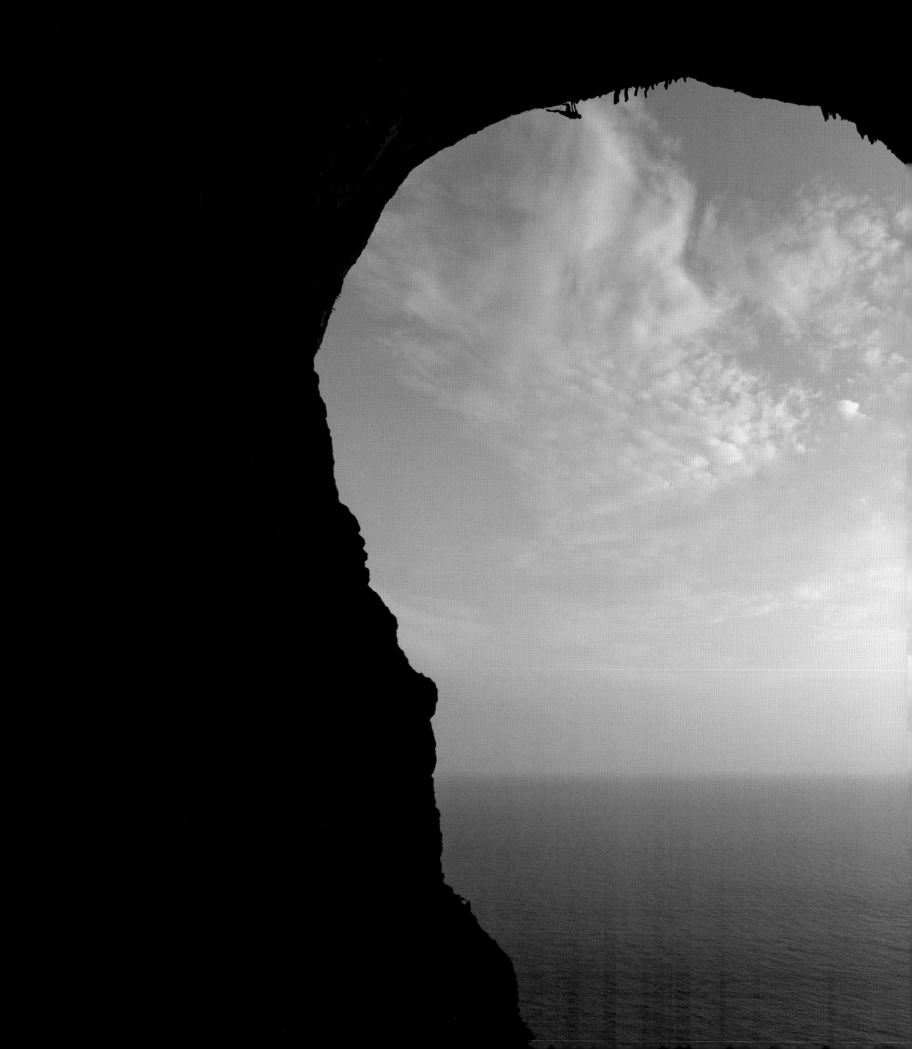

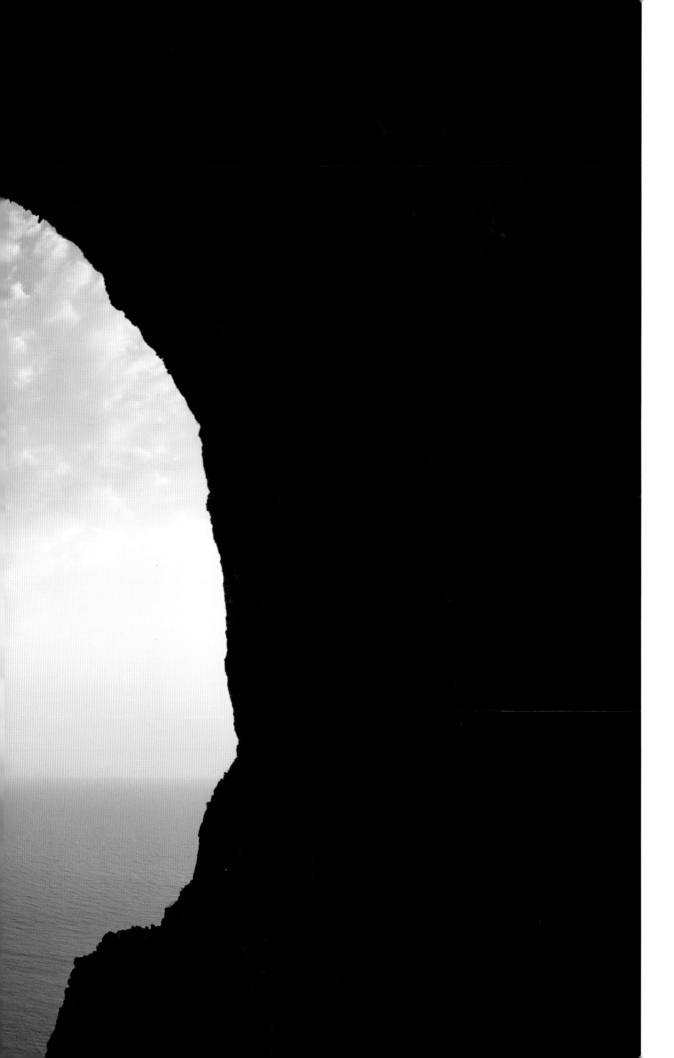

Simon Montmory high on *Typhoon* (7c),
Crystal Cave, Telendos Island. It's a big
cave, you need a 100-metre rope to
lower-off these routes.

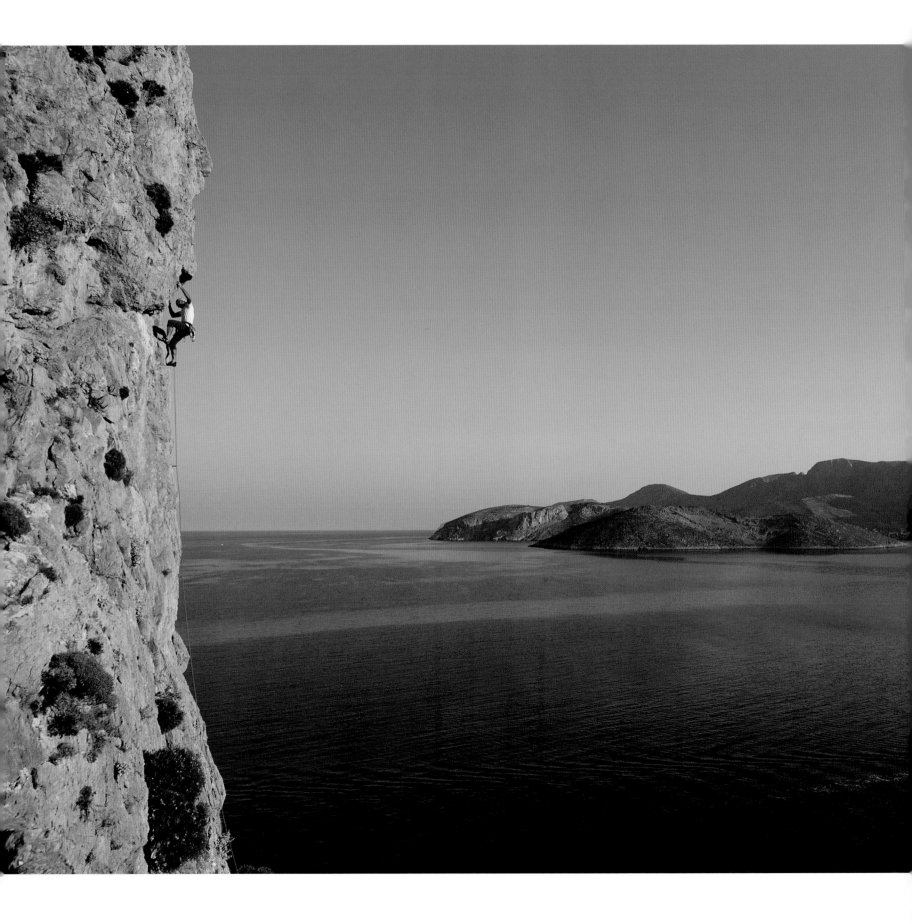

Claude Remy taking a break from new routing for *Pillar of the Sea* (6a+), Kasteli.

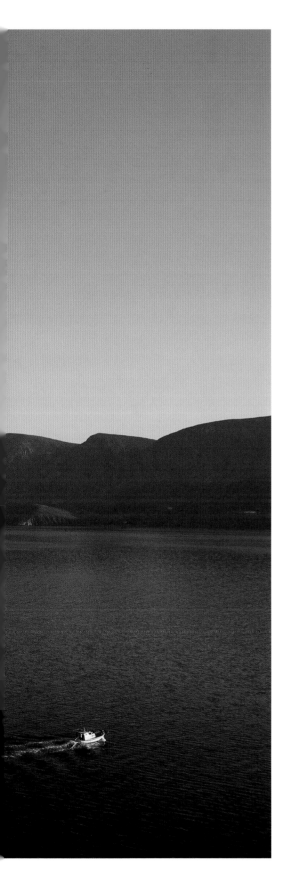

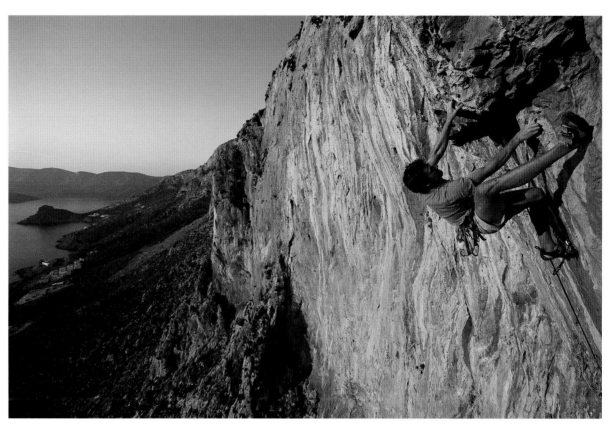

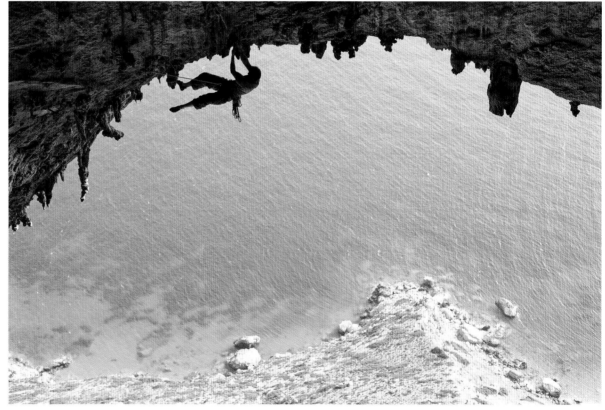

⤊ Simon Montmory working his project which later became **Trous dans l'air** (8b+), sector Kalydna.

⤊ Olivier Michellod sorting through the stalactites high up in Crystal Cave for an onsight of **Es Pontas** (7c), Telendos Island.

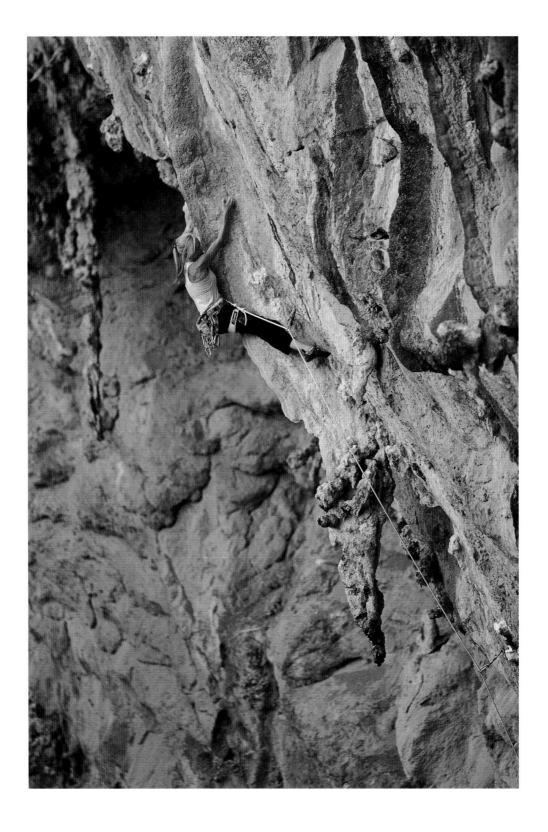

⬆ Ride ´em cowgirl! Monique Forestier onsighting **Laurent... y´ a quelue´ un** (7c+) at Sikati Cave.

➡ Maja Vidmar lapping out on the extraordinarily sustained 40-metre pumper **Fun de Chichunne** (8a) in the Grande Grotta.

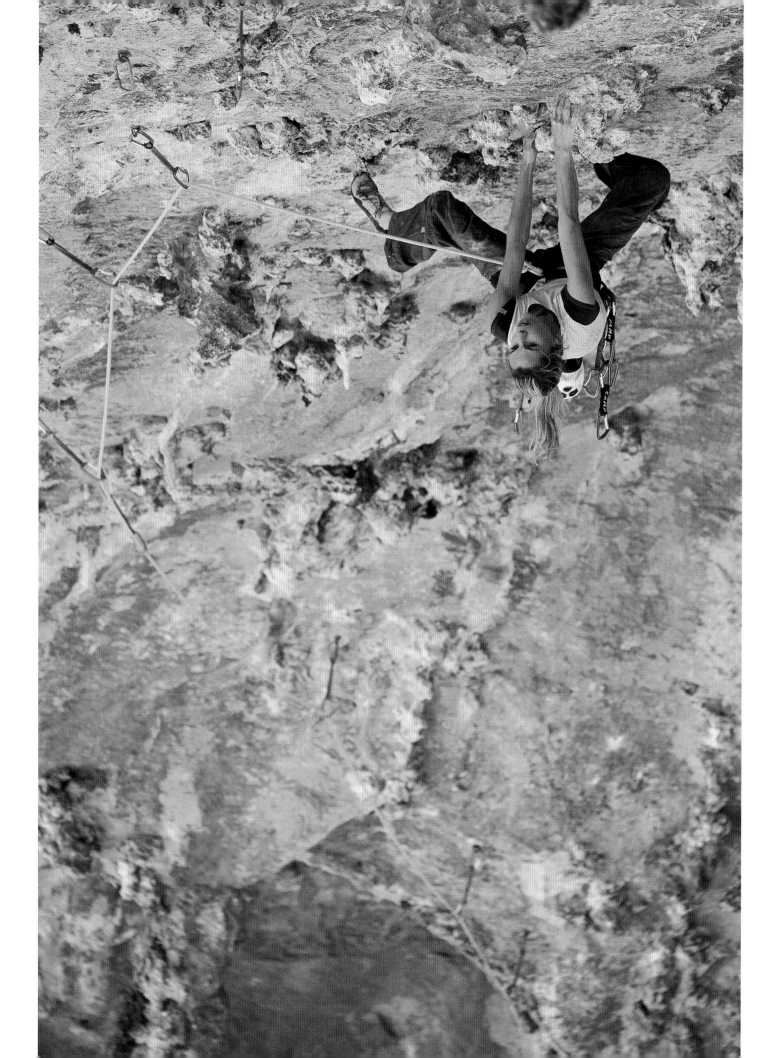

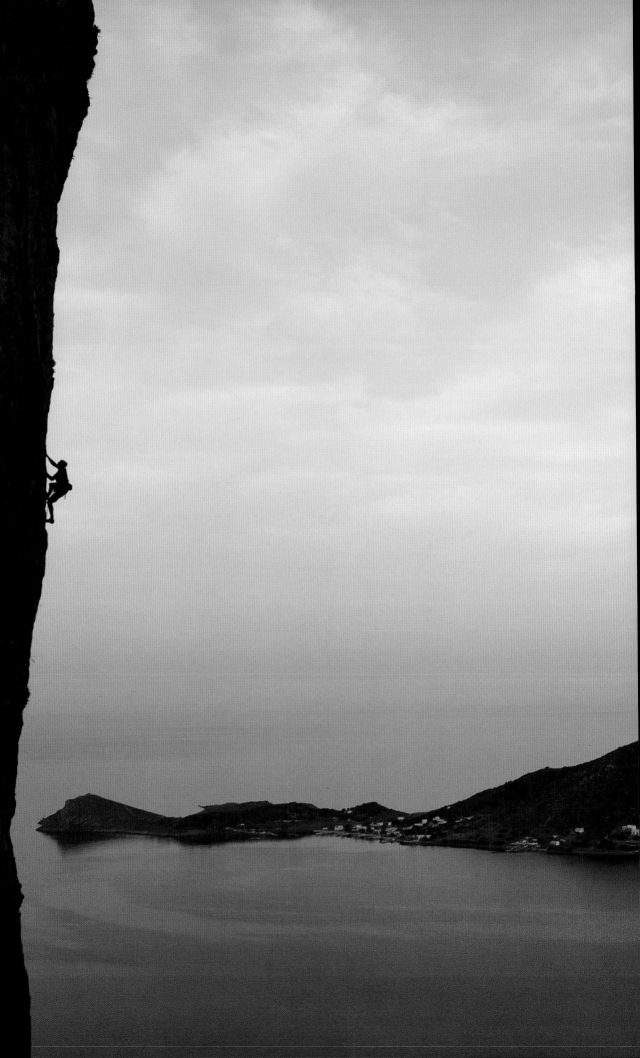

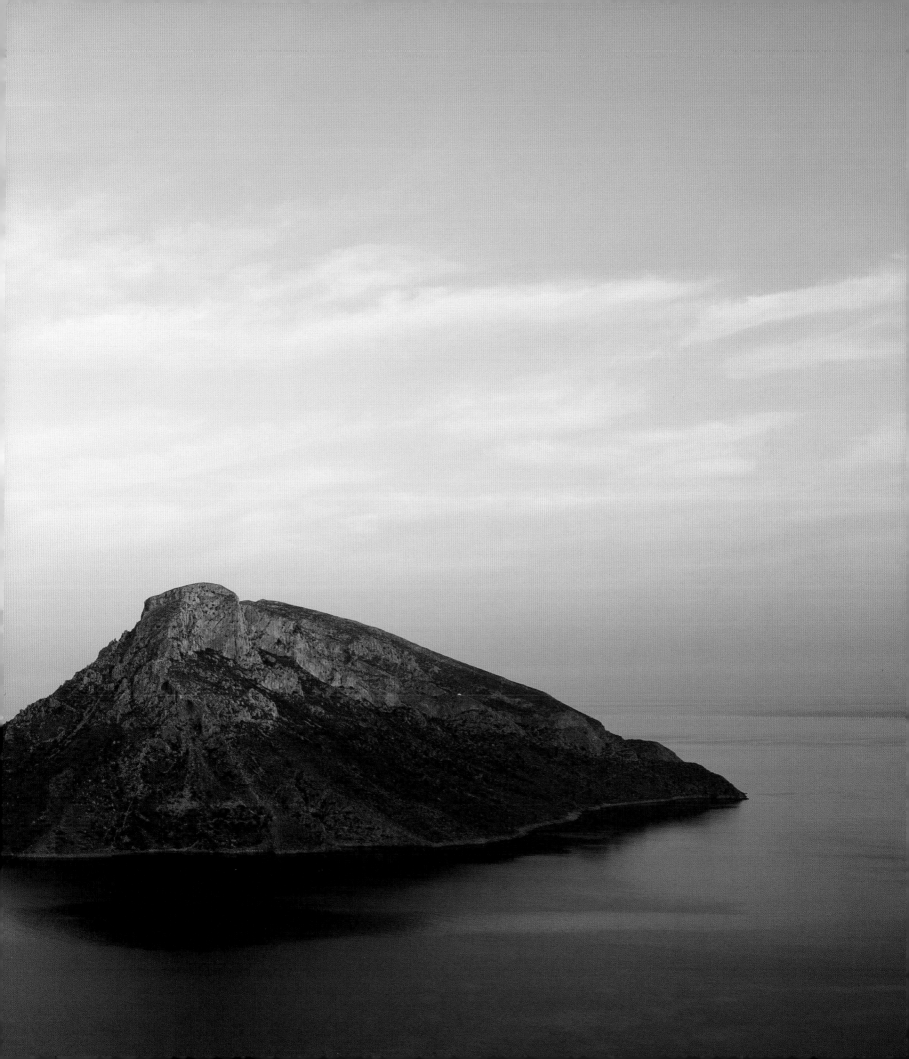

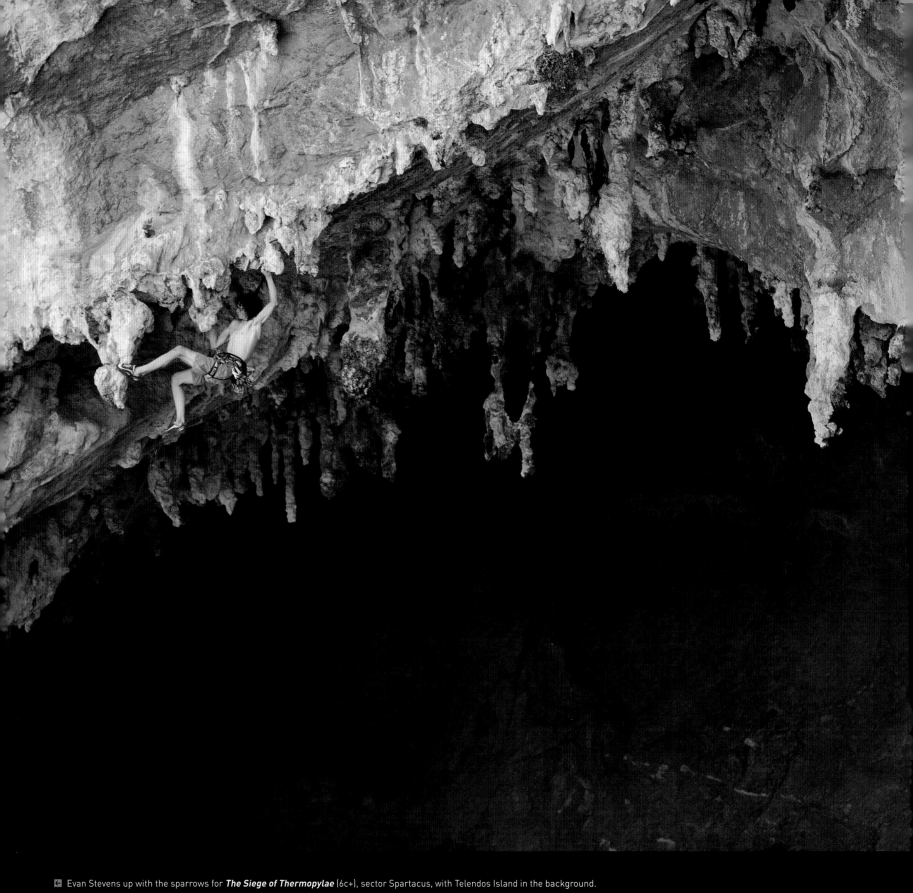

◄ Evan Stevens up with the sparrows for **The Siege of Thermopylae** (6c+), sector Spartacus, with Telendos Island in the background.

↑ Adam Ondra flashing **Jaws** (8c) whilst putting the draws on, Sikati Cave.

⤵ Earlier the same day, Adam Ondra making the first ascent of the hardest route in Greece: **Los Revolucionários** (9a) at sector Odyssey.

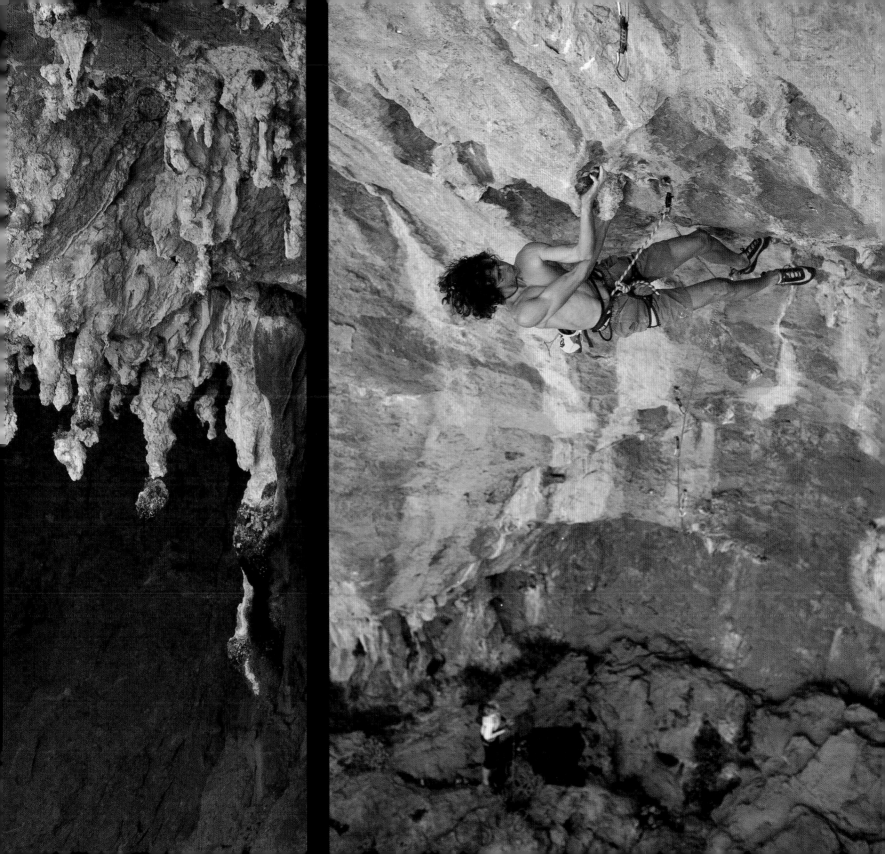

Evan Stevens weaving his way through
the Grande Grotta's stalactite jungle,
on *Priapos* (7c).

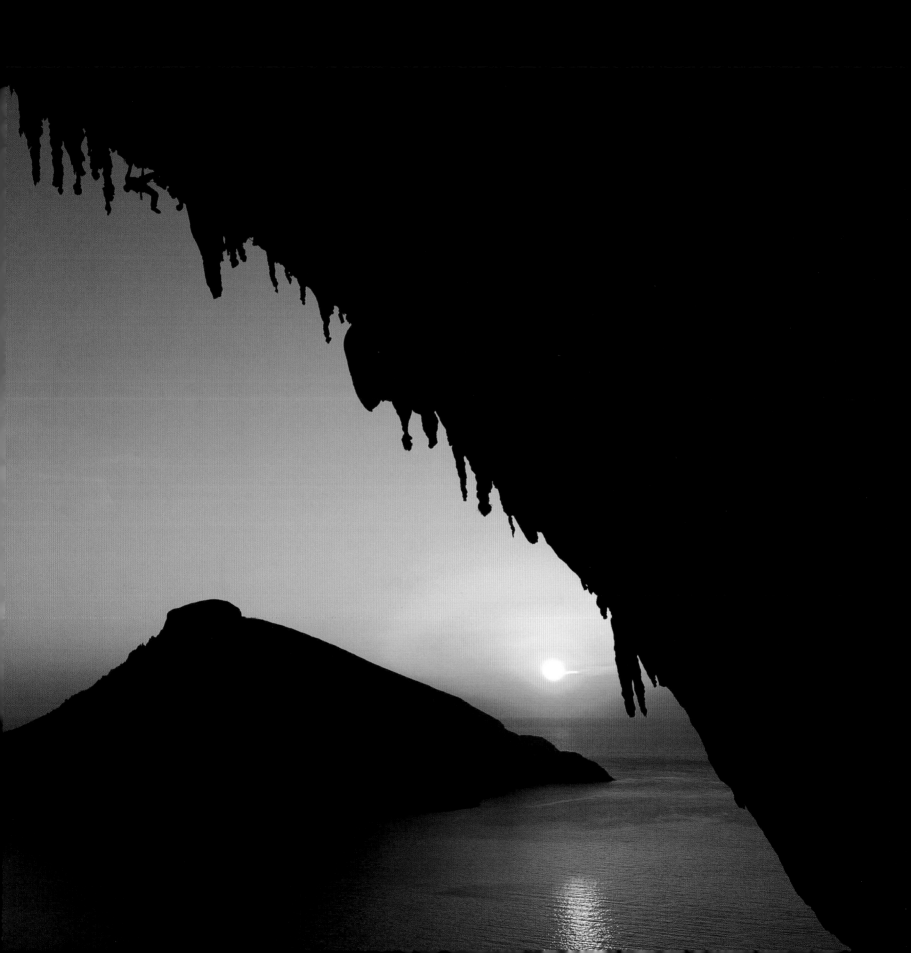

The ninety-minute taxi from Guilin's airport was a terrifying rollercoaster ride where my runaway cart weaved uncontrollably through a congested and dimly lit freeway. When it finally came to a grinding stop I landed in Xian Qian Street, a vibrant slash in the heart of Yangshuo's tourist district. I was confronted by hot air laced with wok fried garlic and chilli and an eclectic mix of music — Bon Jovi, Deborah Harry and the Ministry of Sound boomed from the bars. The street was strewn with tipsy tourists and the overhead fluorescent lighting, in a tangled mess of spaghetti, set the mood.

The region of Yangshuo is carpeted by a checkerboard of vibrant green fields punctured by thousands of sabre-toothed towers mirrored in rice paddy fields and the meandering Li River, an image so alluring that you could simply cut it out of the sky, frame it and hang it on your wall.

With over 20,000 karsts (limestone towers) littering the area it's no surprise that 20 crags are only a stone's throw away, each one unique and most just minutes from the road. As their names suggest, Butterfly Spring is easily recognised by the distinct 15-metre high sculptured butterfly bolted to the rock, Wine Bottle Cliff supposedly resembles a wine bottle, and Riverside Crag resides on the banks of the Li River.

While these crags provide variety, the star attraction is Moon Hill, a magnificent arch measuring 230 metres high and spanning 410 metres. It was Todd Skinner and other Americans who put Moon Hill on the map in the early 90s when they established six routes there. Now the twenty plus routes offer exquisite intricate climbing combined with pure aping through a jungle of tufas on the steeper inner arch. The views from Moon Hill are staggering; a scene straight out of an ancient Chinese painting, the unwavering towers fading off into the hazy horizon.

Moon Hill might be the area's most famous crag, but White Mountain is the best for harder sport routes. It has a commanding presence looming above a grove of apple trees, gentle farmlands and grazing water buffalo. The cliff is 60 metres high, 200 metres wide and steadily over-hanging, making it ideal to hide from the sun and rain. Some routes are steep and physical with lots of open-handed slopers and large spans, whereas other routes offer more balancey climbing.

The choice of crag is a luxury and between them they offer a smattering of moderate single pitch sport routes at all levels; starting from a pleasant grade 4 up to 8c+, with the majority of routes falling between 6a and 7a. Some longer routes, like the five-pitch **Happy New Year** (6b) on The Thumb, add some spice for a great day out.

The region of Yangshuo is a well established tourist destination popular with Chinese and westerners alike, it's a gentle introduction to visiting China. With perfect rock, rest day activities, souvenir shops, bars and an exotic location it all adds up to a fresh, multi-faceted climbing experience — somewhat similar to Thailand's Krabi but fresh and growing. Since initial development, locals and other nationalities have added several routes, now tallying over 200, but new route potential is massive and the area is destined to become even more popular.

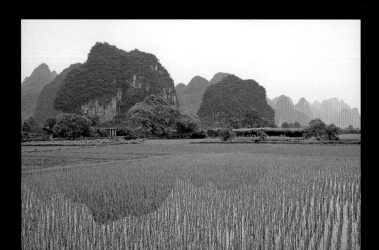

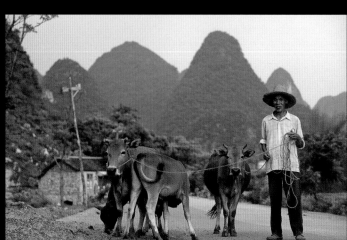

⬆ Rice paddies near the Yu Long River, with The White Cliff on the left.
↗ On the road near Yangshuo.
➡ Olivia Hsu tackling the inside arch of Moon Hill with **Over the Moon** (5.12c).

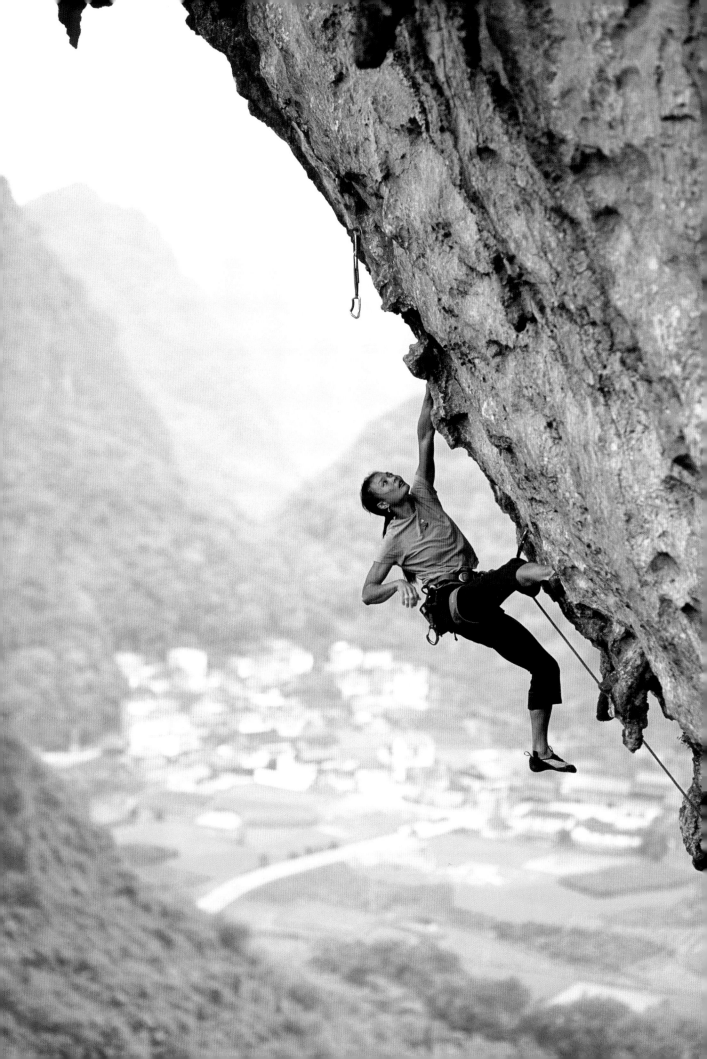

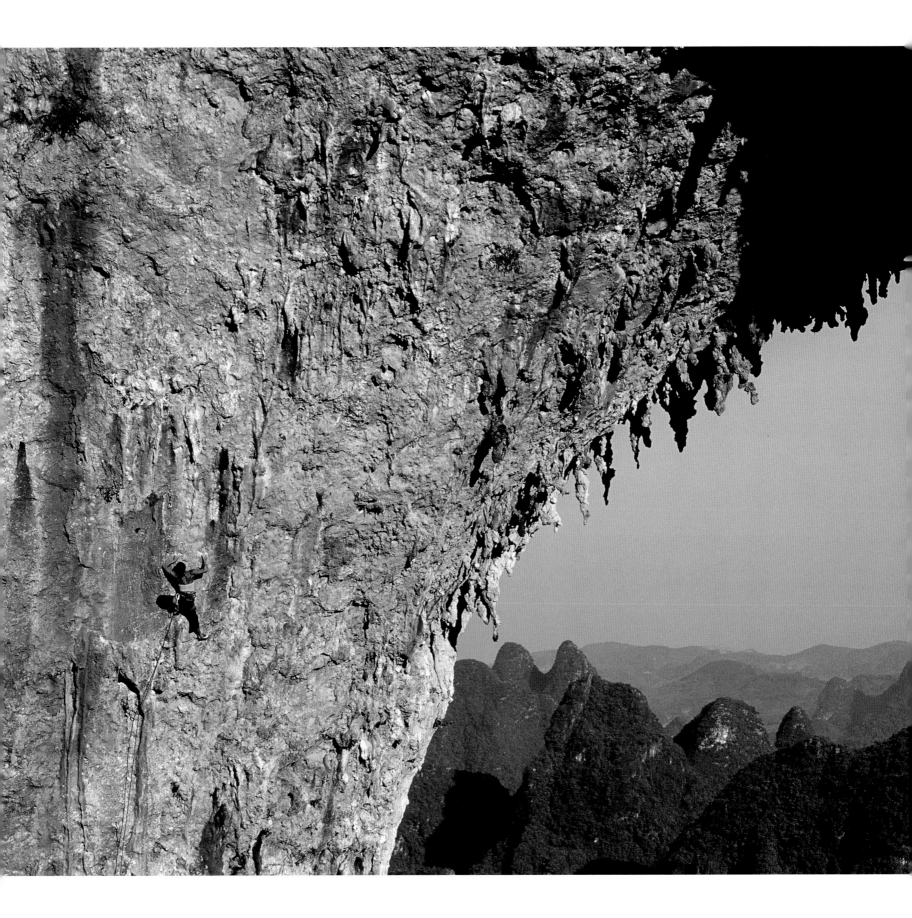

⬆ Olivia Hsu working the intricate sequence of **Red Dragon** (5.13d), Moon Hill.

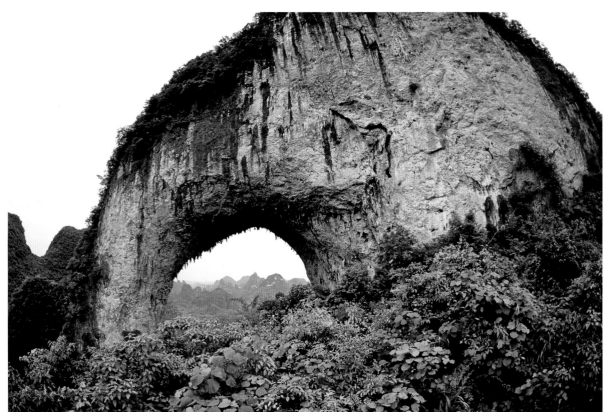

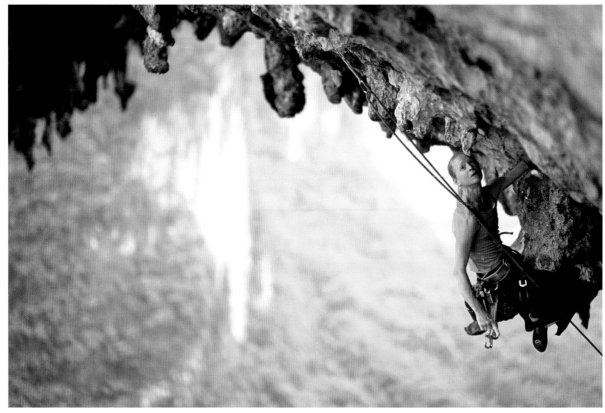

⬈ Moon Hill with Ryan Gormly leading **Artemis** (5.11a) up the middle of the white right wall.

⬈ Monique Forestier figuring out a perplexing sequence on **Over the Moon** (5.12c), Moon Hill.

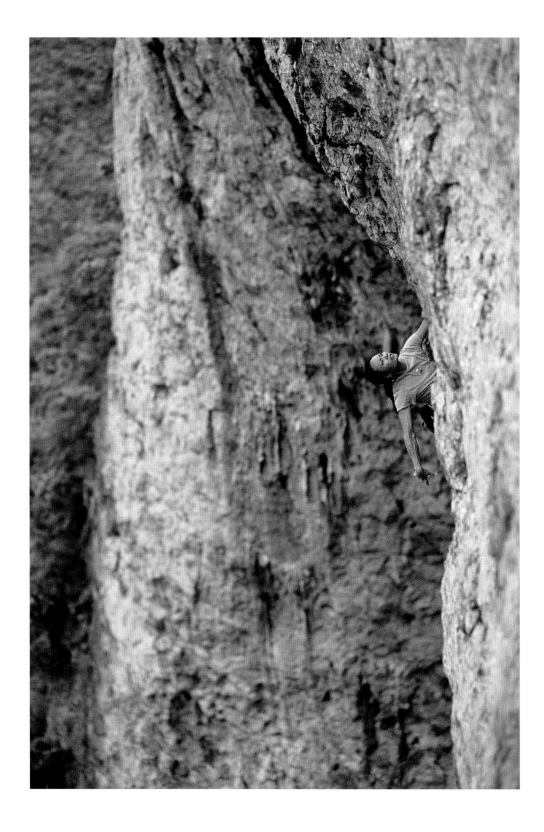

⬆ Olivia Hsu taking one last shake before the final dash to complete **Over the Moon** (5.12c), Moon Hill.

➡ Simon Wilson having a uniquely Chinese experience on a 5.10b sport route at the "Butterfly Spring" tourist attraction.

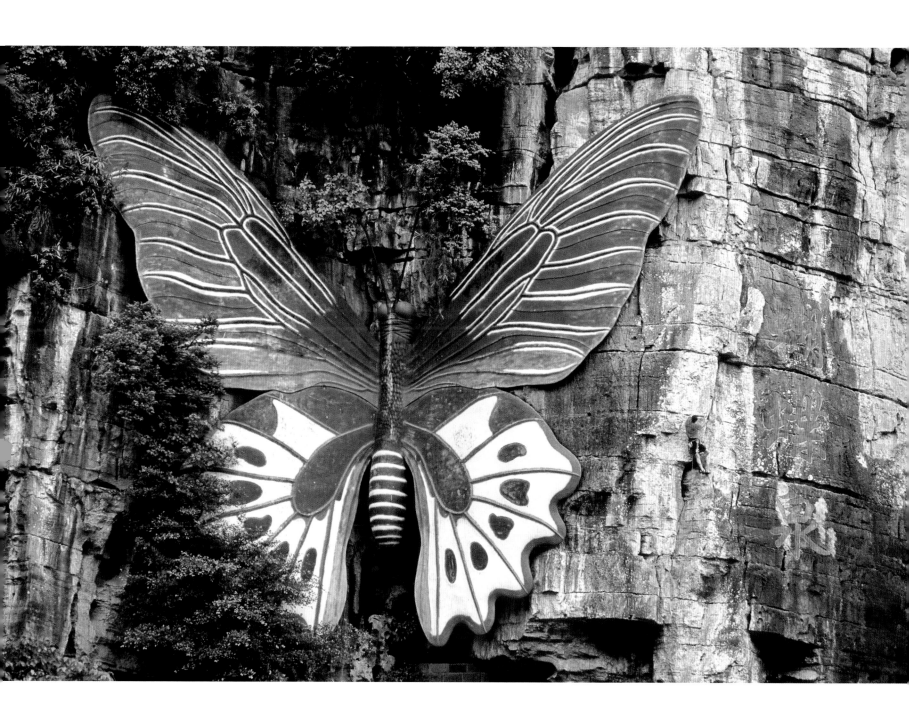

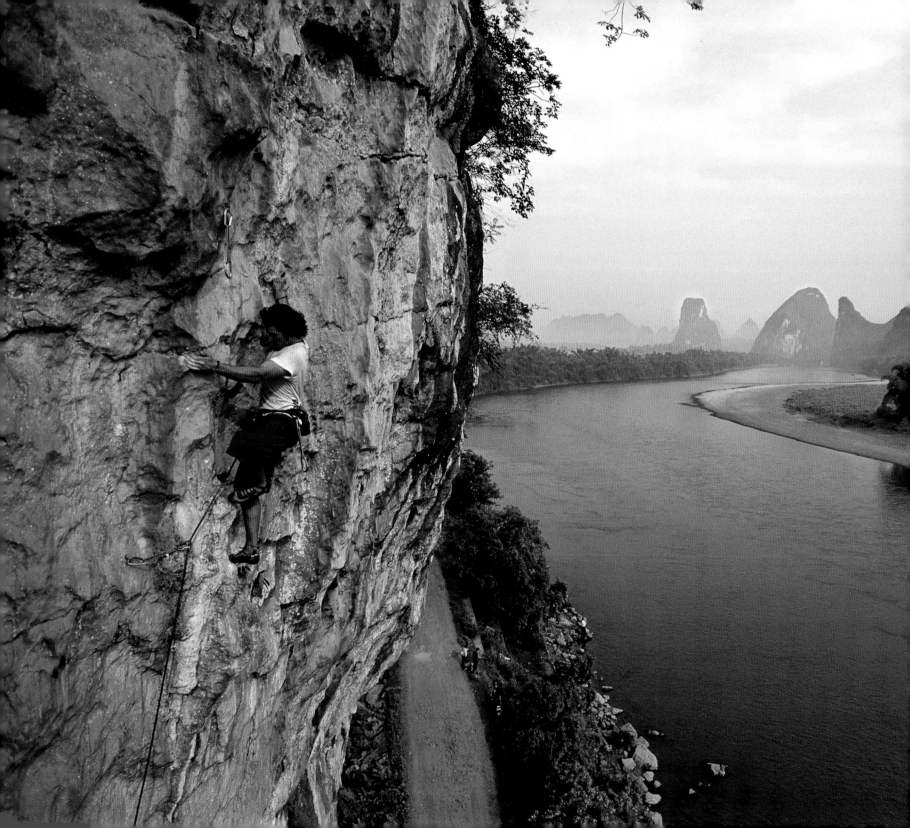

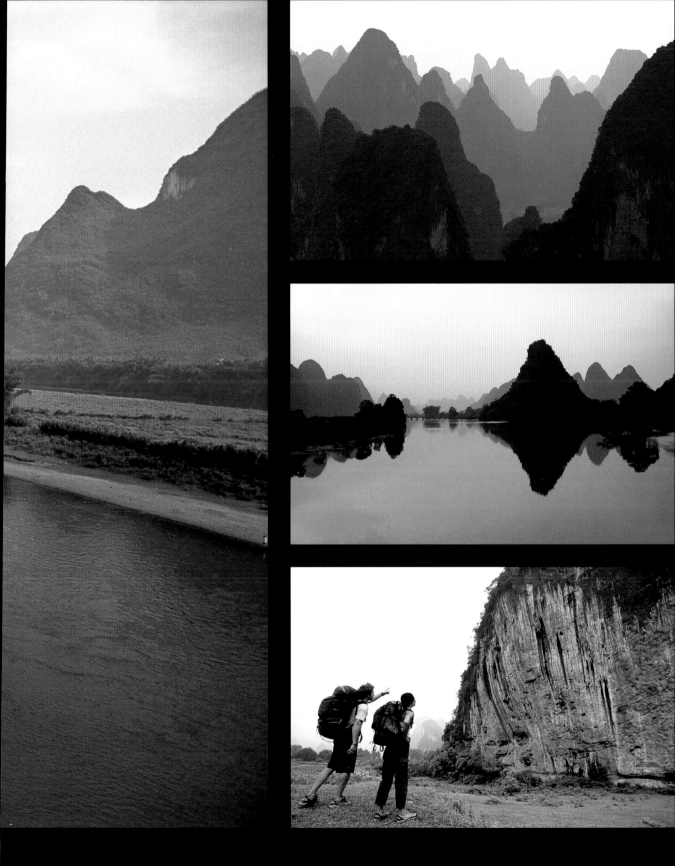

The "karsts", they seem to go on forever.

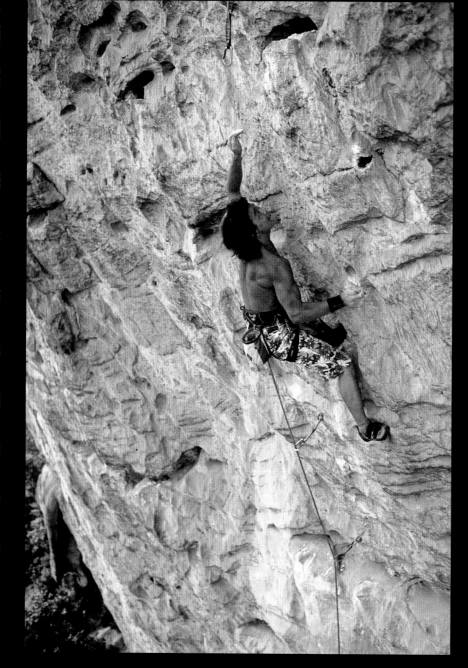
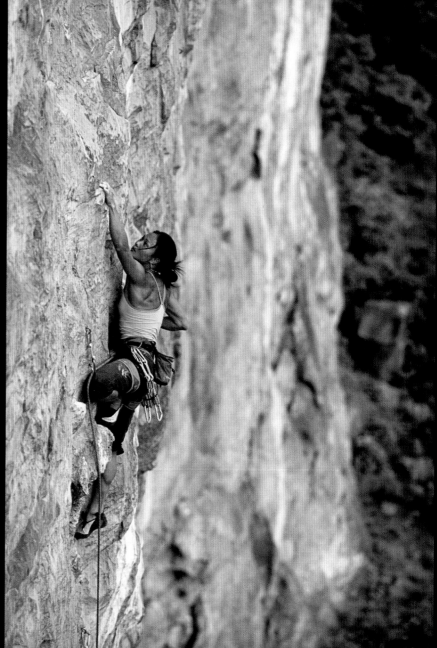

⬆ Local climber Liu "Abond" Yongbang standing strong against a *Gang of Four* (5.12d), White Mountain.

↗ Olivia Hsu unrelenting against *The Wall of Attrition* (5.11c), White Mountain.

➡ Olivia Hsu keeping the *Devil Sticks* (5.12b) in play. White Mountain.

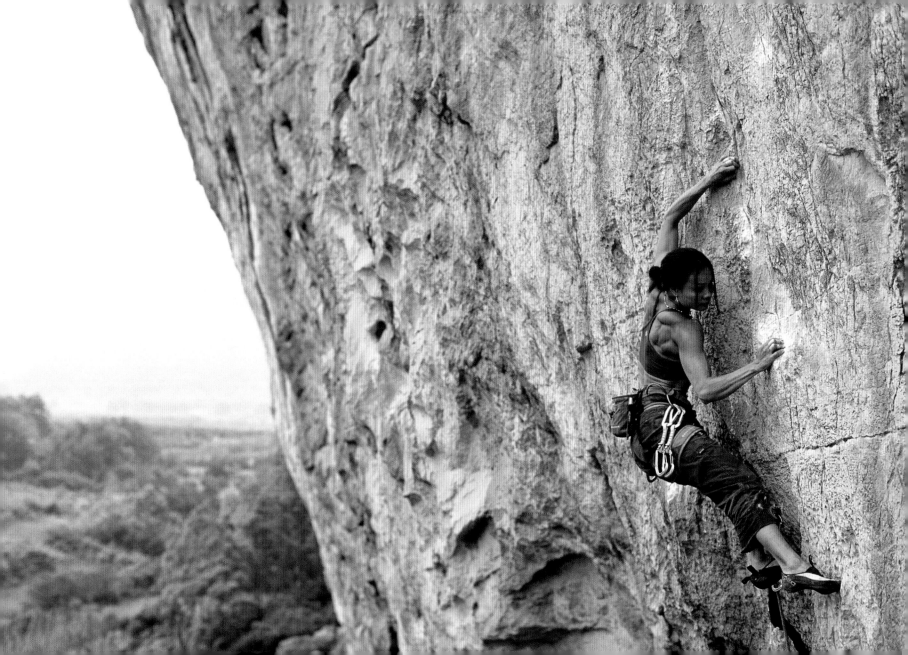

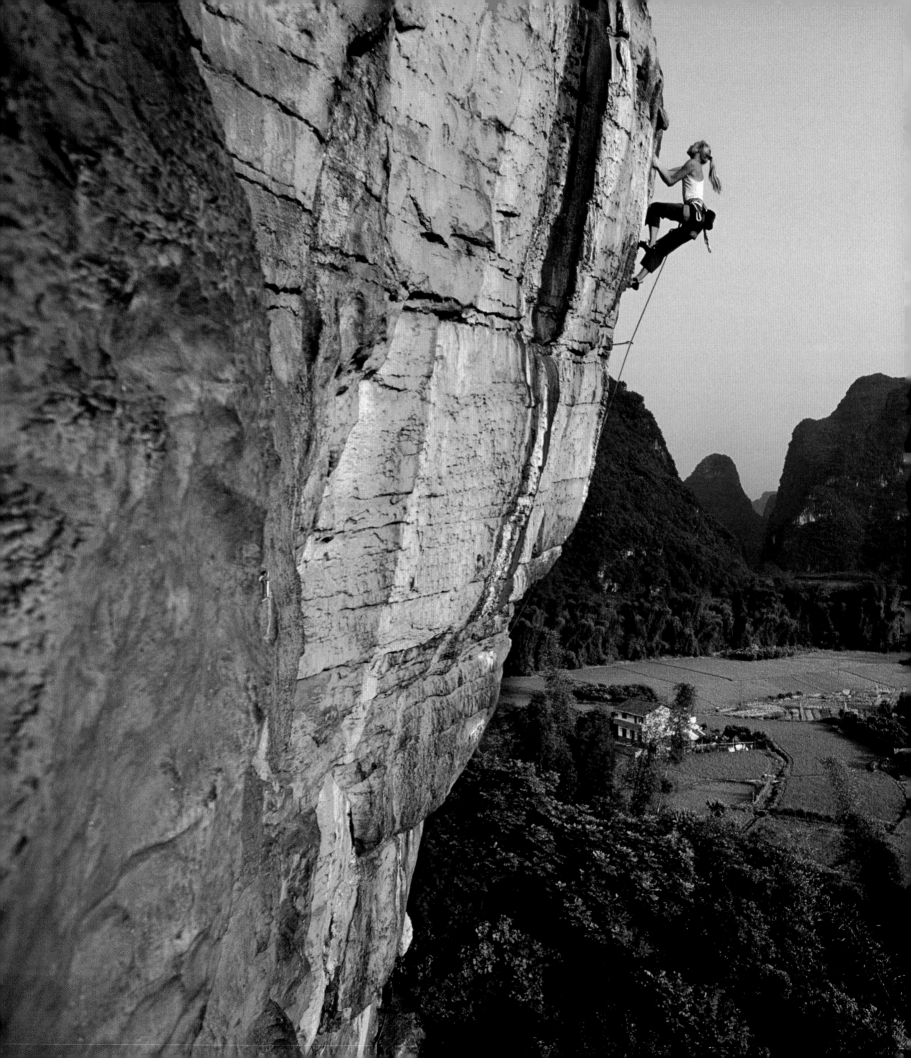

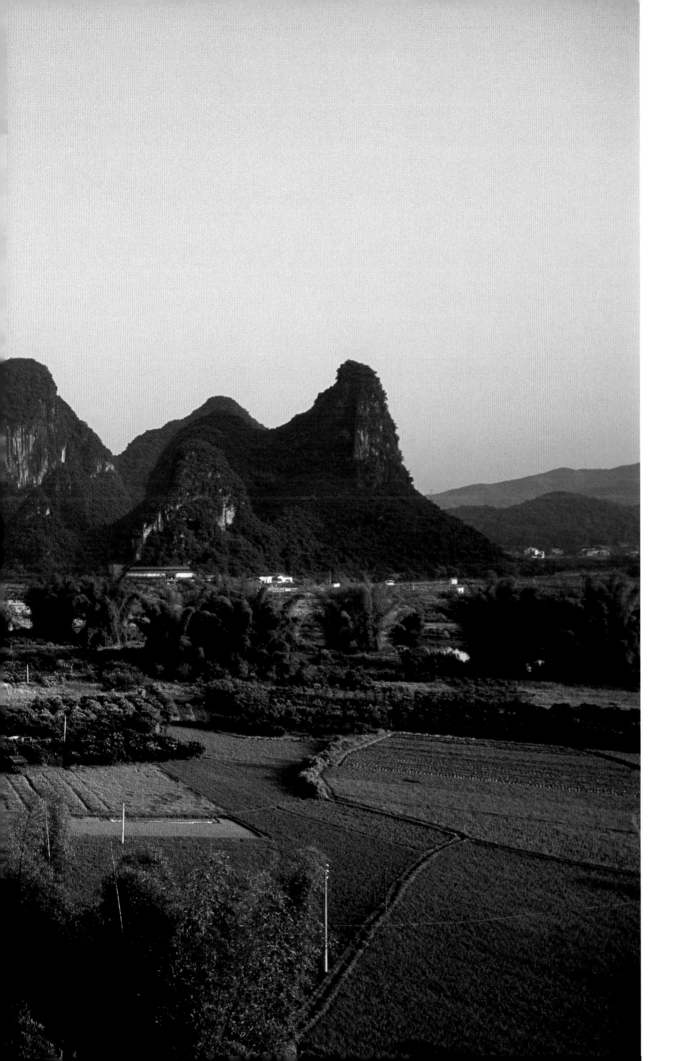

Monique Forestier tickling the tufa on the varied and technical ***Nine Deep, One Shallow*** (5.13d), Banyan Tree Crag.

Legend has it that fearless dragons protected the people of northern Vietnam from invaders by spitting thousands of ungraded diamonds into the sea. Nowadays, the glistening emerald-green waters of Ha Long Bay are studded with 2,153 brilliant-cut limestone karsts and it's no surprise that the Bay is a tourist hot spot, and a 'must-visit' for climbers.

Arriving in Vietnam is a rush of cold blood to the head, a full body awakening that leaves your eyes spinning in their sockets. One minute, you sit frazzled in heavy Hanoi traffic, next minute, your eyes have taken on a tranquil gaze as you sit calmly slurping a mango smoothie in a Cat Ba Island café, a peaceful base camp for Ha Long Bay, 133 kilometres south of Hanoi.

As with Yangshuo, Todd Skinner was instrumental in kicking off climbing development in Ha Long Bay, when he visited with Lynn Hill, Paul Piana and Scott Milton in 1996. They showed the world the area's potential and that access was possible, and although it was several years before it started to become a popular destination they certainly got the ball rolling.

There are numerous roped climbing options available in the Bay, some are standouts. Saigon Wall is an immaculate stand alone incisor of rock; straight out of the boat and up the guts of the enamel fang. And on The Face, another wedge of rock piercing the waters of the South China Sea, lies *License to Climb* (7b, extension 7c) and *The Face* (7b+), having candle-dripped tufa-like features providing perfect hand-sized pinches, it's a pure delight. And over at Tiger Beach, the four-pitch *Screw Loose* (6b) is a sensational all-encompassing journey through a cavernous lair, corkscrewing

its way up and around an eight-metre hanging stalactite before spittng you out onto the face for two more pitches.

For an easy day cragging, without a boat, look no further than the breathtaking Butterfly Valley. Situated on Cat Ba Island itself, it offers 56 bolted routes catering for most climbers (grade 4 to 8a+). My favourites include: *Roots Reggae* (4) which involves monkeying up the root system of a gargantuan tree, *Windchime of the Ants* (7a) a three dimensional odyssey weaving its way through two suspended stalactites, and *Monarch* (7c+) a climb that tickles a flake resembling the right wing of a butterfly.

In recent years deep-water soloing (DWS) has popularised the area. With so much rock you would be hard pushed to visit all the crags, so here is a quick tour. "Toot toot, all aboard!" Our traditional 'junk's' first stop on the DWS groove train is Unemployment Wall, home to *The Diving Board* (7a), a test piece where you have to mount and dive from the horizontal stalactite to score the full points. Next stop, is the larger Hawaii 5-0 Wall; it easily caters for a boat-load of frenzied climbers. Next station, Turtle Cave. This is not for the fainthearted, the traversing line takes the brim of the cave and climbs down the stalactite hanging like a fang from its lip, ten metres above the turbulent turquoise broth. For an optional stop, call into *Streak of Lightning* (7c) an eye-catching splitter crack that happily devours any body part then spits it back out again. Be sure to make the most of high tides if DWS is the primary reason for visiting Ha Long Bay.

The bay offers enormous untapped potential. If you are really psyched organise your our own boat to search for that one carat solitaire.

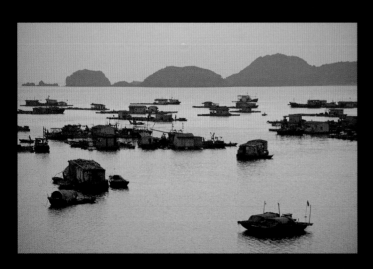

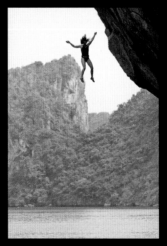

⬆ Floating homes off Cat Ba Island.
◲ Like a duck to water, Tamara Sepetauc fearlessly embracing her first ever deep-water solo. Fisherman's Way.
➡ Now what? Lee Cujes on the wrong side of *The Diving Board* (7a), Unemployment Wall.

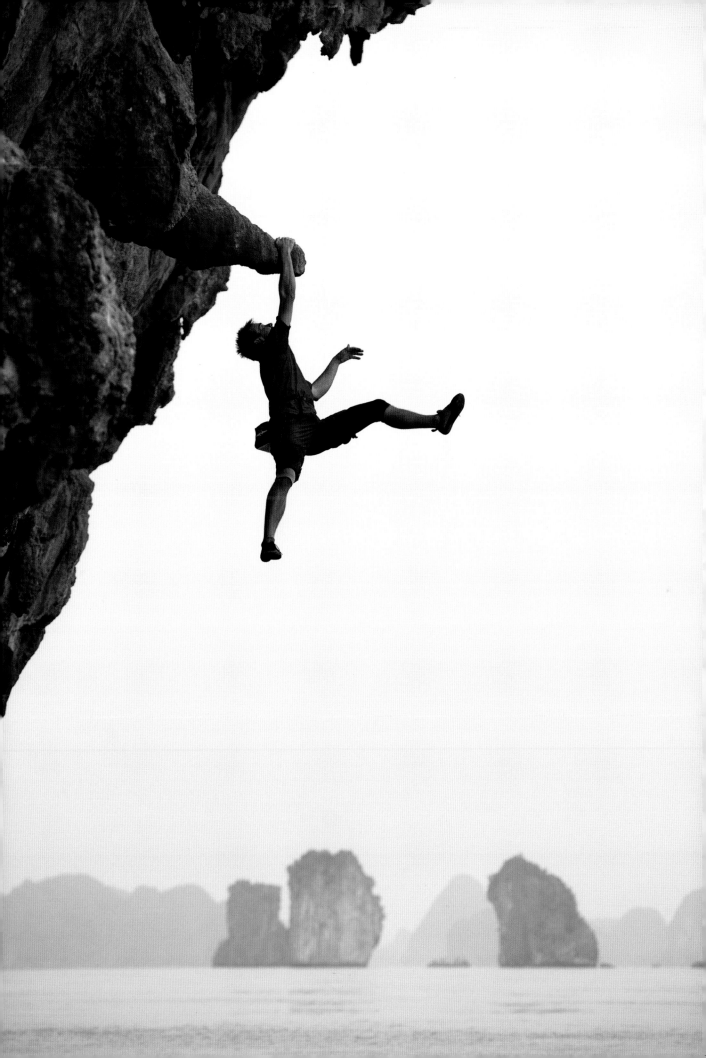

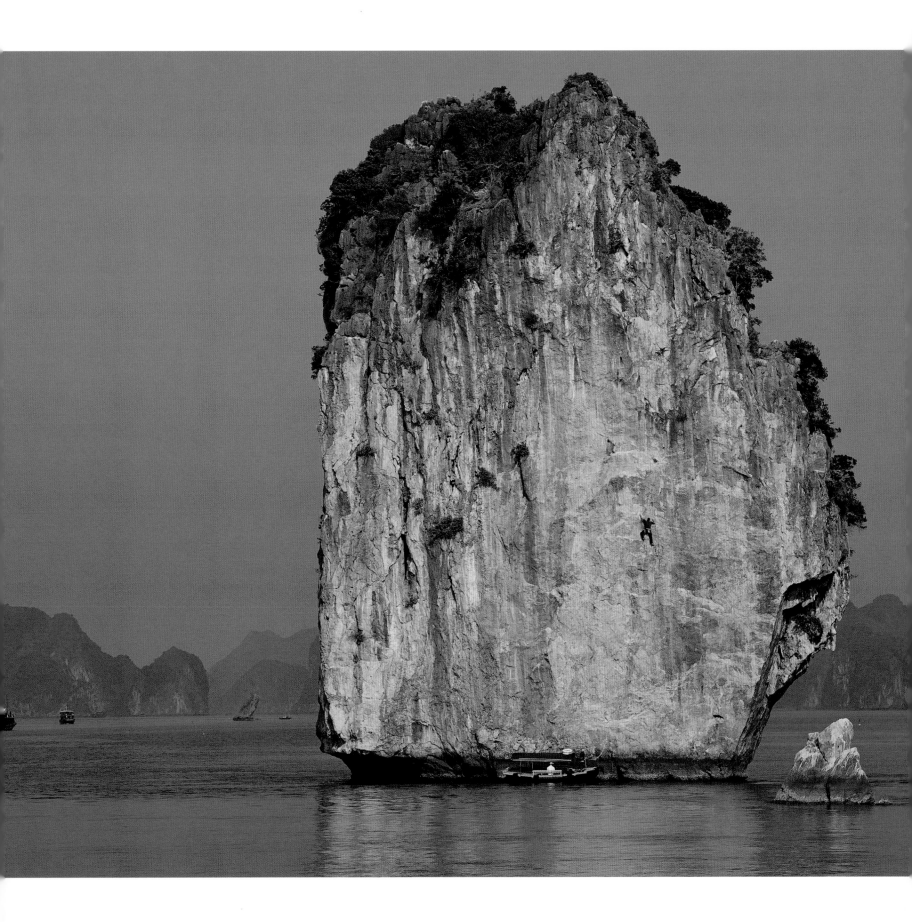

Lee Cujes leading the rebolted **Saigon Wall** (7a) on the incisor of the same name.

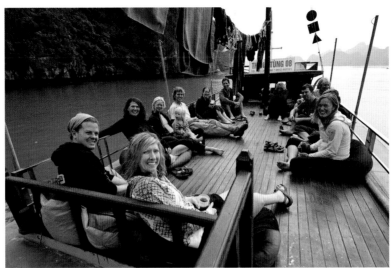

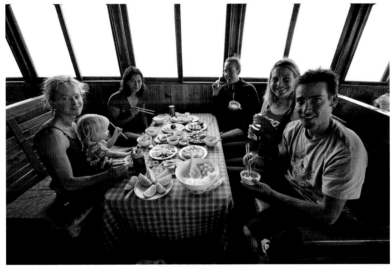

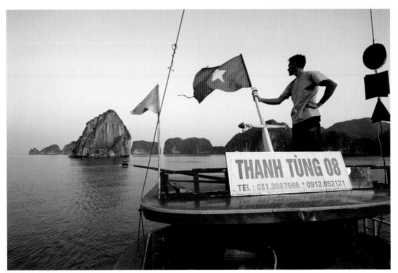

A contented crew after a days cragging and DWS near Tiger Beach.

Junket on a junk? Lunch time on the "Slo Pony Adventures" boat.

Lee Cujes heading home happy after making the first ascent of *Licence to Climb Harder* (7c) on The Face (in the background).

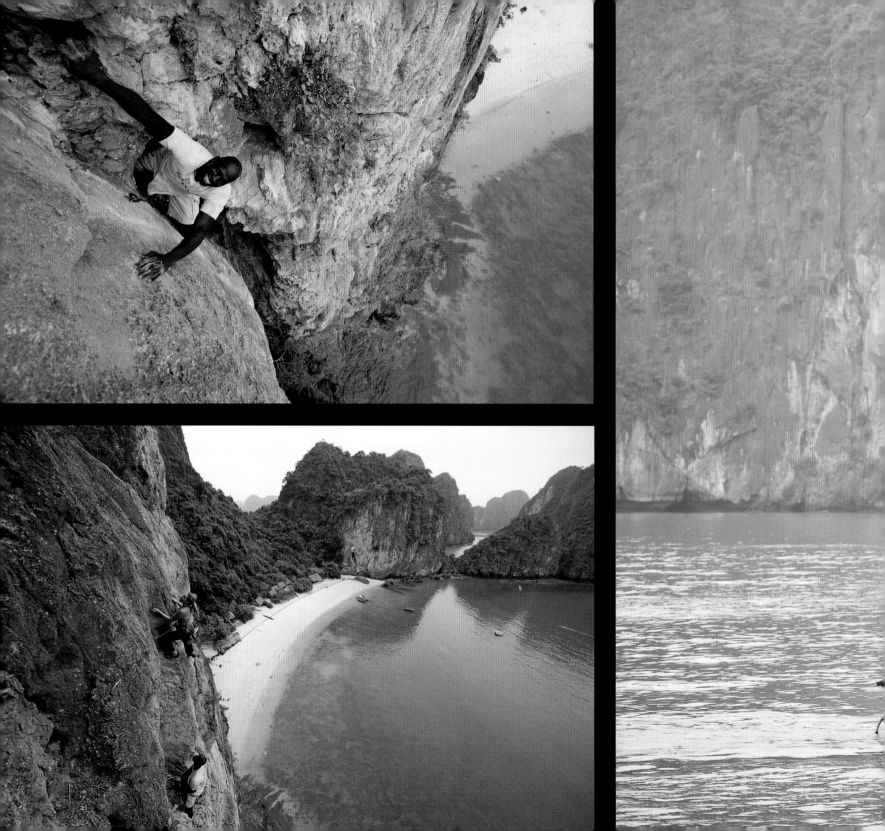

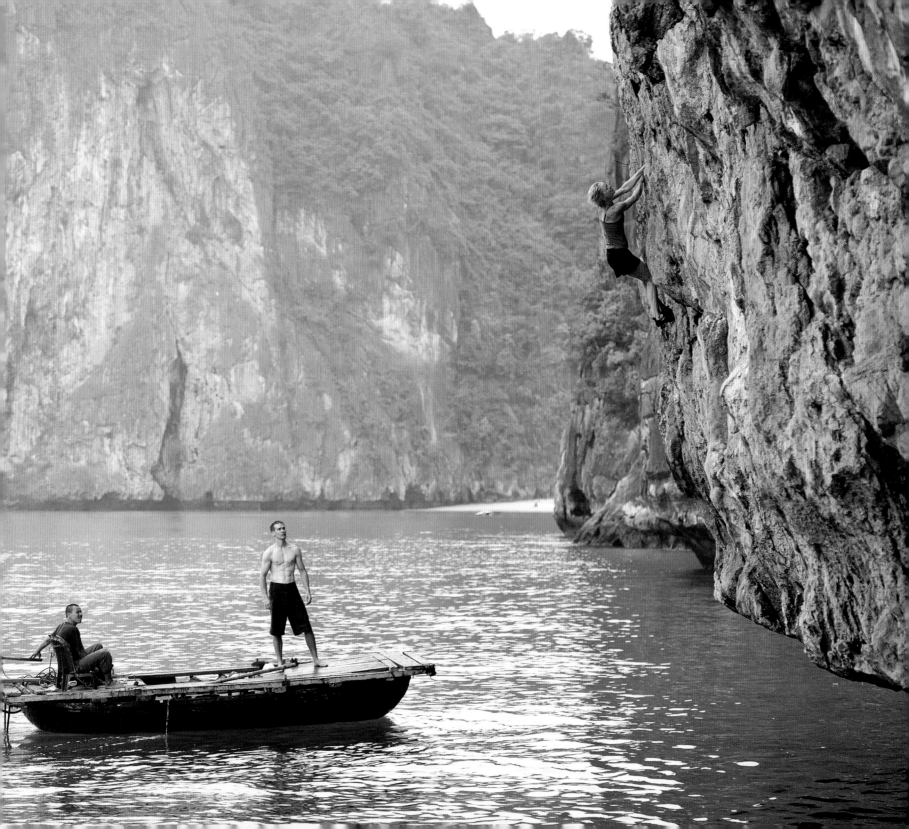

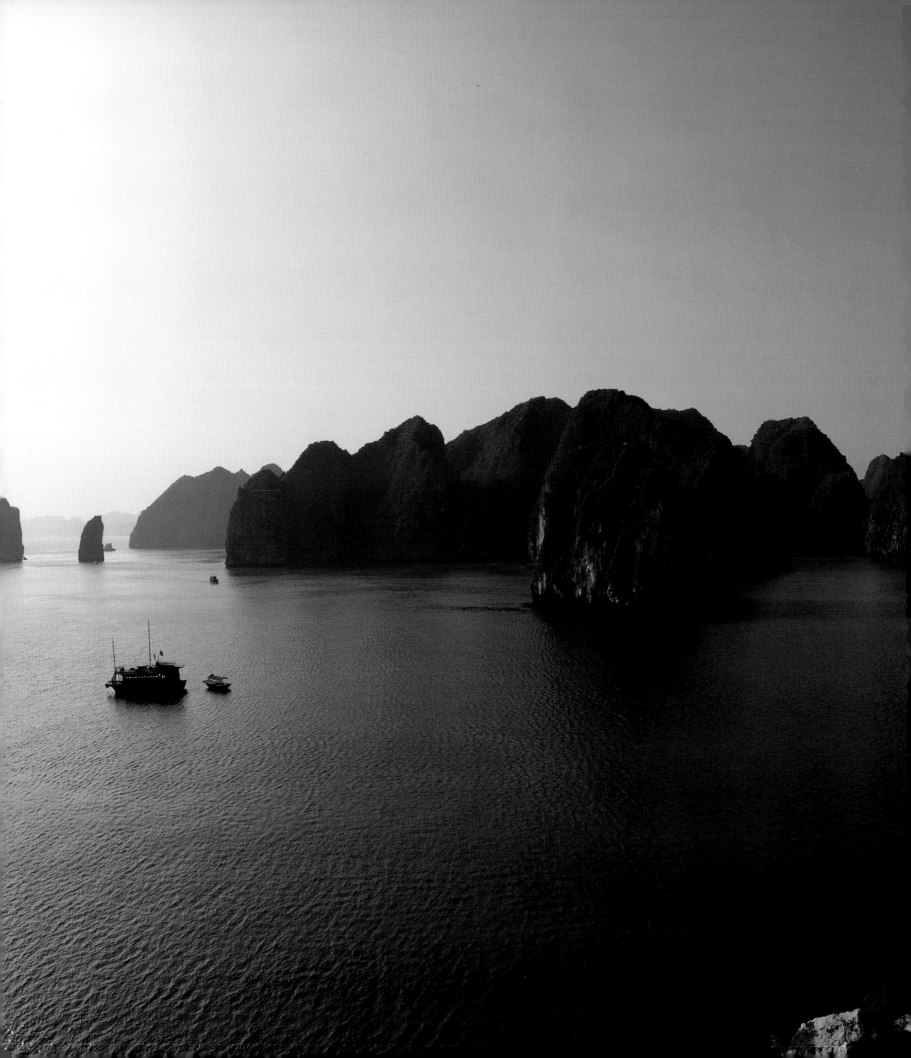

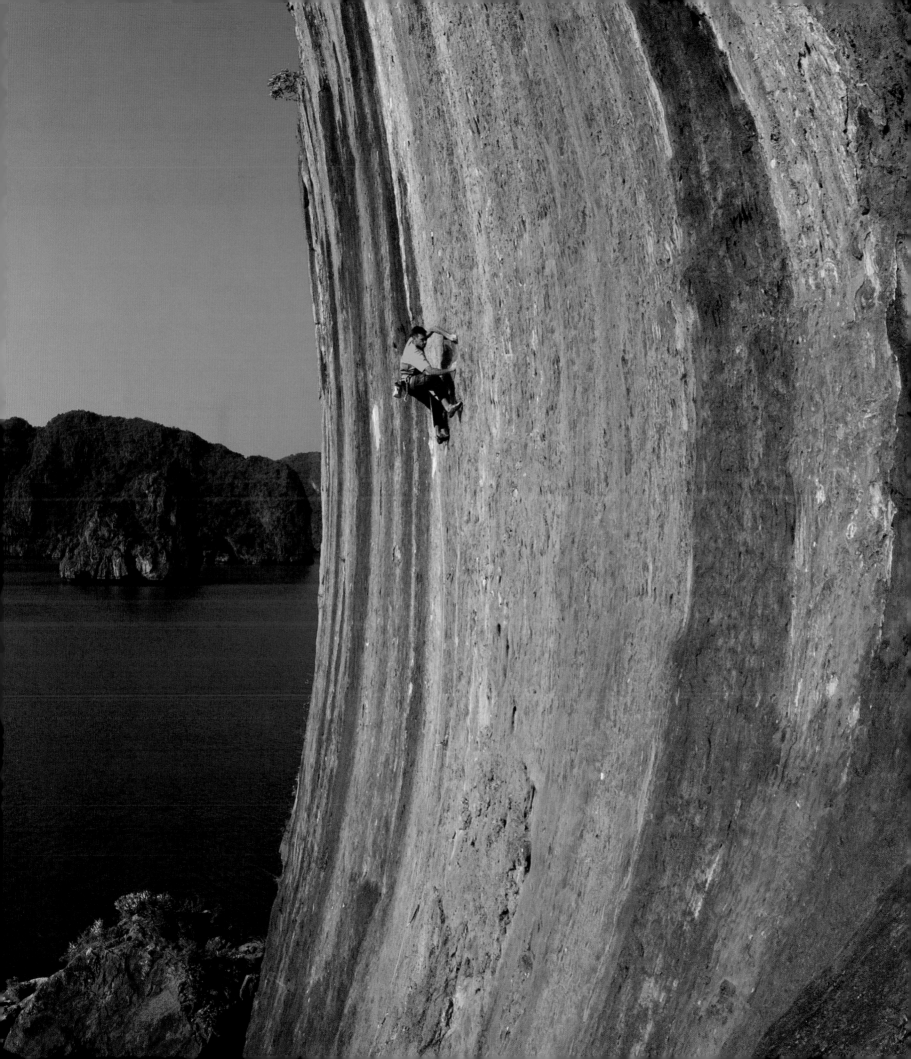

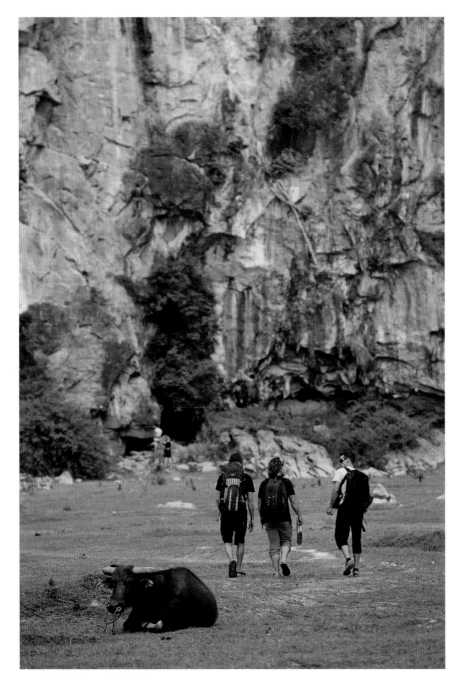

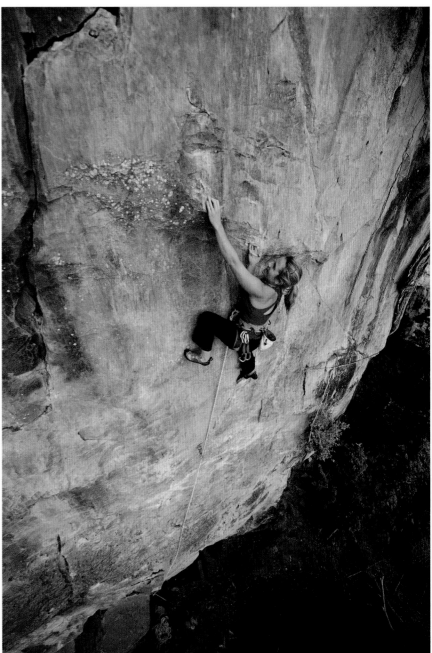

← Lee Cujes making the first ascent of **License to Climb Harder** (7c), an extension to **License to Climb** (7b) on The Face.

↑ It's just a short walk to Butterfly Valley Crag (Lien Minh) on Cat Ba Island.

↗ Sam Cujes on **Elephant Man** (6c), Butterfly Valley Crag.

→ Onslo "Slo" Carrington throwing himself at his project at Butterfly Valley Crag.

⇒ Lee Cujes fighting to hang the fingerlocks on his excellent new route **Monarch** (7c+), Butterfly Valley.

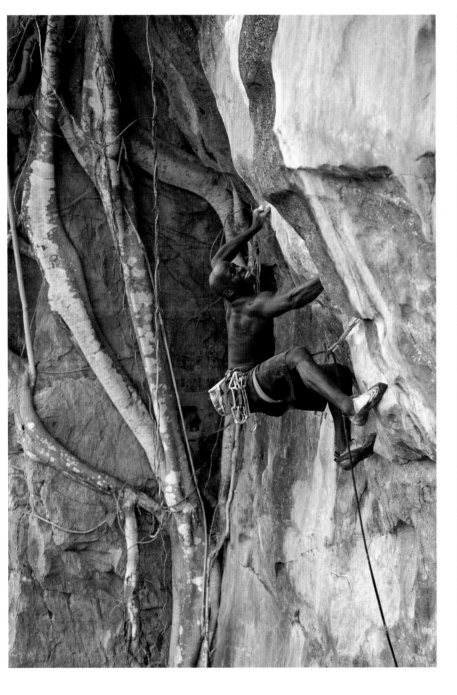

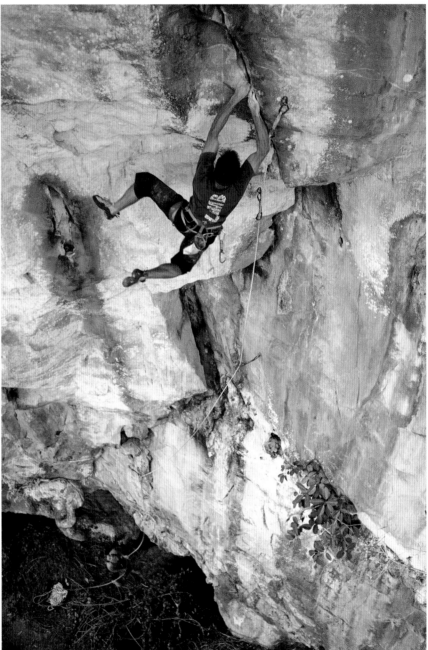

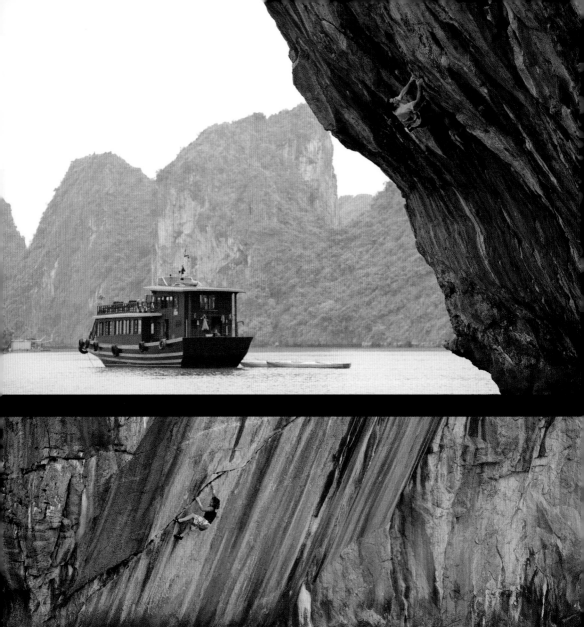
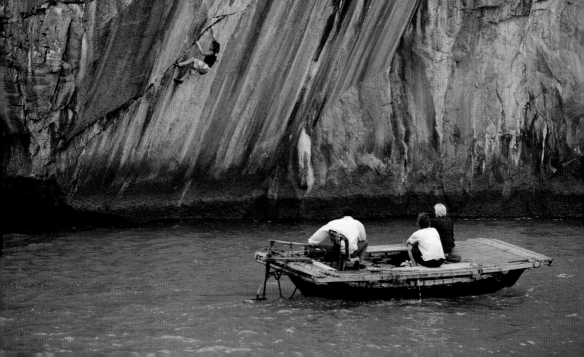

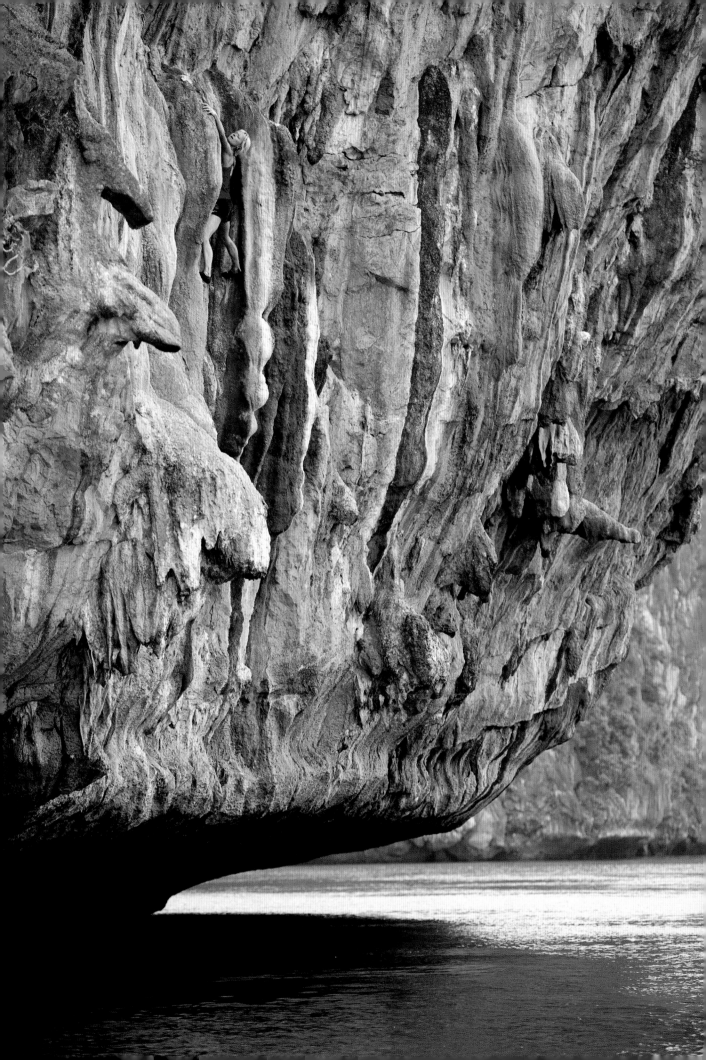

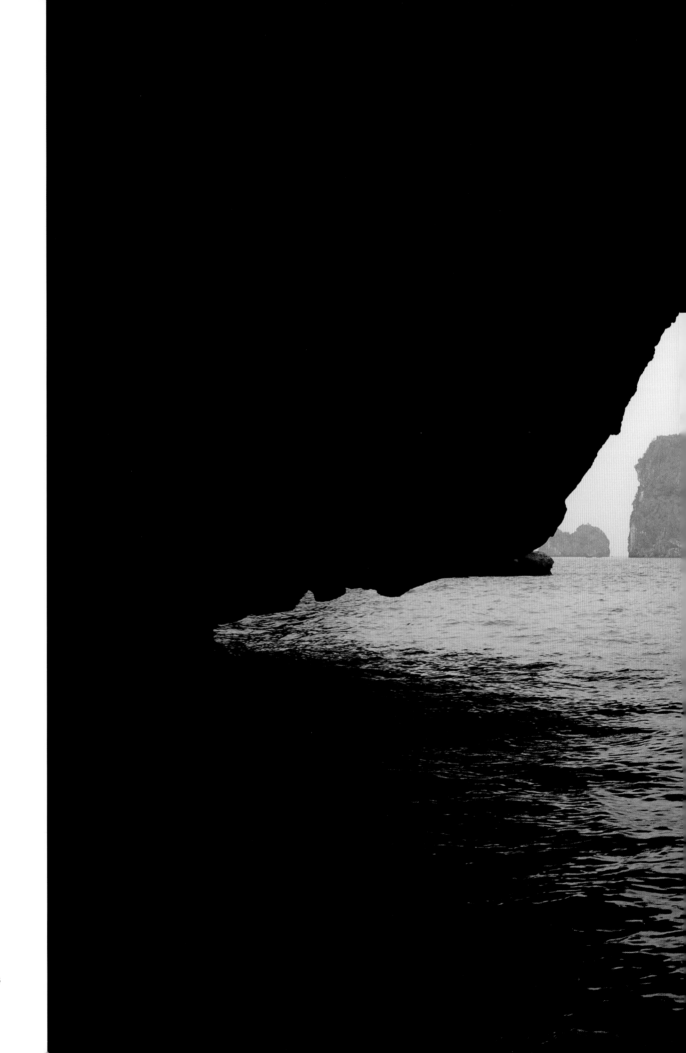

Monique Forestier considering her options after completing a tricky deep-water solo (which comes in high from the left) out to a stalactite at Turtle Cave.

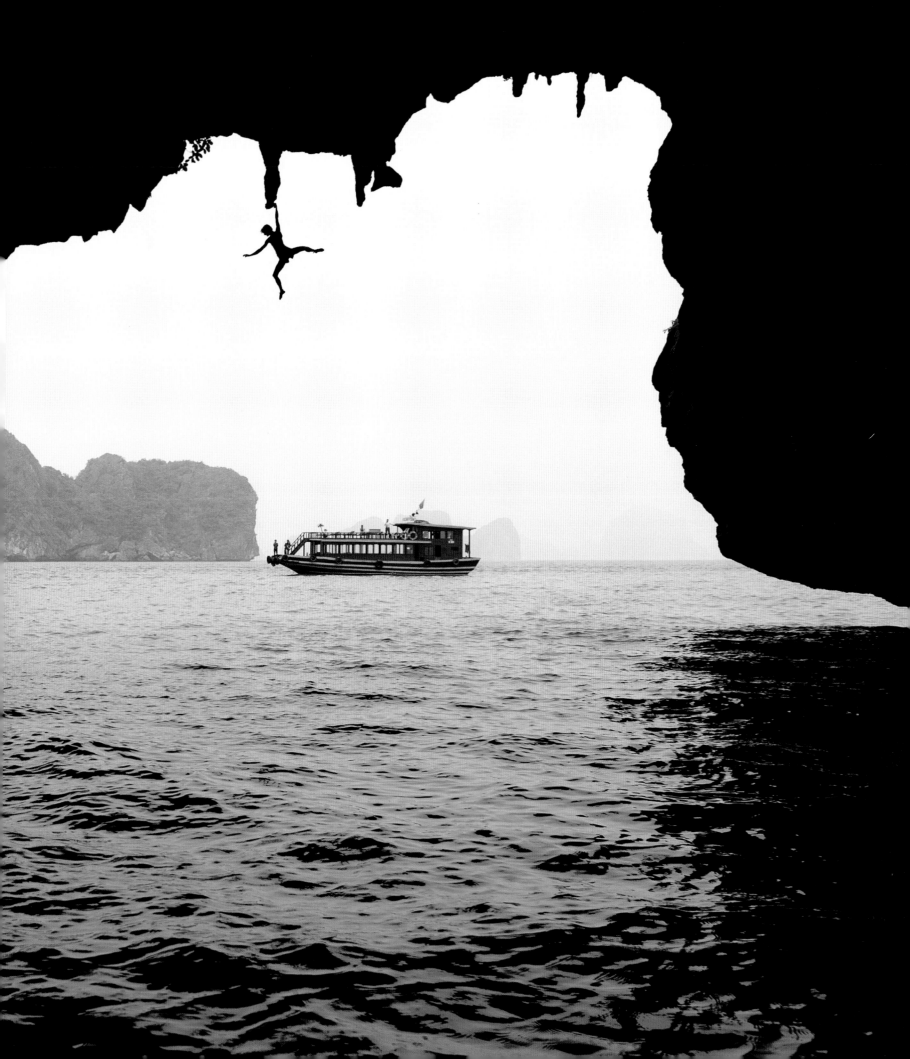

HONG KONG

Hong Kong, one of the world's buzzing metropolises, has an everlasting effervescence that bubbles all day long and sparkles all night. The climbers who live here share a special secret — the knowledge that there's more to the area than big city skyscrapers and infinite shopping malls. And for these climbers, the crags scattered around the region offer more than just an escape from the hustle and bustle for a few hours, they offer a lifeline.

Like most things in Hong Kong, many of the crags are accessible by MTR (underground railway) so mastering this mode of travel is the key to maximising your visit. This in itself can be somewhat of a challenge and amusing; let's just say that with our three-month-old daughter, we turned some heads in the subway with her bouncinette haphazardly pitched on top of our crag packs.

Climbing in Honkas Bonkas is just that, bizarre. You climb on natural rock but the surrounding environment is man-made. Nature precariously holds its ground, perhaps fighting a losing battle against modern development, where not even a matchbox size plot of land is left undisturbed. Climbing is a super surreal experience, you can feel the eyes piercing your back, and over your shoulder, off in the distance, an army of concrete soldiers stands to attention, watching and waiting for their next command.

The rock here is mostly granite or volcanic tuff and many of these crags only exist because the hillside they sit on is so steep and unstable that development is kept at bay. Landslides are common and needless to say their prevention is paramount. Soho crag, perched high on a hill overlooking central Hong Kong, is basically bolted together so it doesn't wipe out the concrete army below like pins in a bowling alley. The rock features diagonal seams, acid drops, bird beak rooflets and credit card edges and makes for interesting enough slab sport climbing.

Lion Rock, so called because this monolith resembles a sleeping Lion in profile, sits proud on a ridgeline bordering Kowloon and the New Territories. It has over 20 multi-pitch routes: both sport and traditional. The view from the top can be either marvelous or, more likely, a thick humid haze. The climbing is certainly lofty and worth the walk.

Hong Kong's most popular crags are situated on Tung Lung Chau, an island accessed by public ferry only on weekends. The main area, Technical Wall, offers 33 routes and comes with its own rock-viewing platform, perfect for watching a theatrical live performance of vertical dance.

All up there are 20 or so crags and bouldering spots in the area. You probably wouldn't visit Hong Kong just to go climbing. But once there, you might be surprised by its diversity and above all its enthusiastic friendly local scene.

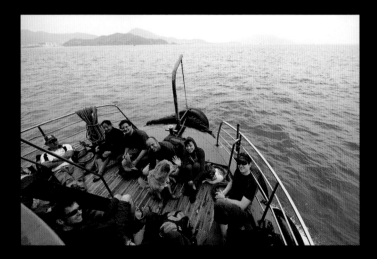

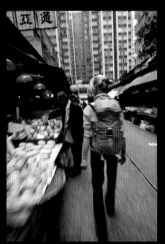

⬆ Some of the regular Hong Kong crew taking the Saturday morning ferry to Tung Lung Chau.
↗ Monique Forestier cruising Yin Chong Street, Mongkok.
➡ Monique Forestier cruising *Peel Street* (6b+), Soho Crag, Central.

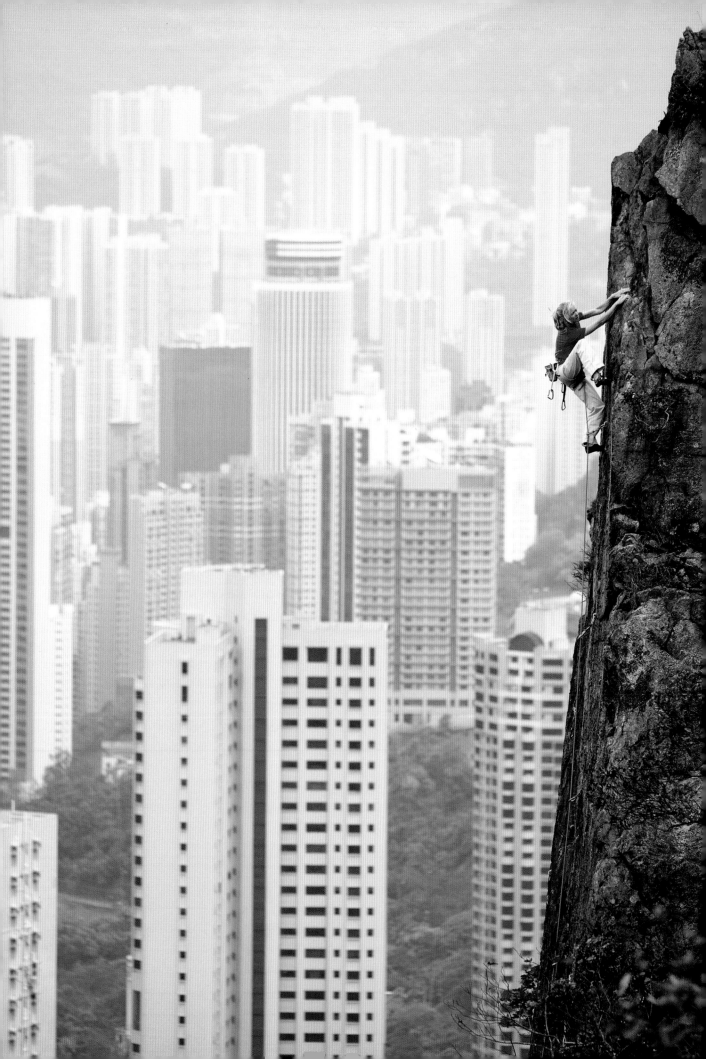

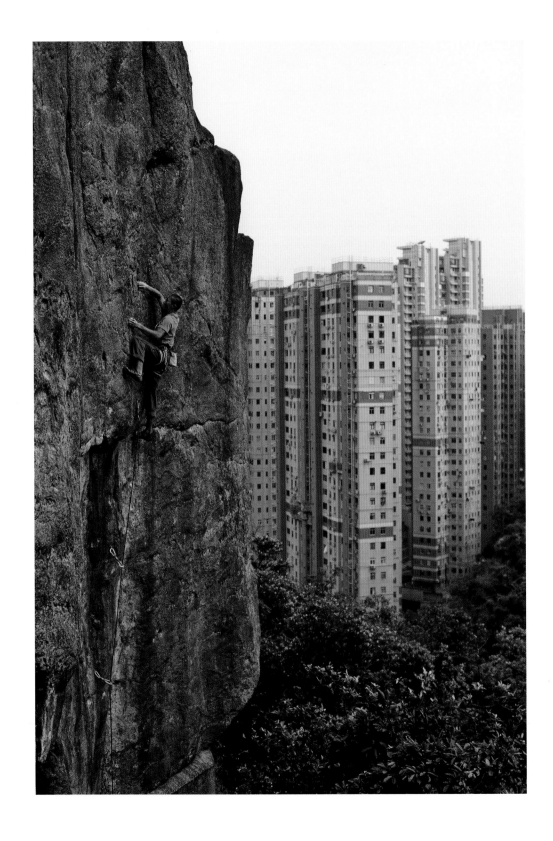

⬆ Ron Chow attempting the eviscerating *Evolution* (8a), Monkey Buttress.

➡ Taki Miyamoto on *Doppelganger* (HS 4c), a moderate trad route up the unusual volcanic tuff of Waterfall Rock, New Territories.

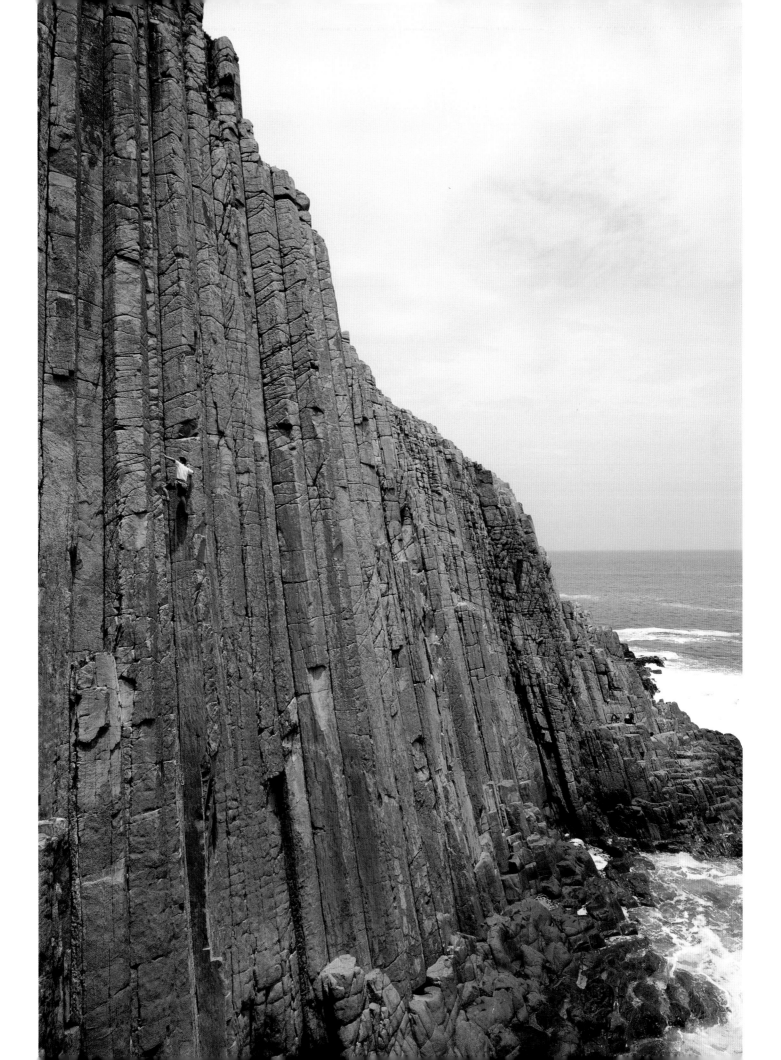

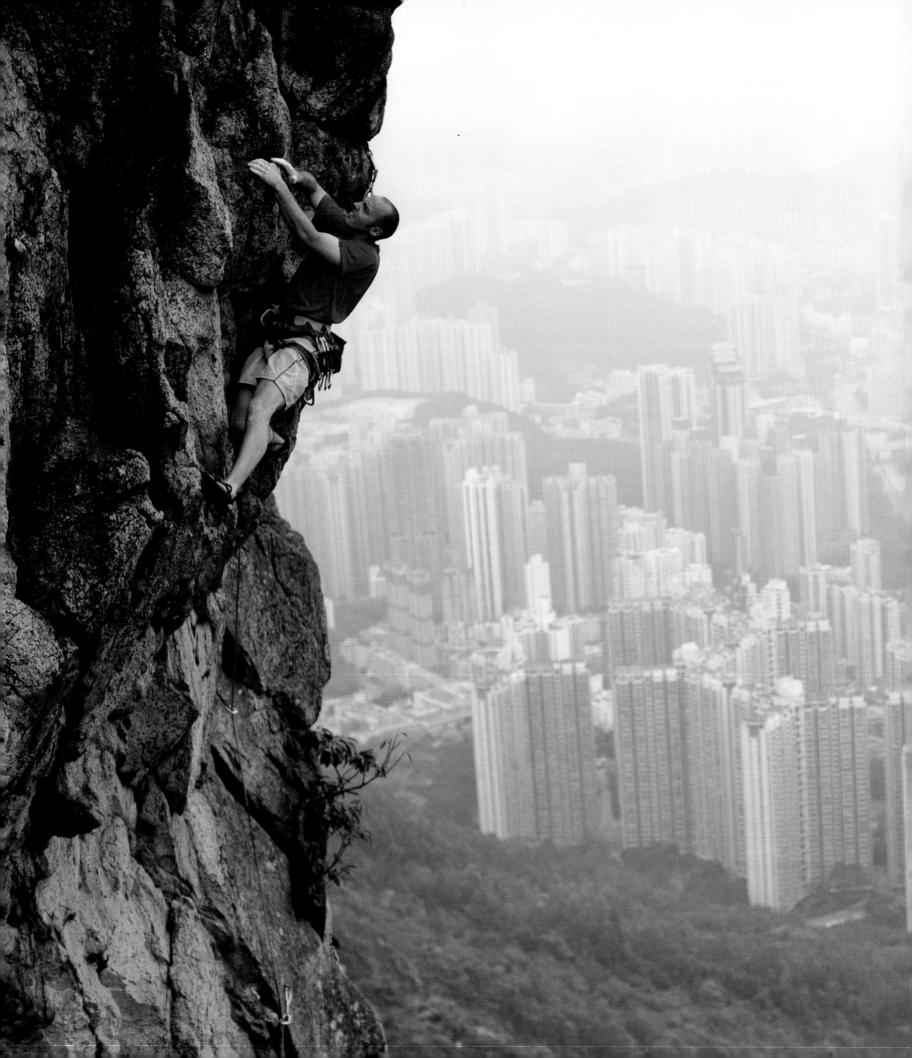

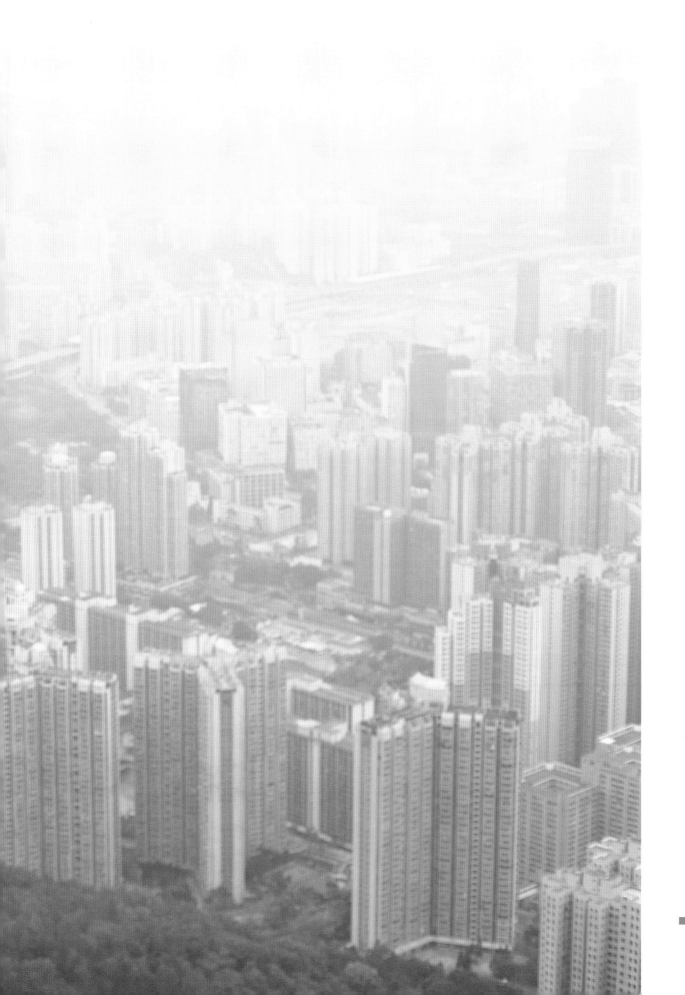

Stuart Millis on familiar ground climbing **Scaredy Cat** (6c+), a variant fourth pitch to **Gweilo** (5+), which he first freed years earlier. Lion Rock.

JOSHUA TREE

Upon arrival in Joshua Tree, the part of the mind concerned with the stresses of modern life can be checked in at the park gates so that the rest of the mind can party on, get freaked out and enjoy the climbing. The simplified surroundings of J-Tree literally extend deadlines, delete inboxes, detangle wrinkles and allow life to flow to a natural rhythm.

Steeped in history, J-Tree's tri-coloured canvas of camel skin boulders, bottle green topped Joshua trees and a brilliant blue sky has for decades provided the ultimate playing field for climbers to practice their art. The first 'Modern' artists to lay paint on the canvas and test their technical rock climbing skills were the audacious 'Desert Rats'. During the 1960s this active but unruly bunch hijacked Hidden Valley and established routes up to 5.9, now latter day classics, many were aided using pitons. The 70s saw the arrival of the 'Postmodern' movement, better known as 'The Stone Masters'; they not only embraced clean climbing ethics (using removable, non-damaging forms of protection) but with their taut torsos they established 5.11 in J-Tree and freed many of the previously aided routes. Some notable classics include: *Illusion Dweller* (5.10b), *Coarse and Buggy* (5.11a) and *Figures on a Landscape* (5.10d). The 80s brought 'les Fauves' (wild beasts) style of climbers. Donning sticky rubber and untamed attires, they let loose on the outer reaching cliffs, sunk bolts (now forbidden) and hang-dogged their way up some very difficult sport routes like *Bikini Whale* (5.12a) and *Satanic Mechanic* (5.12b) to name but a few.

Don't be fooled, J-Tree is huge, and there are no shortcuts; the climbing is often a love / hate affair and it takes time to get a feel for the place. Getting lost is a given, how many times depends on the length of your stay and your diligence in sticking to guidebook descriptions. The number of routes exceeds 4,500 and the grade range caters for all. It's no clip up affair; there are some bolted routes but, in keeping with the area, they can feel pretty bold too. Seriously, you go to J-Tree for the ultra classic trad lines.

Nowadays, J-Tree has a classic appeal where climbers come from all over the world to admire and pay homage to what has passed before. J-Tree is a great bouldering destination, Hidden Valley is beautiful, and the sun warmed granite offers a pleasant retreat from the harsh northern winters. The climbing is always stout and humbling but when you reach the top, that's when you can smile, drink up the sun and do it all again.

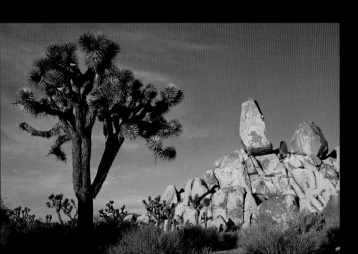
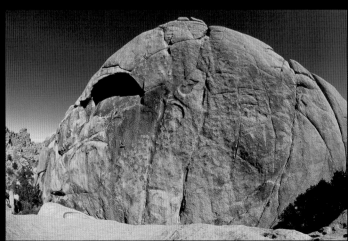

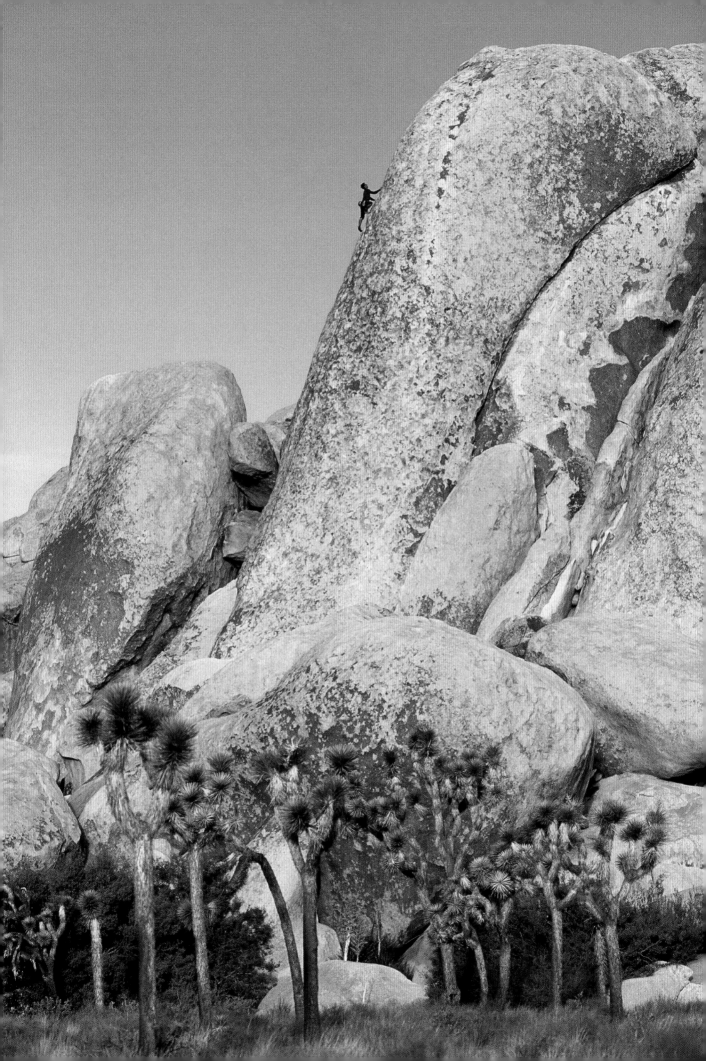

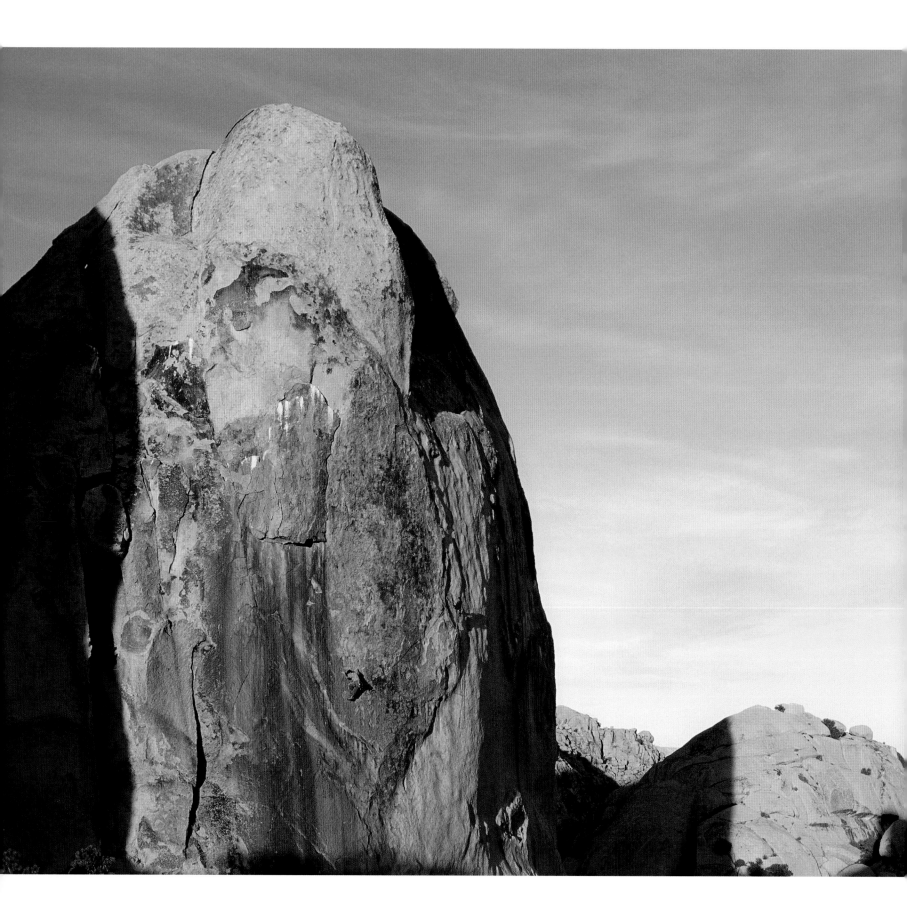

⬆ Greg Loniewski (following) and Kate Rutherford on pitch one of
the classic *Figures on a Landscape* (5.10b), North Astro Dome.

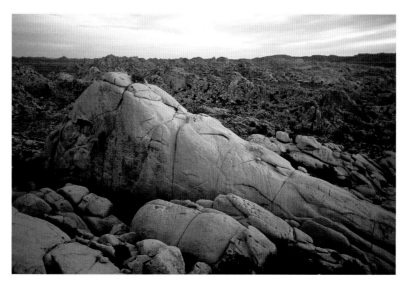

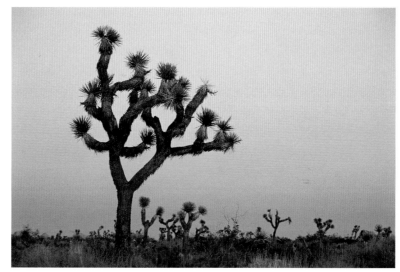

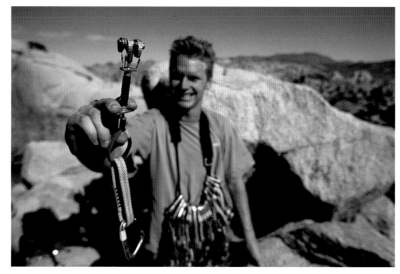

◪ Miles of piles of rock. A view across The Sentinel and Real Hidden Valley.

◩ Joshua Tree sunset.

◪ David Stallard selecting his kit for **Run for Your Life** (5.10b) on the Tumbling Rainbow Formation.

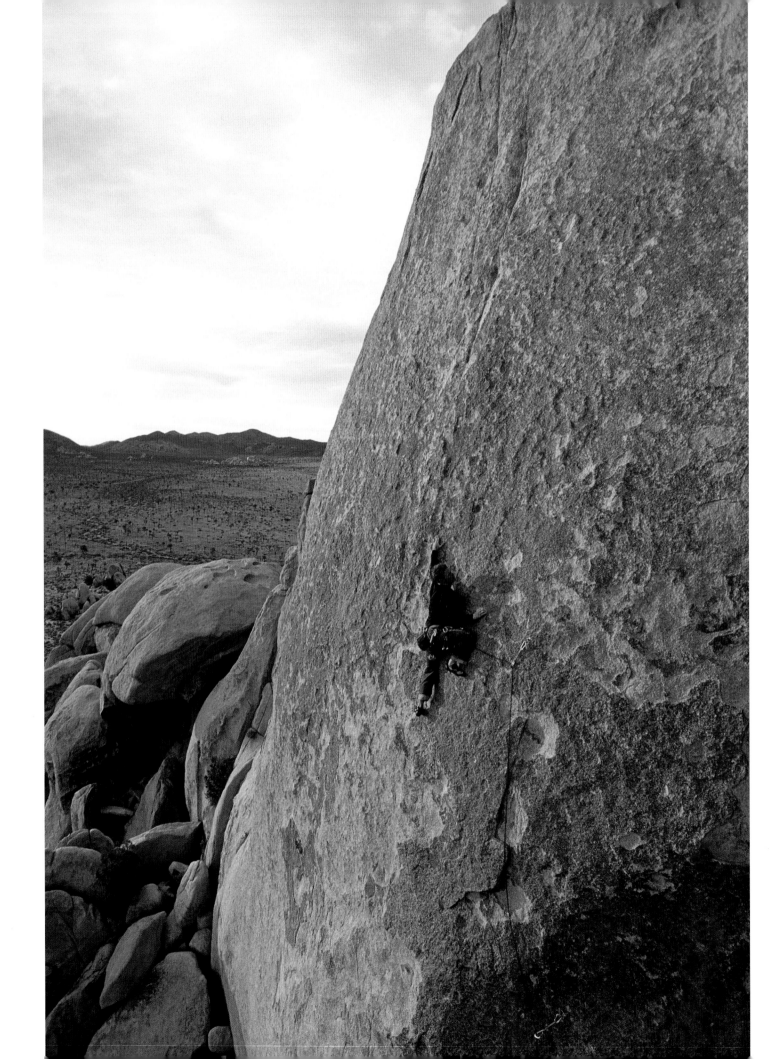

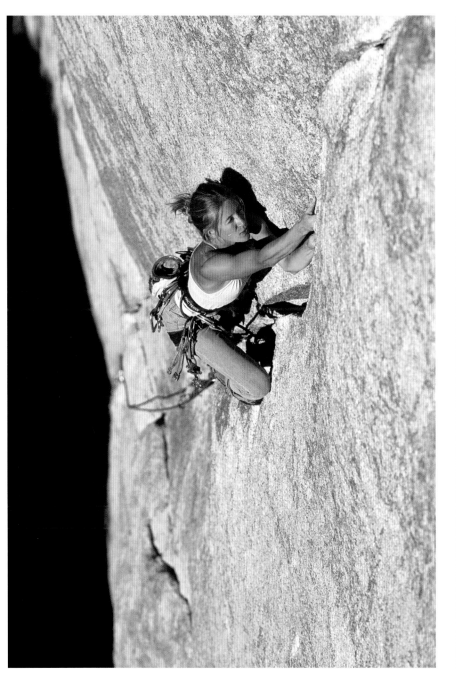

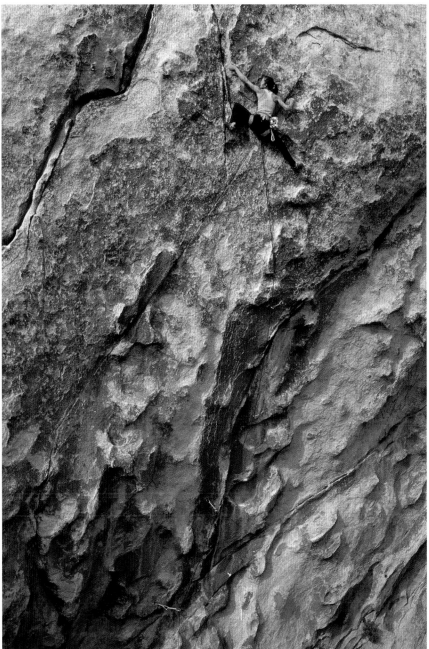

← David Stallard serenely sending **Run for Your Life** (5.10b), Tumbling Rainbow Formation.

↑ Kate Rutherford grooving up the deceptively difficult **Illusion Dweller** (5.10b), The Sentinel.

↗ Monique Forestier putting her pedal to the metal on **Satanic Mechanic** (5.12b), Turtle Rock.

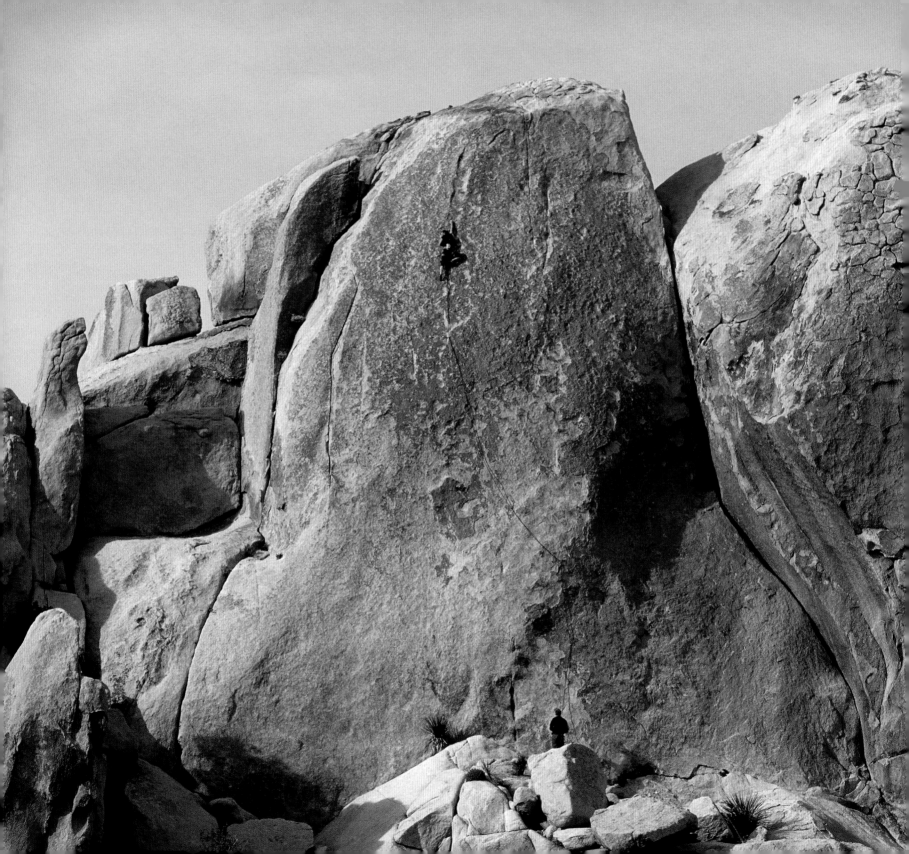

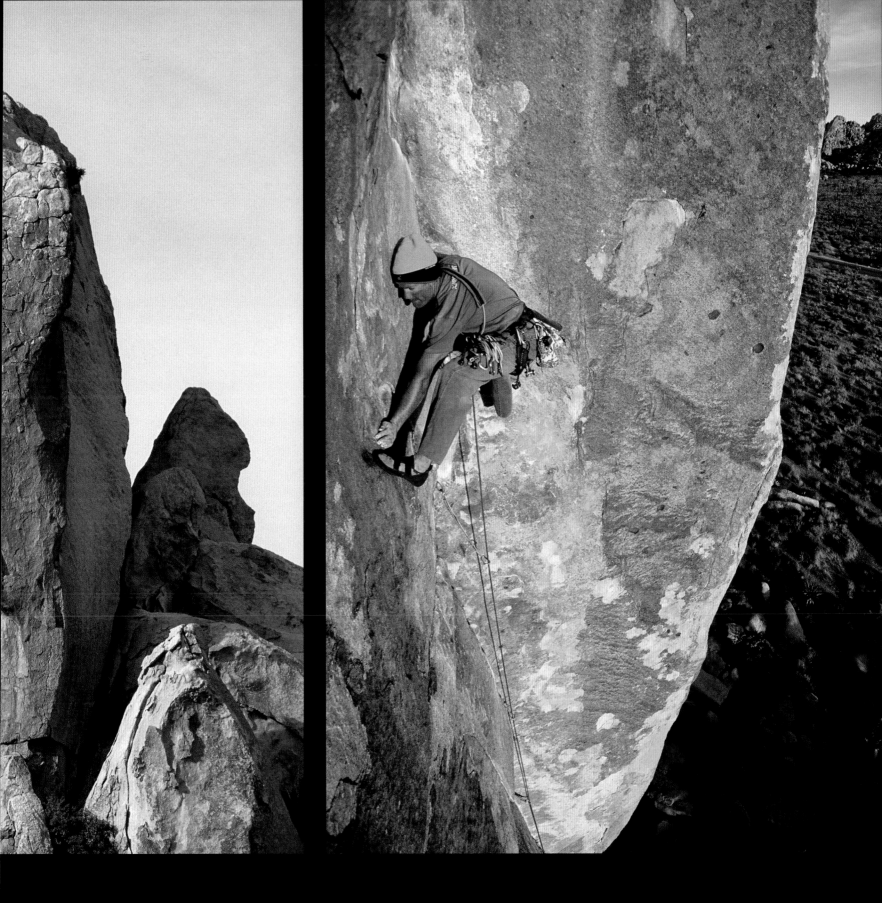

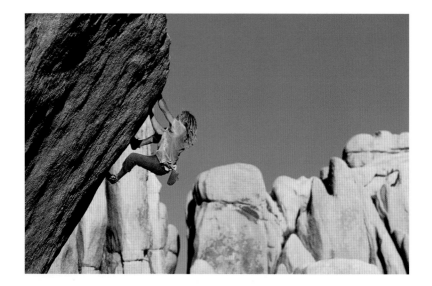

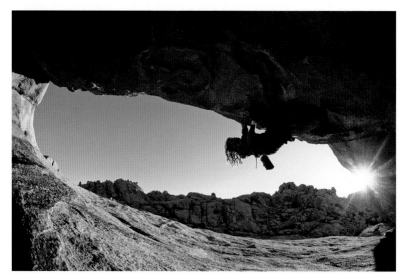

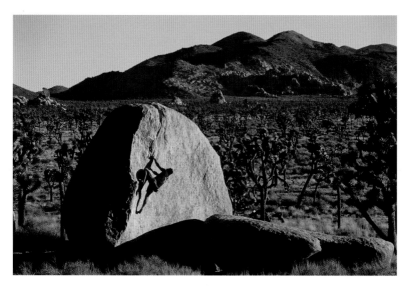

Nicholas Mahmood, *White Rastafarian* (V3 R), in the no-fall zone.

Nicholas Mahmood practicing his wizardry on *Sex Magician* (V7).

Phil Tifo hanging loose on *Classic Curl* (V1).

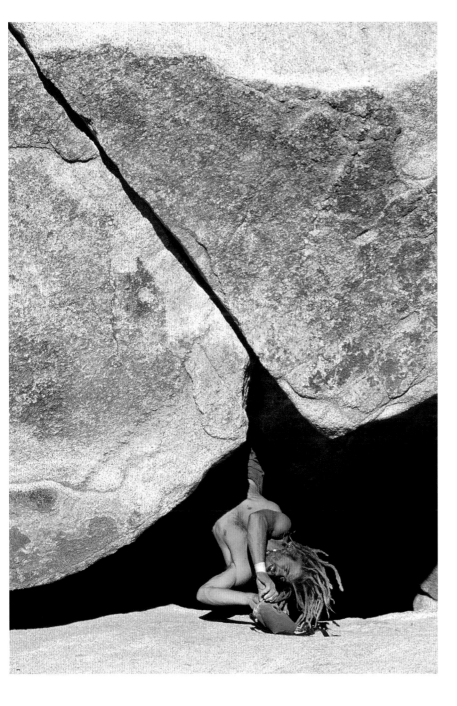

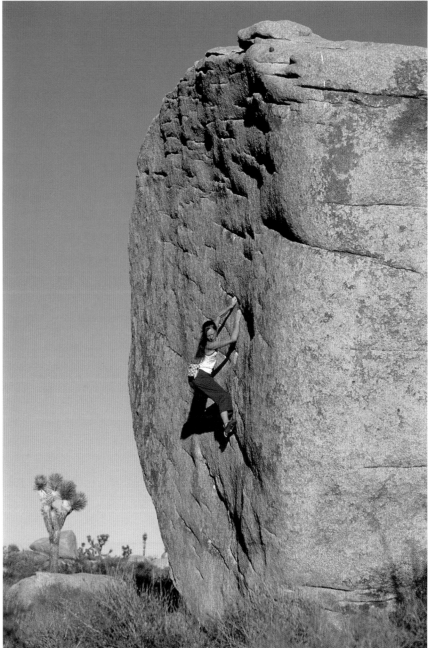

⬆ Kneebar master Nicholas Mahmood dipping into his strategically prepositioned chalk bag on **Pig Pen** (V4).

⬈ Monique Forestier climbing the disconcertingly high **Slash Face** (V3 R).

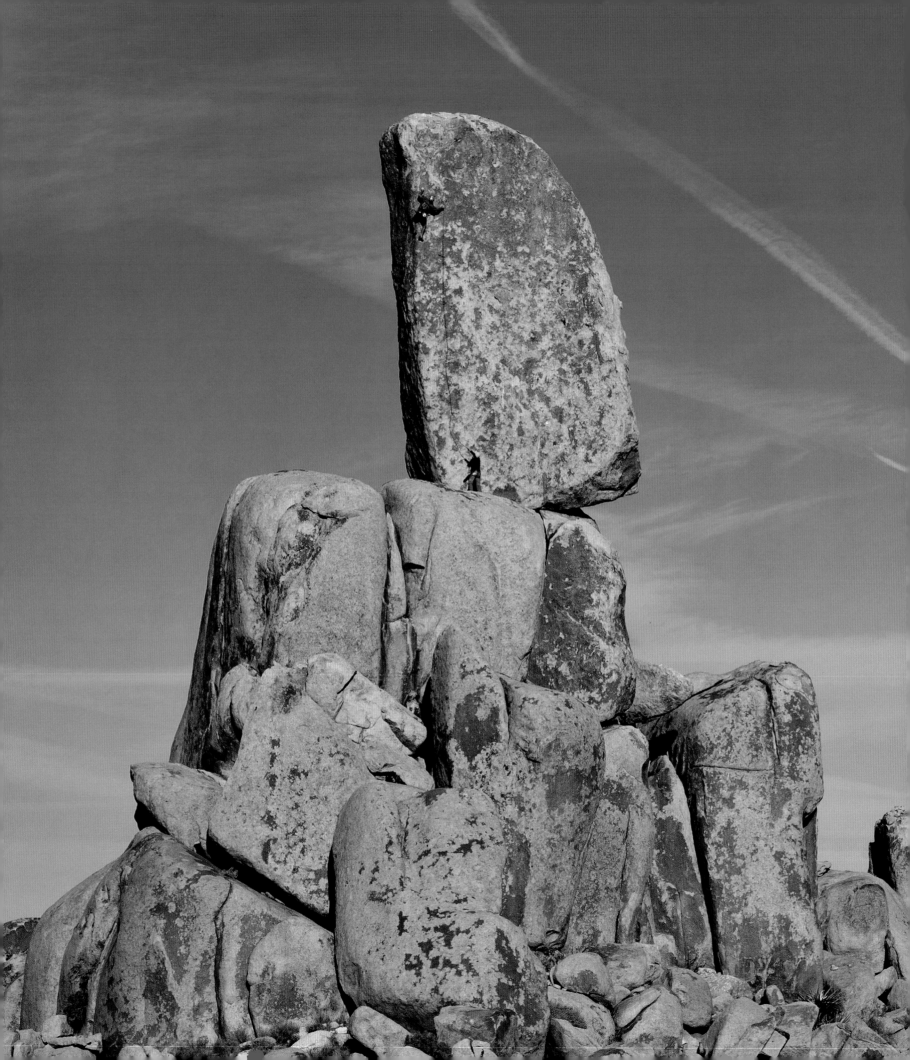

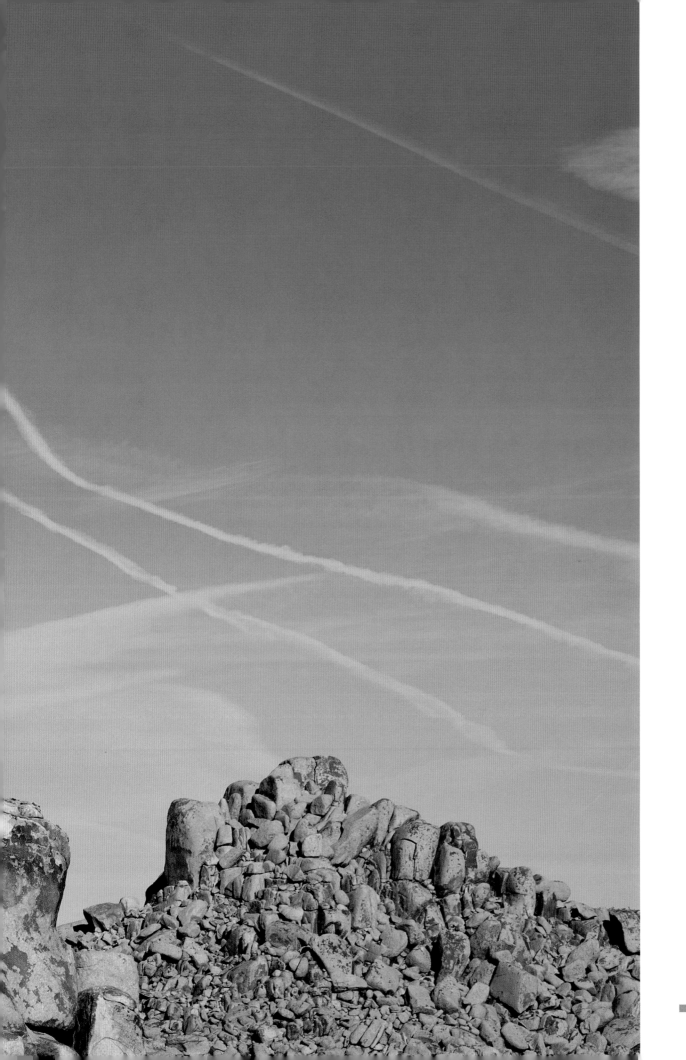

John Durr, with Diana Durr belaying, finding **Indian Giver** (5.12b) no gift. Lost Pencil.

DEVILS TOWER

Before you have even turned your head, as if by magic the plug of rock appears; it literally springs up and says "ta, daa!". The towering multi-faceted columns stand tall over the sweet, luscious meadows playfully dancing in the wind below. The Belle Fourche River silently glides through Ponderosa pine forests, past chipmunks, comic prairie dogs and deer seeking shelter in the Tower's motherly embrace.

Also known as Bears Lodge, the tower is a sacred site for many American Indians and out of respect for their beliefs climbers are asked not to climb during the month of June when religious ceremonies are held.

Devils Tower was declared the first National Monument of America in 1906 and made famous to the mainstream by the 1977 Stephen Spielberg film, *Close Encounters of the Third Kind*. The iconic landmark is distinctly recognisable by its strict geometrical columns which fizz with luminous yellow lichen. In cross section, each hexagonal column can be a few metres in diameter and packed together like honeycomb. And to trad climbers, it's the splitter crack lines and bridging voids between the towers that attract their attention. The 150-metre tall natural wonder, hosts some 220 routes from 5.6 to 5.13a, most of them falling between 5.10 and 5.12.

The summit was first reached in 1893 by Rogers and Ripley, by means of a crude wooden ladder. The tower was first free climbed in 1937 when Fritz Wiessner, Lawrence Coveney and William House climbed the *Wiessner Route* (5.7). The second free route on the tower was the *Durrance Route* (5.6), first climbed in 1938 by Jack Durrance. Nowadays, it is done in four to six pitches and out of the 4,200 climbers who visit the tower each year, about a third seek out this route mainly because it's the easiest means to the summit. Another explanation is that this route is listed in Steck and Roper's *Fifty Classic Climbs of North America*, published in 1979.

Other test pieces which tackle the proudest of lines and have excellent protection include *Soler* (5.9) which was the first aid route on the tower, now a five star two-pitch finger and hand crack in a corner which gets you to within scrambling distance of the summit. Located on the north side is *New Wave* (5.10a) also well-travelled due to its shady position and it has an easy, slabby first pitch that gets top-roped quite often. Then there's *El Matador* (5.10d), a torturous groin-straining workout involving relentless stemming between columns, which are either just within or just out of reach depending on your flexibility and stature. And not forgetting the impeccable *Mr Clean* (5.11a); with over 100 metres of unadulterated finger and hand crack on offer, how can you resist?

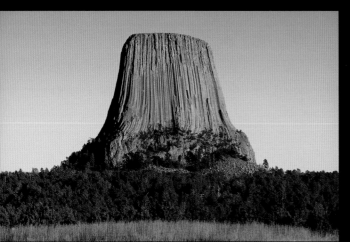
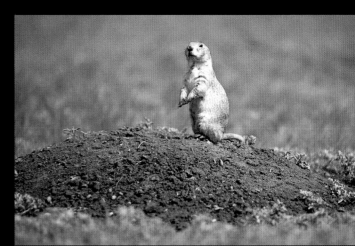

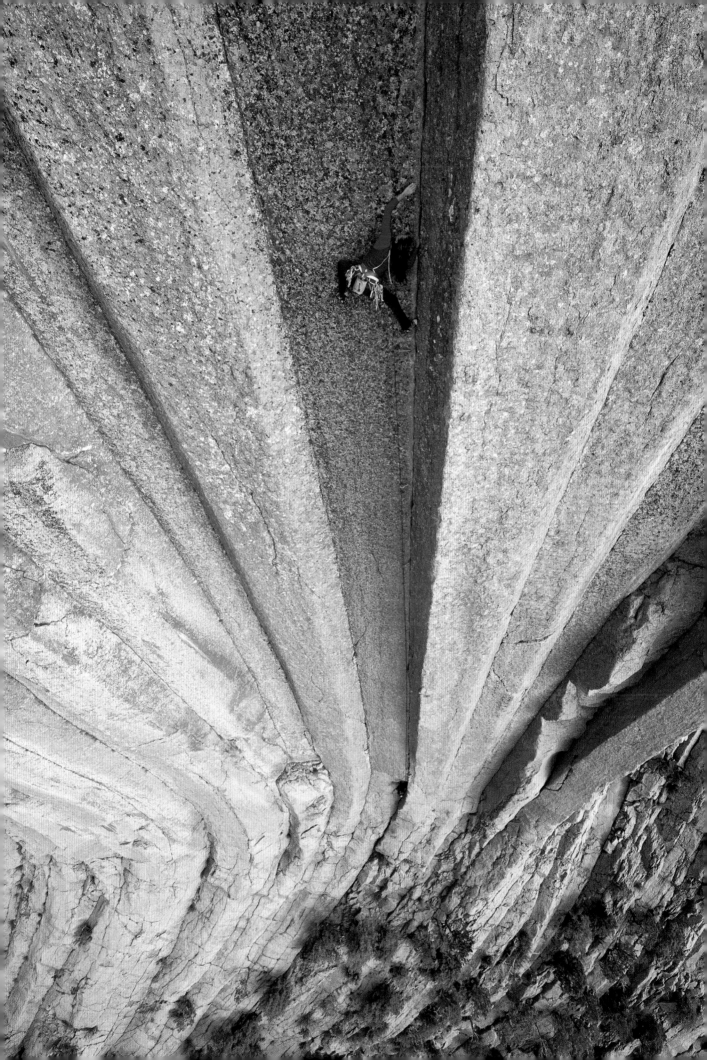

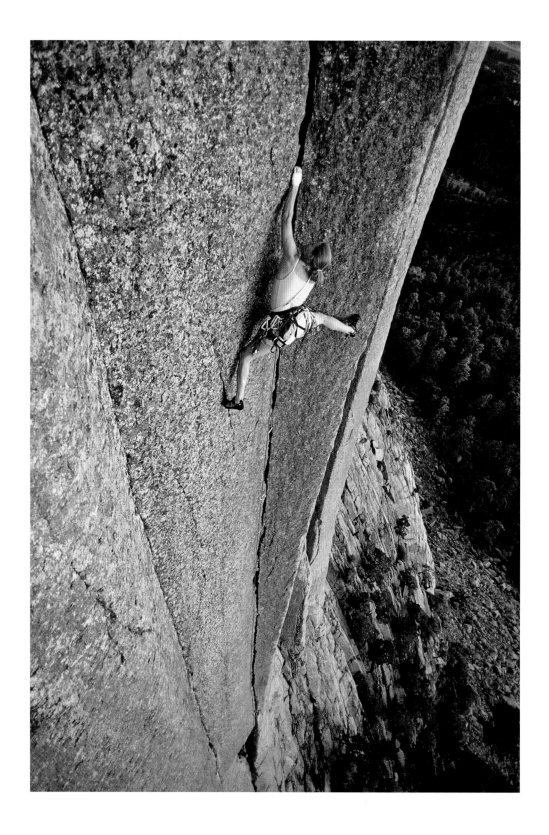

Lisa Gnade on the crux pitch of **Mr Clean** (5.11a). First climbed by Henry Barber and Chip Lee in 1977, the route is easier these days with sticky rubber and cams.

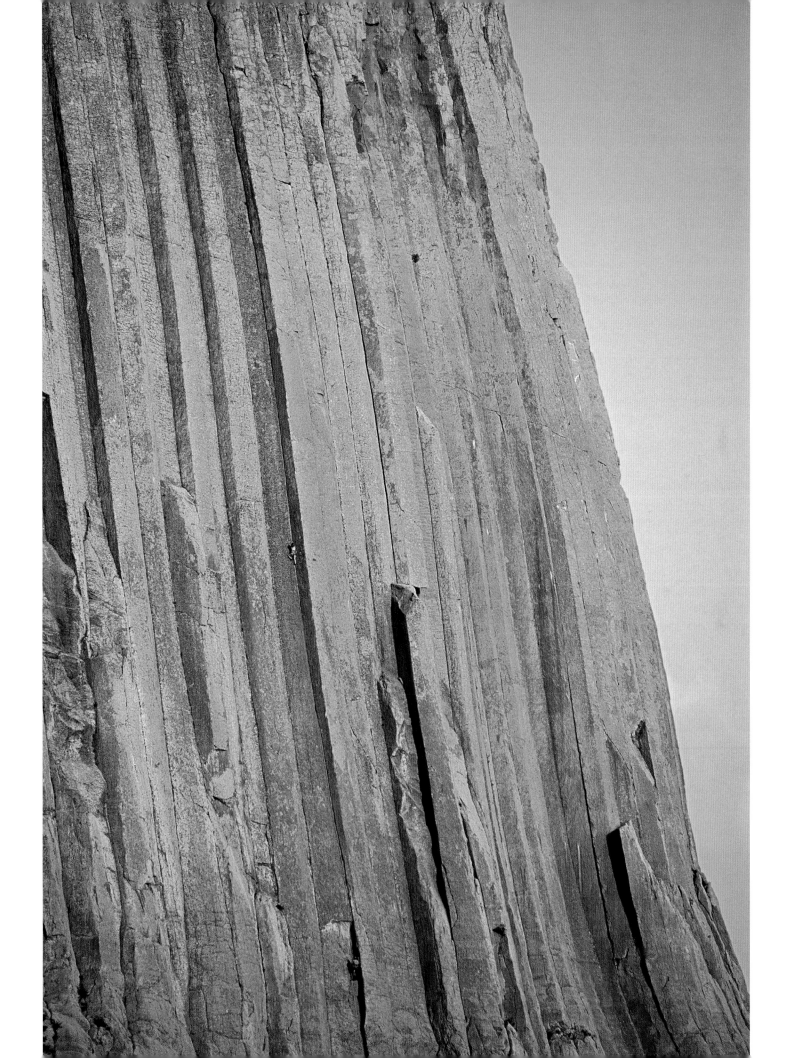

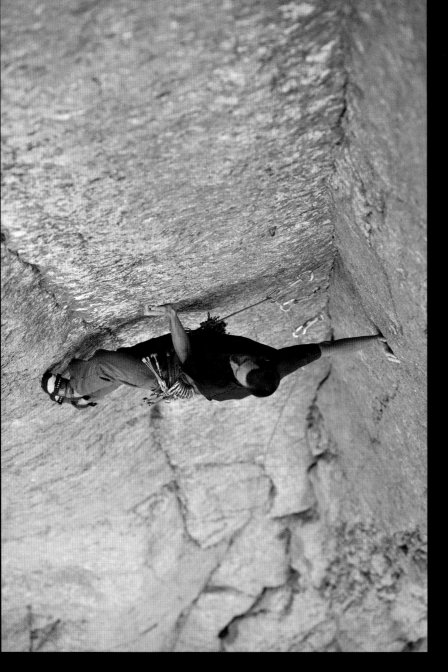
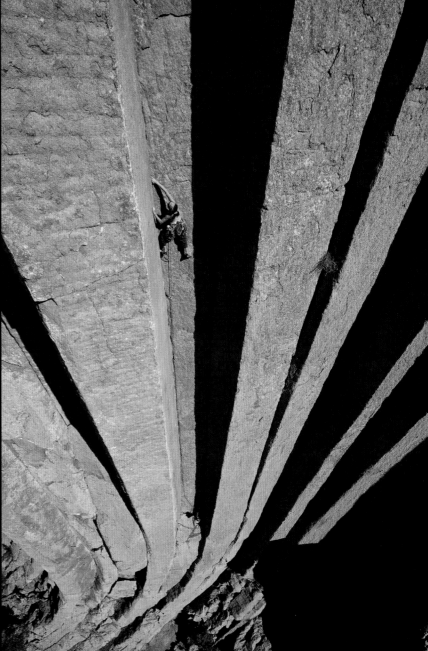

⬆ Sean Nelb battling the tricky crux manoeuver on **A Bridge Too Far** (5.11d).

↗ Crystal Davis on the coverted **El Matador** (5.10d).

➡ Brittany Griffith also on **El Matador**. The route was first free climbed by Bob Yoho and Chick Holtkamp in 1978.

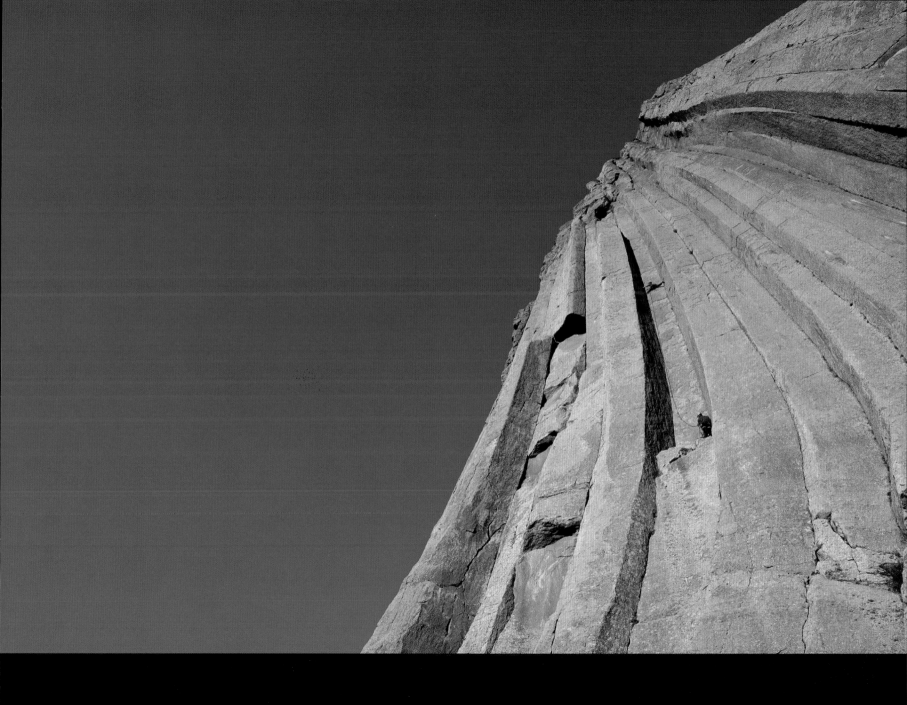

RED RIVER GORGE

Cosily nestled in eastern Kentucky's oil country, the constant whirring of pumps set a regular tempo for the raucous shenanigans in session at the petrified gardens of the Red River Gorge. These sandstone outcrops are splattered throughout the sleepy hollows like dandelion seeds dispersed by the wind. What makes this place so special however, is the wonderful variety and plenitude of rock ensuring that any sport or trad climber will find something to their taste in this lolly shop.

With declining temperatures the leaves put on a spectacular show, a kaleidoscope of colours which burn the hills like unruly wildfire. The downward migration of leaves marks the start of perfect sending conditions and the en masse yearly pilgrimage to the area.

Red River Gorge holds a strong hand of picture cards, with its easy go lucky camping, deliciously affordable pizza, rapid cliff access and a plethora of crag options housing an impressive arsenal of grades. It's no wonder that it is endangered of being loved to death by enthusiastic nomads and locals alike, but it is kept in check somewhat by the short weather window. Most climbing areas are located on National Forest Service land or private land which has suffered past and present closures. In 1996 The Red River Gorge Climbers' Coalition was formed, a non-profit voice of climbers advocating the protection and promotion of responsible climbing and since then they have purchased large tracts of private land to further secure access in the area.

The first route in The Red, as it is affectionately known, dates back to the 1950s, put up by some cavers seeking adventure. Then, during the late 60s and early 70s, the area was frequented by traditional climbers practicing clean climbing ethics up natural lines. The early 80s saw the route numbers reach 300 when a fitter breed of climbers came and set new benchmarks and established numerous bold classics. Then in 1990 Porter Jarrard, armed with a power drill, led the charge to rap bolt some of the featured overhanging rock which didn't take natural gear. Within three years the number of routes skyrocketed to 700 as the area's potential was realised. The discovery and development of The Motherlode in 1994 cemented the 5.13 grade in The Red and rightfully established it as one of the best sport climbing destinations in the country. Today there are over 1600 routes with an almost equal mix of sport and trad climbs.

The route names give a good idea of what to expect: *BOHICA* (Bend Over, Here It Comes Again), *Fifty Words for Pump*, *God's Own Stone*, *Pulling Pockets*, *The Pinch*, *Insanity Ceiling* and *Corner Cutter*... It's a real mixed bag of lollies.

The Red offers mind blowing fun on amazingly featured frictional sandstone. The radical array of holds are a dream to behold; perfect texture and non aggressive. And with angles and aspects available in any configuration you can climb in most weather conditions with any tick list in hand. For me though, the main attraction was the Motherlode, no long reaches, no stopper moves; just all day suckers, endless pumping on positive edges. And to top that, the two-faced Madness Cave, with lines so sweet they lure you in only to suck every last drop of juice out of your arms. One way or another they'll leave you hanging on the end of the rope, the question is whether you had enough in the tank to clip the anchors in time.

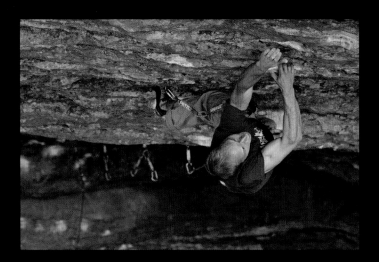

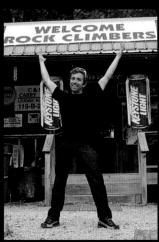

1 Ryan Pall coming within a whisker of onsighting *Omaha Beach* (5.14a), Madness Cave, The Motherlode.

2 Timmy O'Neill giving a good ol' Kentucky welcome at the beer trailer.

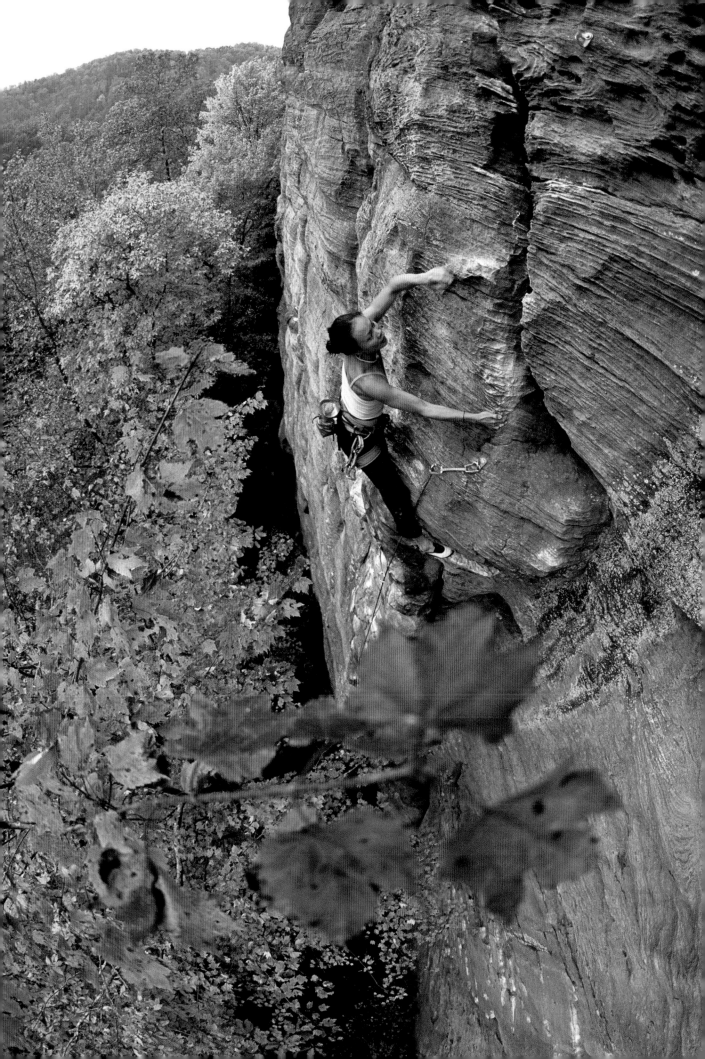

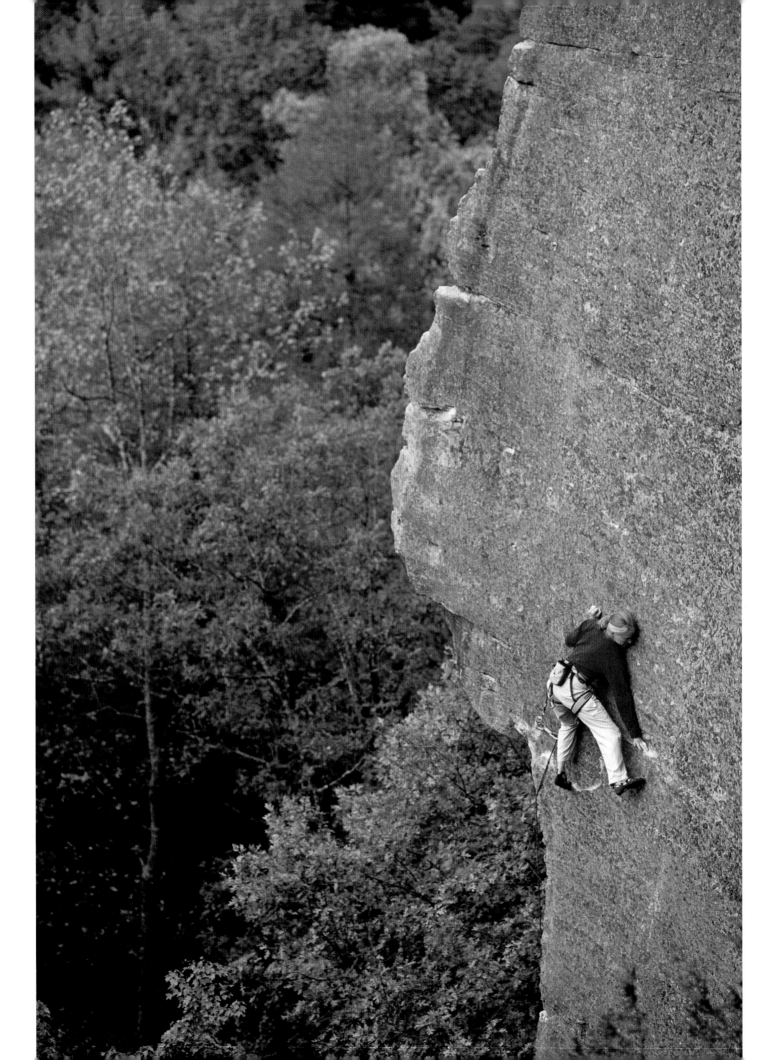

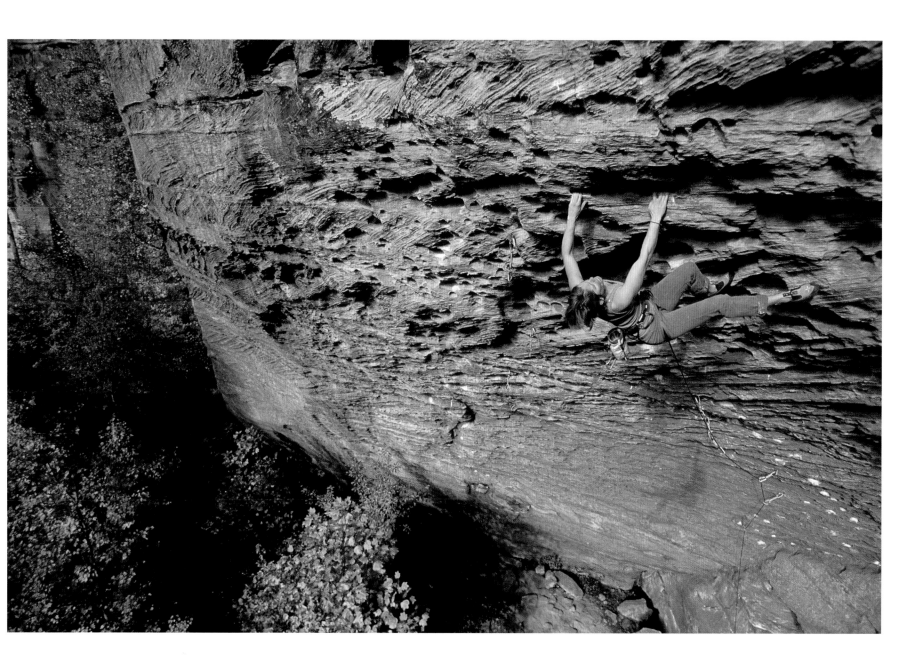

◁ Lisa Gnade working out the inobvious **Prime Directive** (5.11b), Funkrock City.

⬆ Whitney Boland straightening out the tangles on **Ultra Perm** (5.13d), Bob Marley Crag.

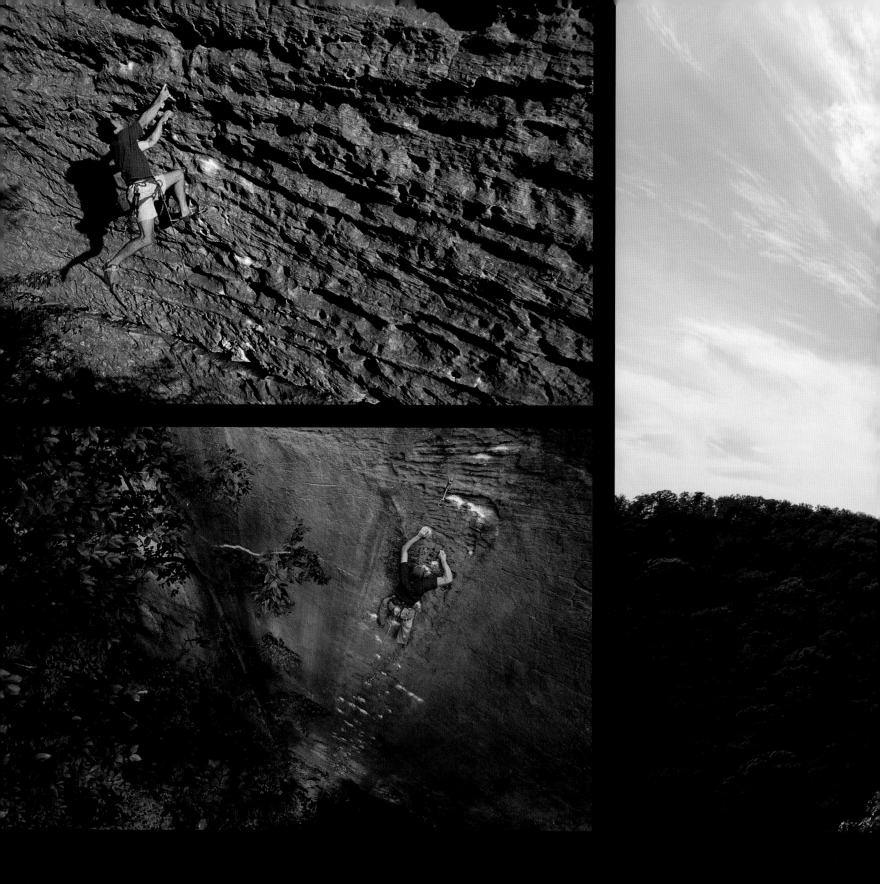

Greg Child not hanging around for **The Return of Chris Snyder** (5.11d), Roadside Crag.

Alex Kobes squeezing the hard but delectable drops of **Orange Juice** (5.12c), Fuck Rock City.

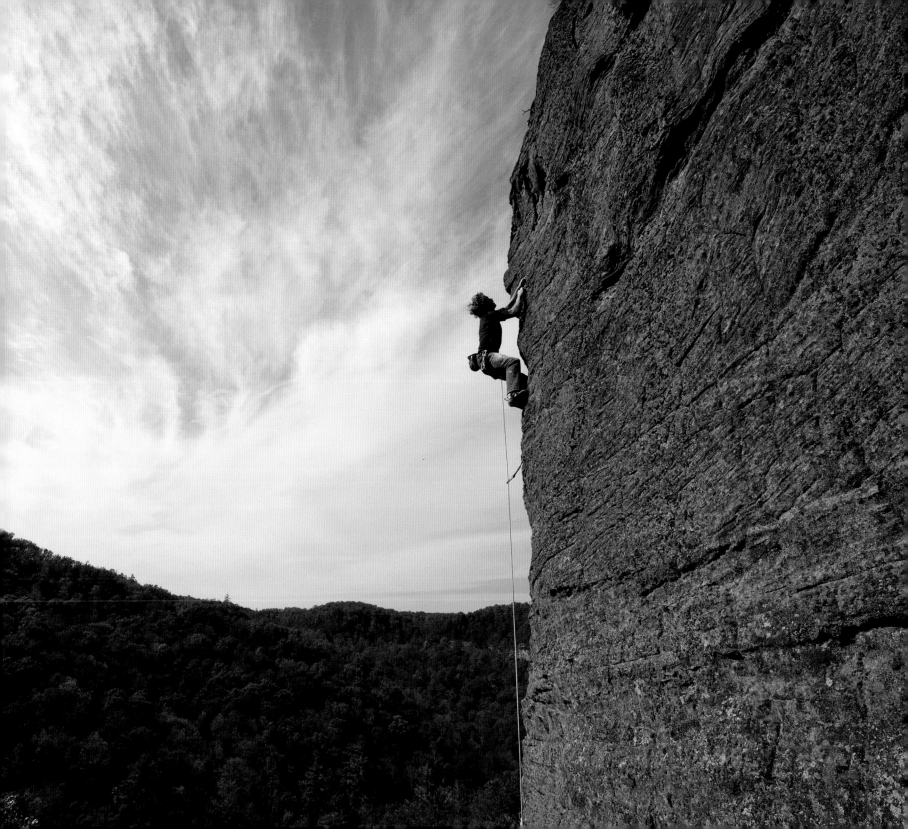

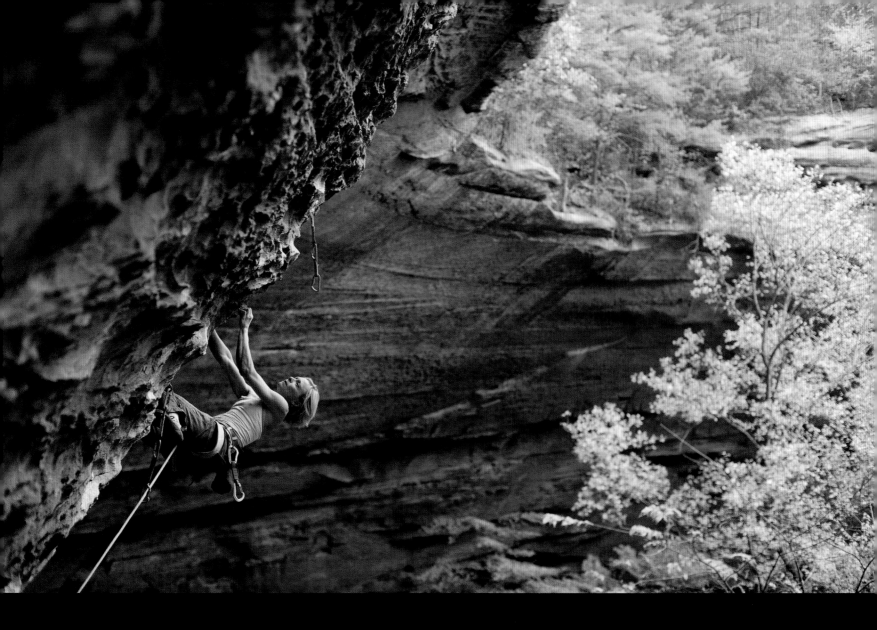

↑ Monique Forestier on her route *Kaleidoscope* (5.13c) at Drive-By Crag.

↳ Whitney Boland persevering past *Flour Power* (5.13b) into its extension *Pushin' Up Daisies* (5.13c), Madness Cave, The Motherlode.

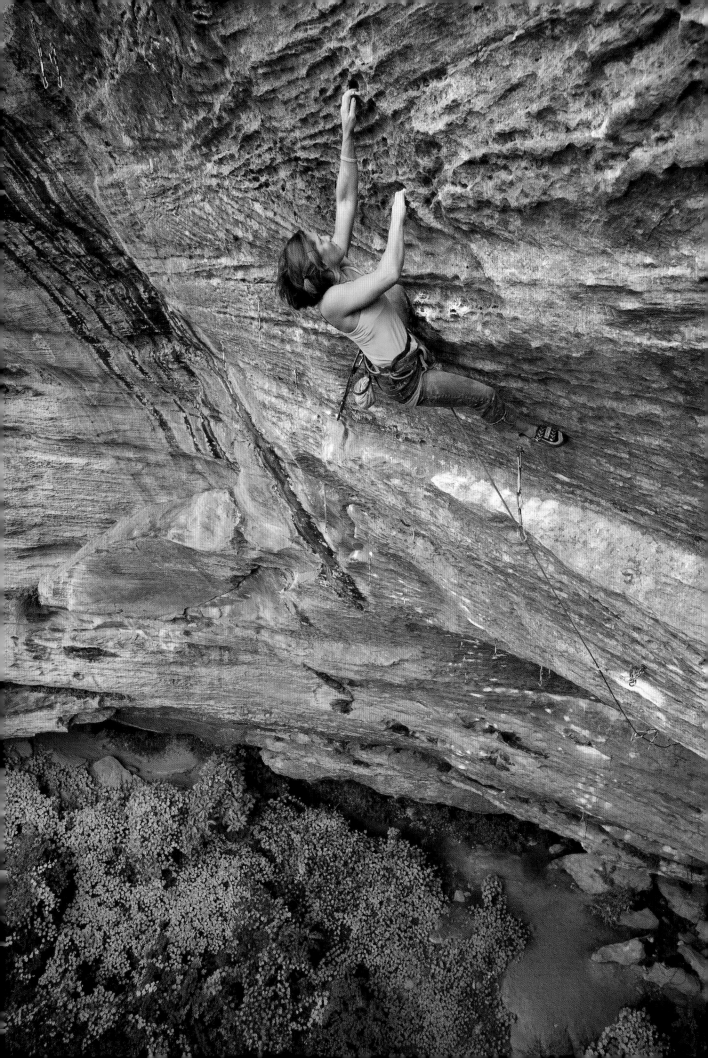

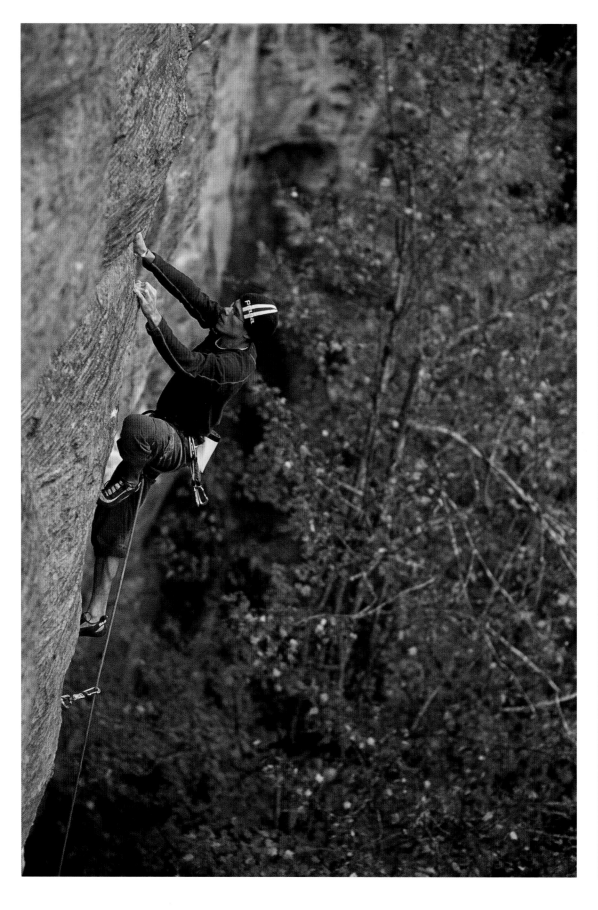

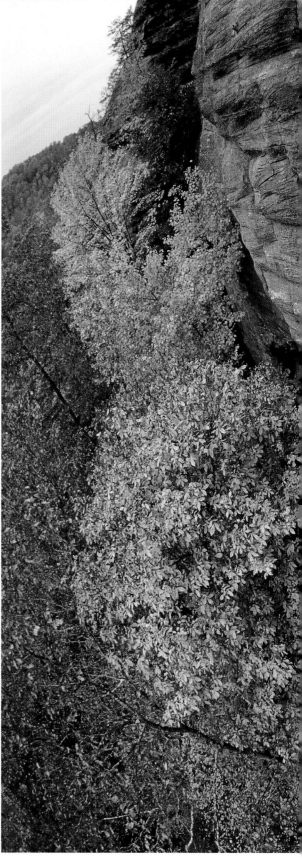

↑ → No worries for Bentley Brackett on **Hakuna Matata** (5.12a), Drive-By Crag.

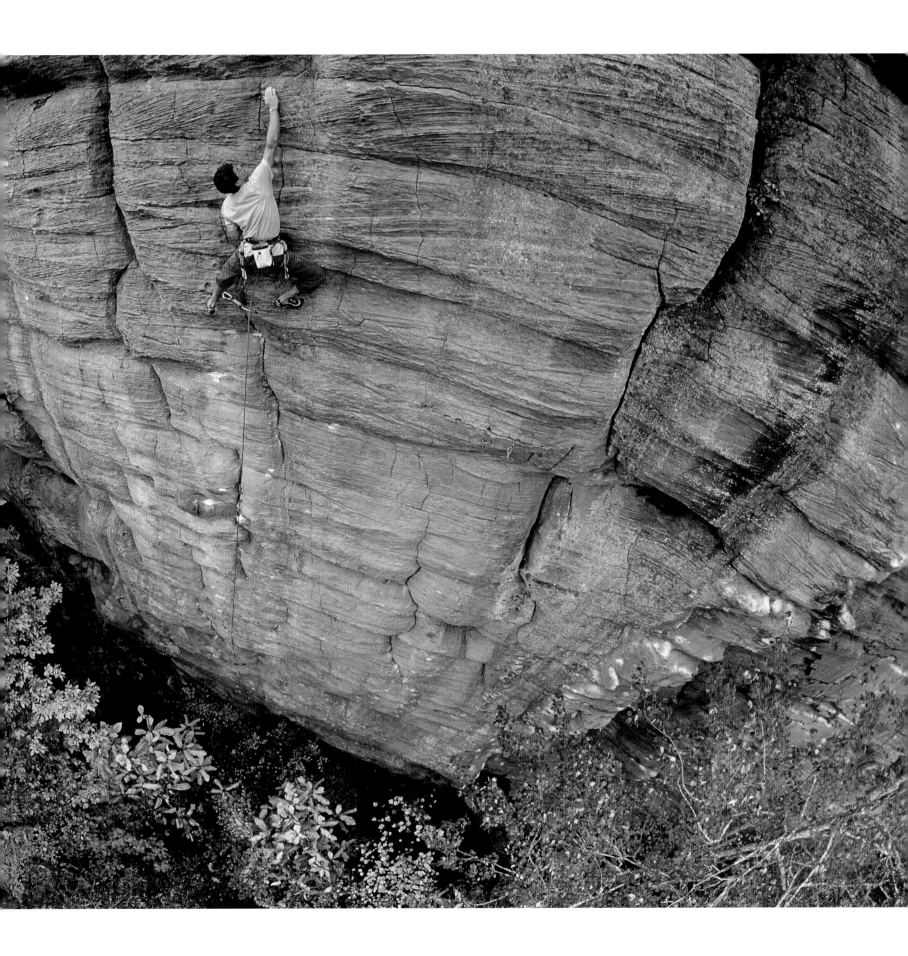

THE DARRANS

My nostrils fill with crisp pristine air, the skin on my face contracts and my senses are heightened. We are in a prehistoric wilderness, the land that time forgot — forgot to bulldoze and develop that is — a wilderness unto its own. It's a Jurassic adventure park with ancient rainforests clinging to vertical cliffs, chiselled valleys carpeted with emerald felt, thunderous cascading waters fed by snow capped peaks. Delicate ecosystems are symbiotically supported by natural infrastructure of massive proportions. What an astounding place!

The remote Darran Mountains not only provide the scenic backdrop to the majesty of northern Fiordland, they also provide endless opportunities for adventurous climbers to explore and conquer.

This rugged collection of granite peaks is home to many classic alpine rock routes. The venerated *North Buttress of Mt Sabre* (17) is undoubtedly one of these, first climbed in 1968. Situated on nearby Moir's Mate is another test piece, *The Bowen-Allen Corner* (17), established in 1972. Also becoming popular is the six-pitch *Lucky Strike* (20), recently opened in 2010.

Being one of the wettest regions in New Zealand (receiving a whopping eight metres of rainfall per year), recent development of sport crags down the Cleddau Valley — The Chasm, Babylon and

Little Babylon — has provided a much needed wet weather option when climbing at higher altitudes is out. At present there are 110 routes collectively, making it the highest concentration of hard sport routes in the country. For many climbers these crags are not so much an alternative but the main drawcard.

Paul Rogers and Steve Walker led the charge in 1993 when they established *High Ideals and Crazy Dreams* (22) at The Chasm. Babylon waited till 2002 to see some action when Bruce Dowrick and Gwilym Griffith-Jones put up the three pitch *Birdsong* (26). Then in 2006 Little Babylon was spotted from the air, perched just above Babylon, it received more attention than a new born and was almost entirely bolted in that one summer. The first routes there were *Weta-Cide* (23) and *Rua Tahi* (25); now it hails high-end work horses like *The Giving Tree Extension* (32) and the super strenuous *Colossus* (33), the latter likely being the hardest route in New Zealand.

One can hear the sweet chirps of forest birds intermingled with calls of desperation as climbers latch or don't latch their crux hold. It is tough to imagine in such an unblemished setting that only a few kilometres down the raging river, the famous Milford Sound churns the masses through its stiles for tourist packages offering boat cruises on the fiord, scenic flights, seal spotting, diving, and the like.

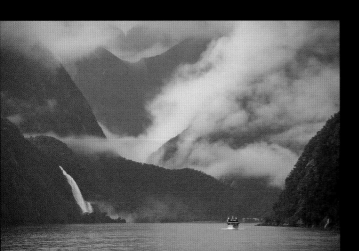

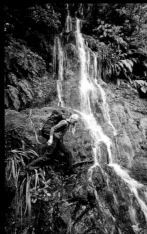

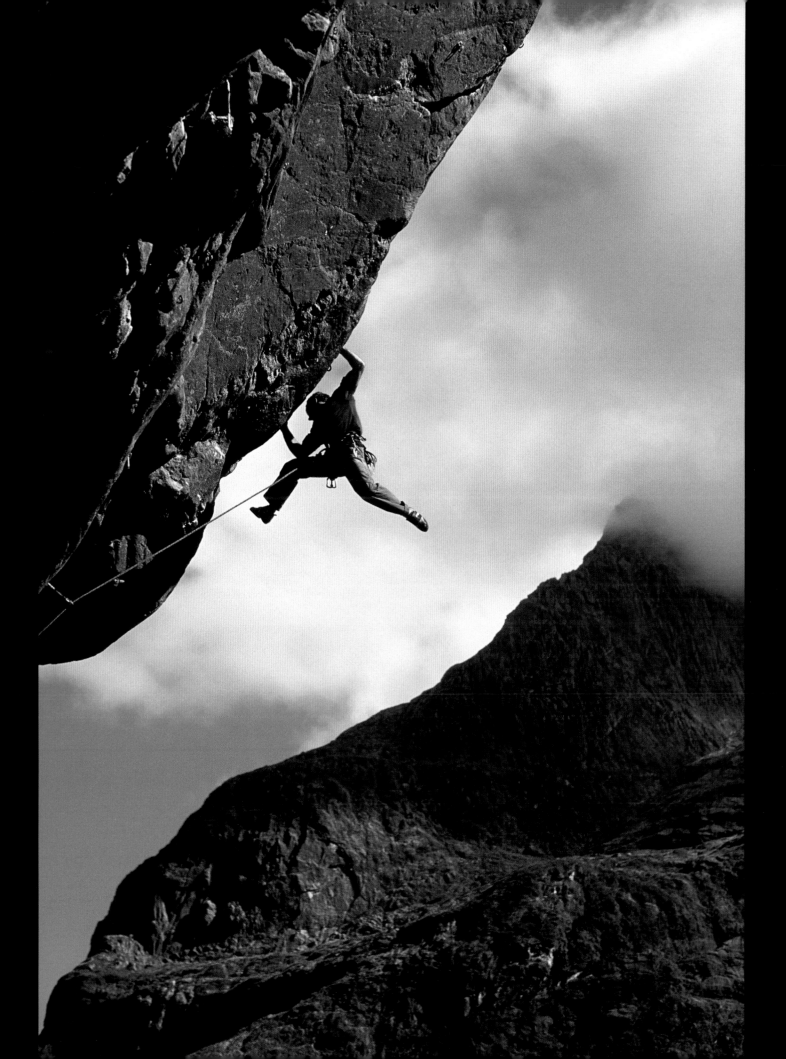

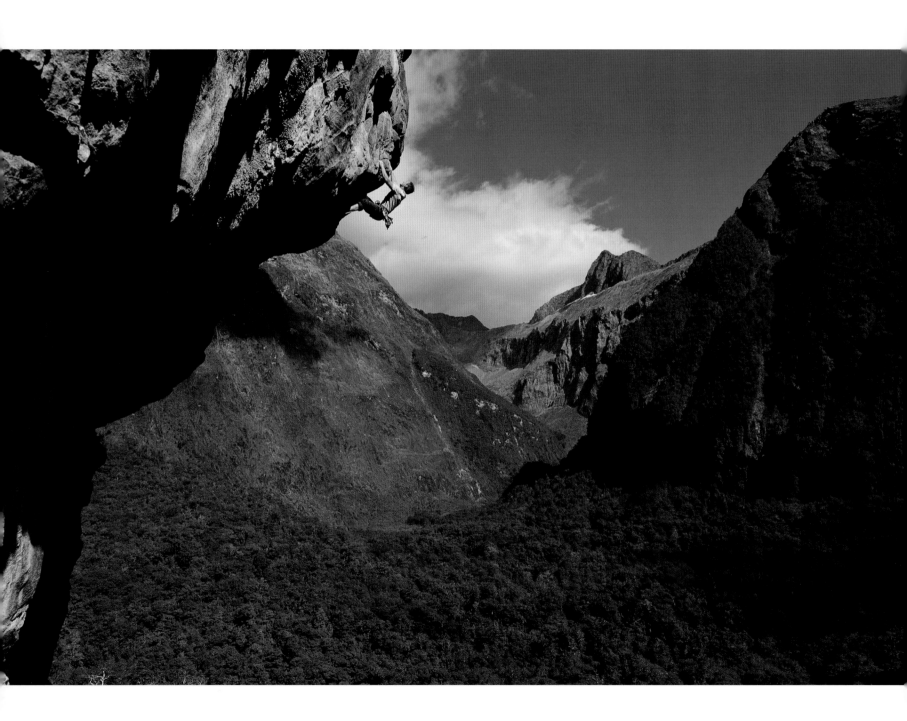

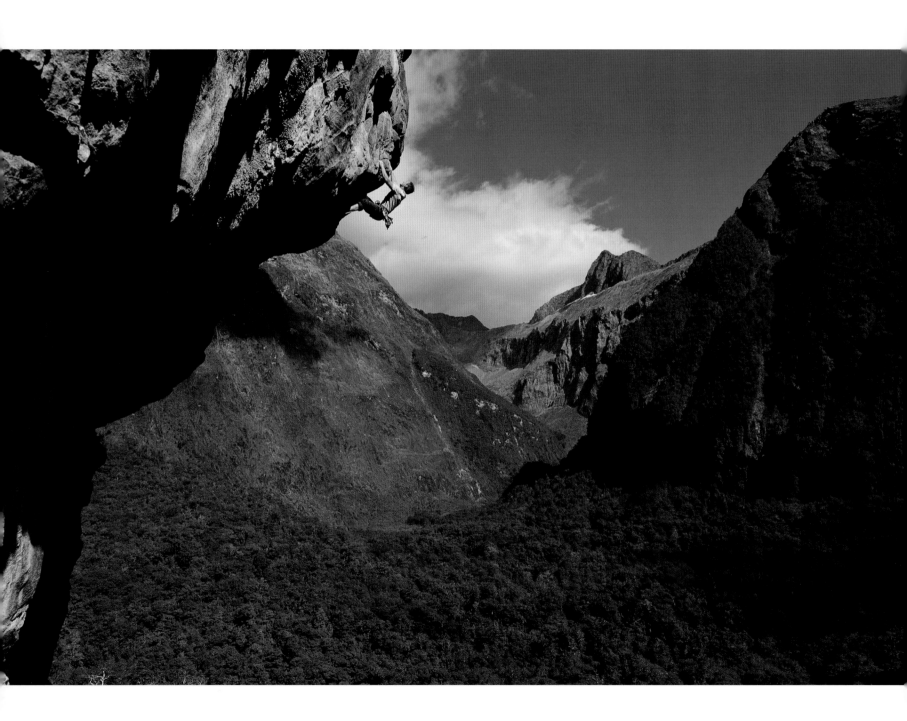 Matt Evrard attempting the magnificently positioned *Contact Neurosis* (29), The Chasm.

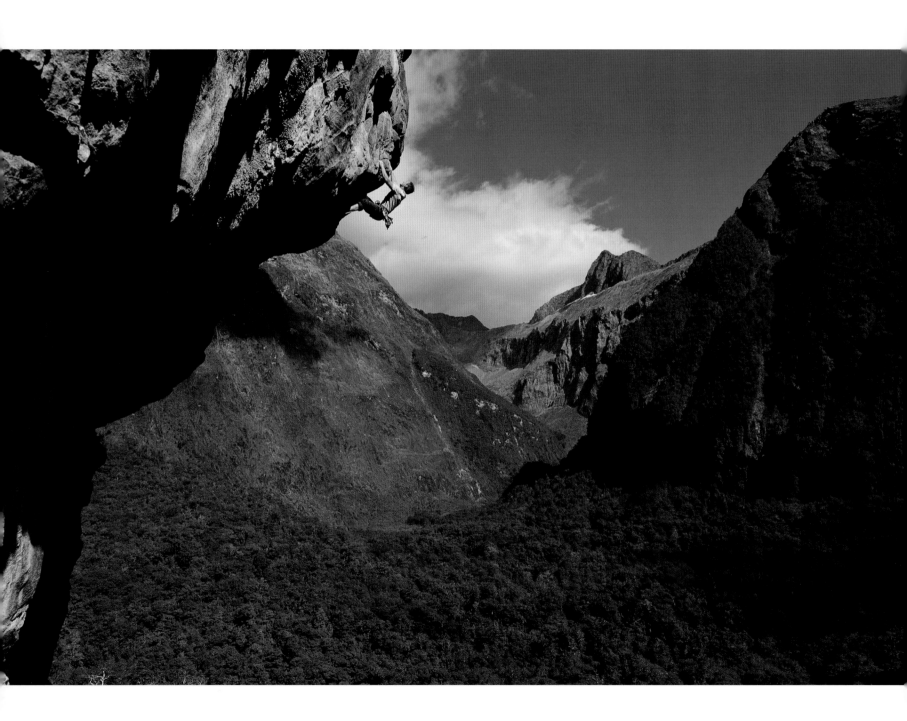 Brian Alder wrestling the juggy dyke (with a heart-breaking finish) of *Buster Milford* (27), The Chasm.

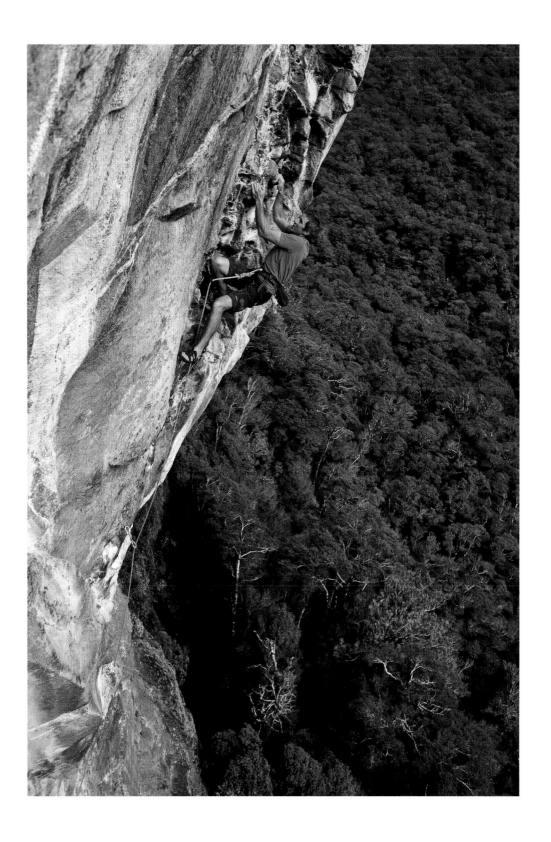

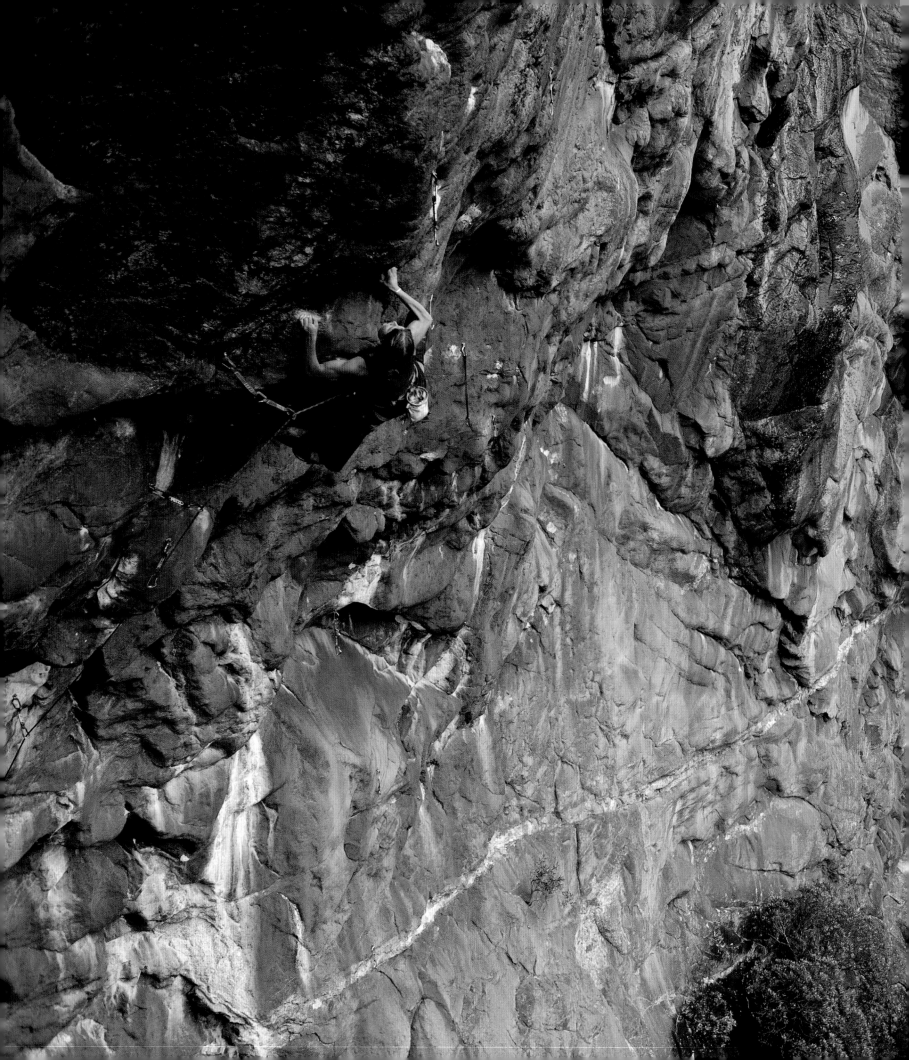

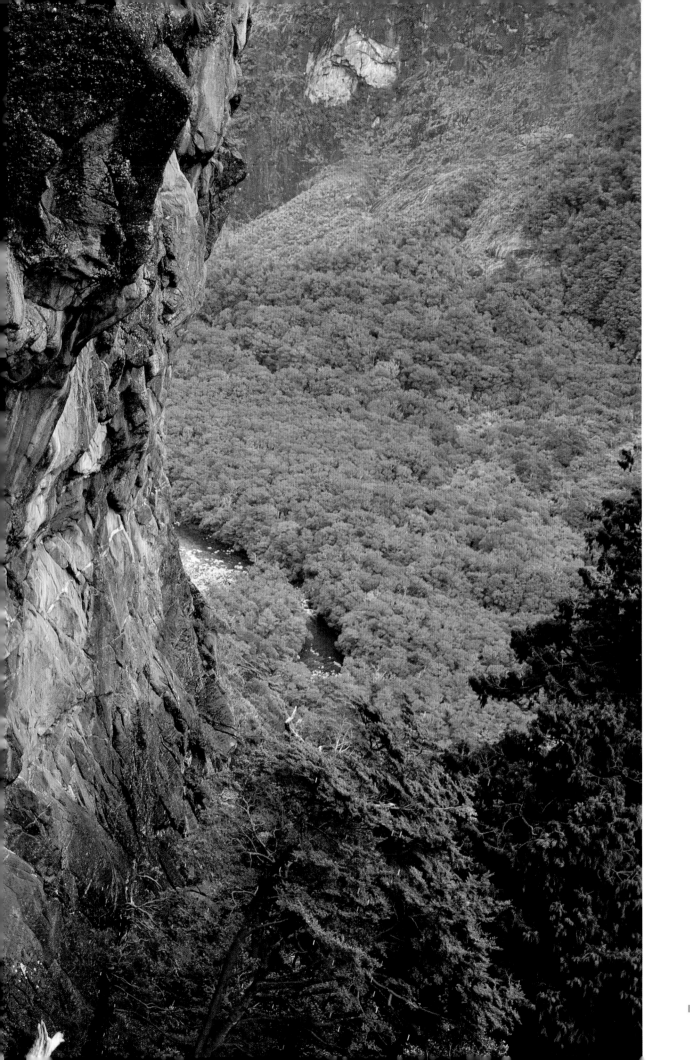

Mayan Smith-Gobat stepping up to a giant fight with **Colossus** (33), Little Babylon.

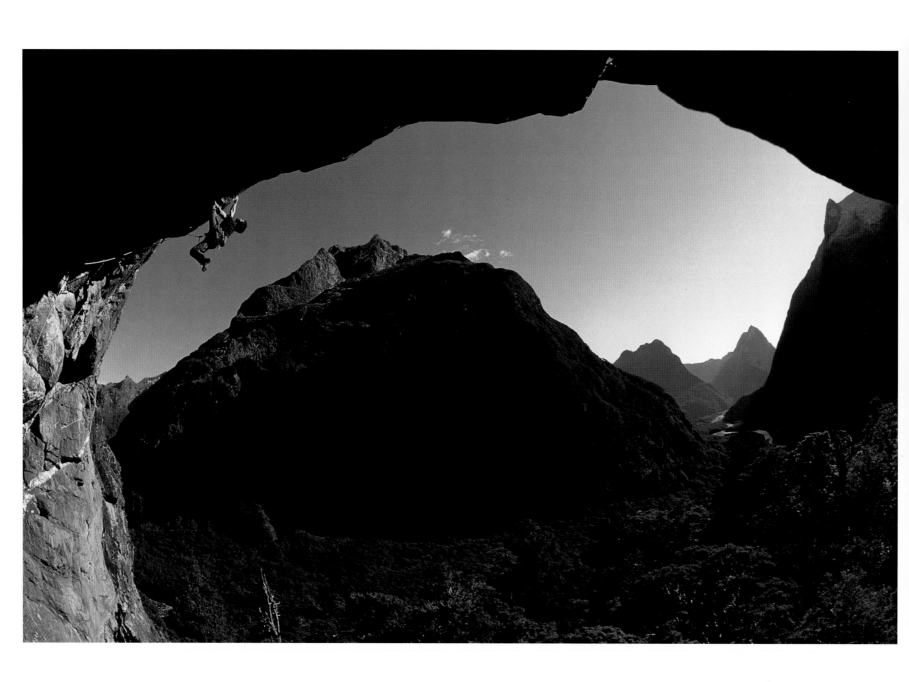

⬆ Bruce Dowrick high on *Jesus Built My Hotrod* (27), Little Babylon.
➡ Jon Sedon low on *Fuel* (29), Babylon.

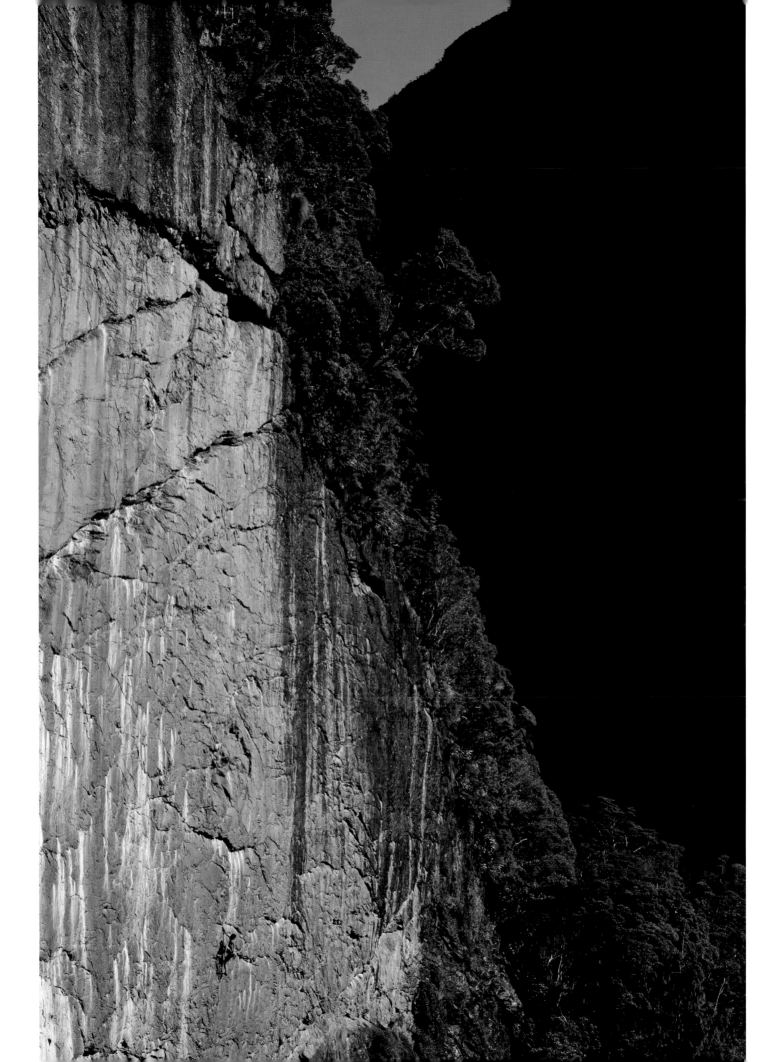

owned by the Royal Australian Navy. During weekdays it is used as a training and weapons range, but on most weekends and holidays it is open to the public to explore the original lighthouse (1899), take in the vertigous views across the Tasman Sea, and if in luck, witness the migrating humpback whales frolicking just off shore.

For the vertically inclined, it's exacting geometry seats over 500 climbs on rock of varying quality. Looking down from above, the peninsula has been cut out by dressmaker's pinking shears, its zigzag cliff profile allows for climbing out of the wind and sun in most conditions.

On the rock the perfect plumb line of verticality, over 100 metres high in parts, surge up from the cobalt depths to ensure never ending heart pumping action. As is the norm here, most routes are rap-in-climb-out affairs on 'mixed' gear.

and snap you back to reality, quick smart.

The superlative Windjammer Wall has been splendidly sea-sprayed with oodles of three star classics. A popular introduction to the area, with bomber gear placements, is the exemplary *Grey Mist* (17) which psyches you up for more. Perhaps then consider the classic cracks of *Icebird* (19) or *Windjammer* (19), or *Walk The Plank* (24) with its fearsome hanging flake.

Eventually my path led to *Liquid Insanity* (23), with an incessant easterly whipping through my headspace and the bombarding waves below it was an unnerving ride. Sea-cliff climbing is perhaps not for everyone, for me it adds another dimension to just clipping bolts; but I couldn't do it all the time. When the area is closed or you've had enough of the churning; the seas below and your stomach within, then head to Nowra.

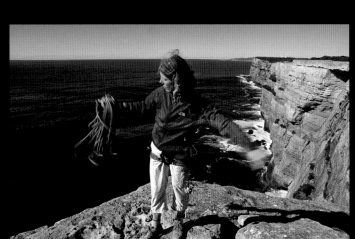
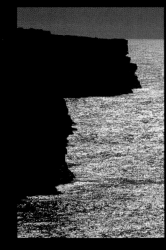

⬆ Sky, sea, cliff and climber: Abby Watkins.
⬈ And looking the other way — up the coast.
➡ Abby Watkins not quite at the end of *Our Terminal World* (25).

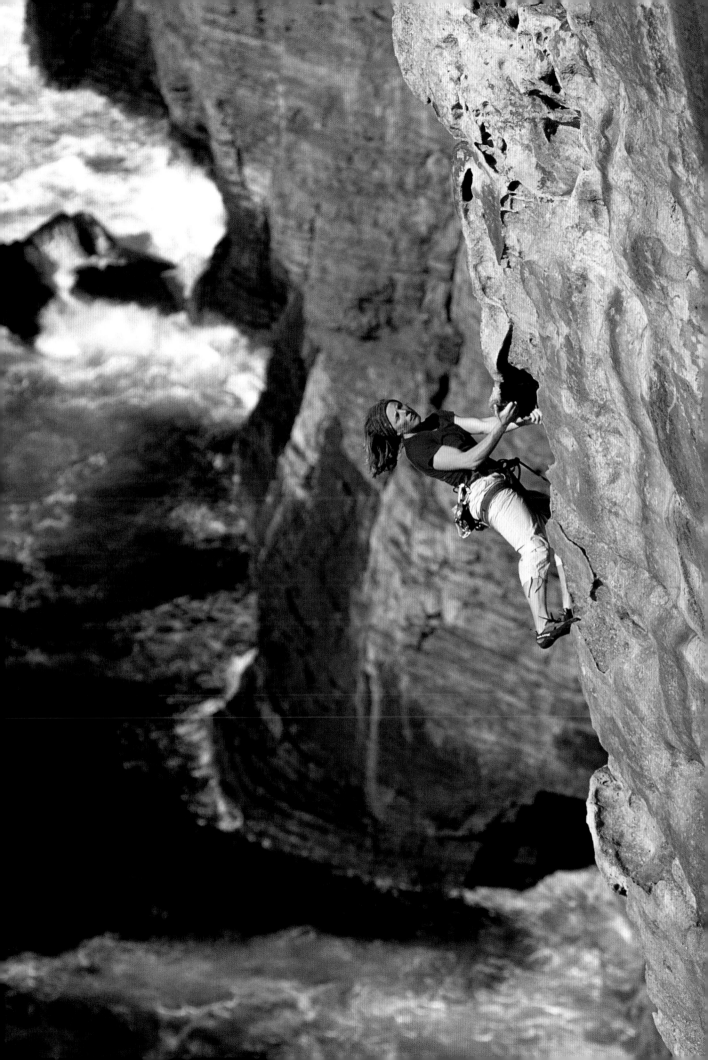

Lee Cossey has downed his spinach and is now eating up *Choy Sum* (23), a neglected delight on Popeye Wall.

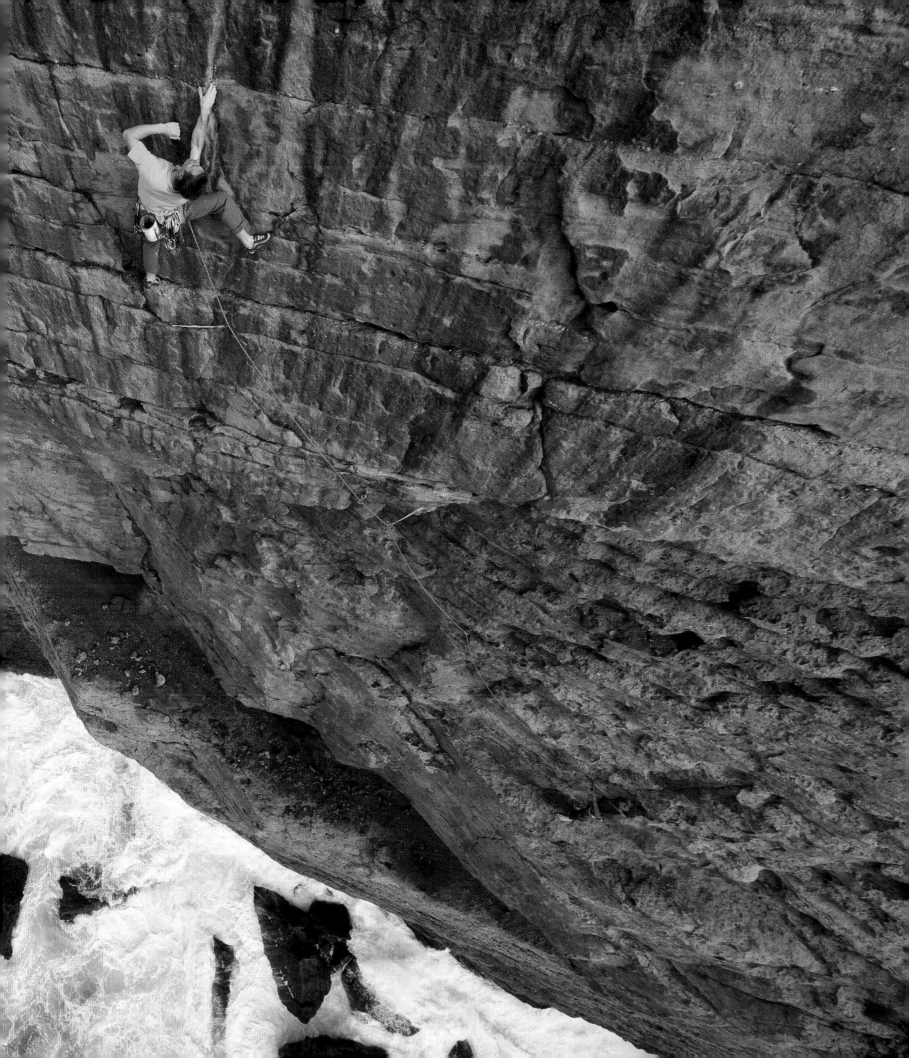

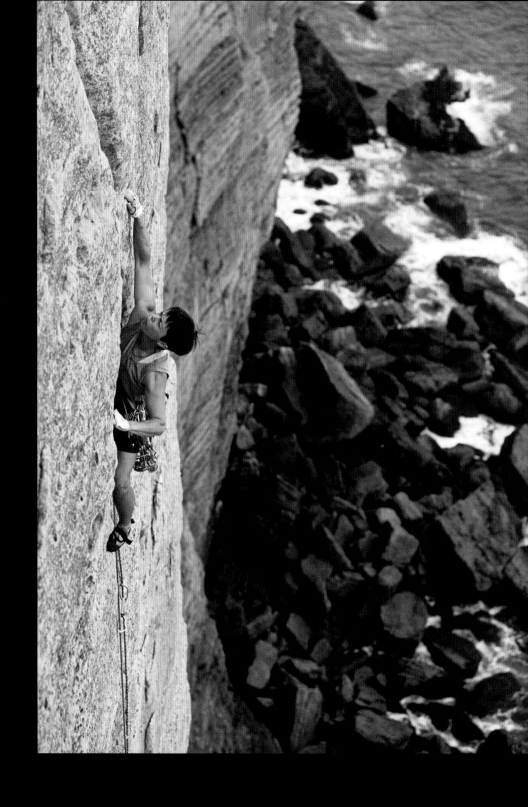

Robyn Cleland smoothly riding out some **Heavy Weather** (19), Windjammer Wall.
Ben Cossey out there on the crazy **Liquid Insanity** (23), Lighthouse Area.

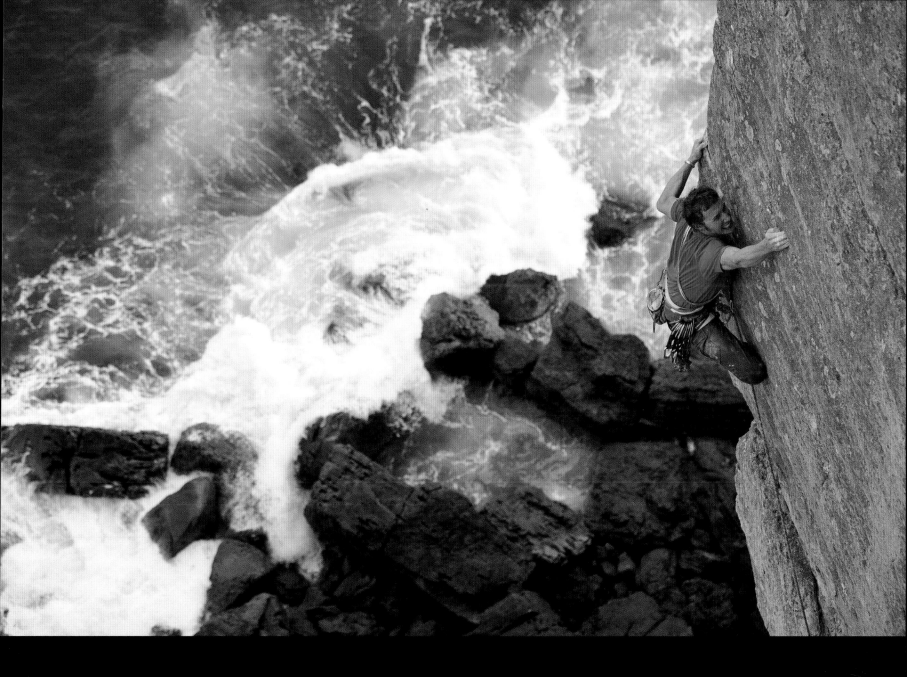

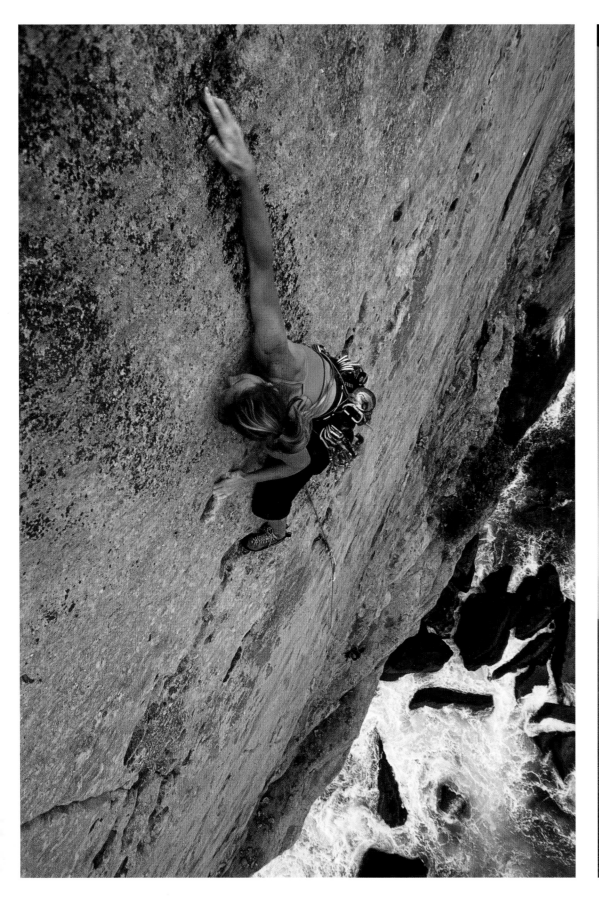

⬆ Nicole Lowres on the timeless *Retro* (21), Popeye Wall.

➡ Monique Forestier, *Superstyling* (25), over Jervis Bay on this sandy six-metre roof at Bayside.

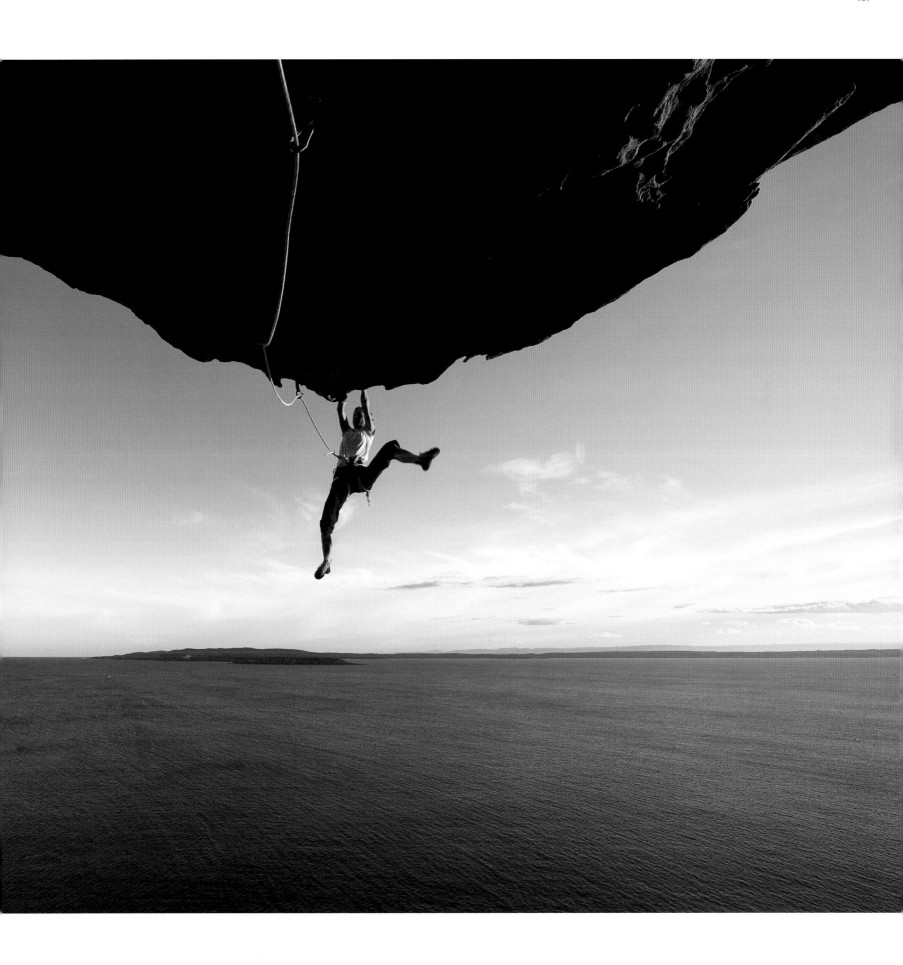

Short or tall, straightforward or convoluted, enjoyable to downright petrifying, the Tasman Peninsula's wild and woolly coastline is home to a range of enticing excursions. Adventurous souls will be in their element with the exceptional possibilities here.

The area is home to some of Australia's highest sea cliffs. Take Mount Brown's lofty main face which has two hundred metres of rap-in-climb-out pant filling action. It requires spirit, skill and speed to squeeze one of the committing crusades into a day. Word on the street is that *Talk is Cheap* (24) and *I've Heard it all Before* (23) are the routes to do here. The rock looks like baggy elephant skin and these routes tackle the full cliff in ten impeccable pitches.

For steep sporty fun, the Paradiso's black dolerite is decorated with bolts for clip and go action. The oddly oriented holds may not be instinctive to read but they make for intriguing climbing. The sun bathed rock platform at the base of the cliff can lure you into a false sense of comfort. Just metres above the tumultuous Tasman Sea, a freak wave can swallow your belayer right out of the blue.

The Tasman Peninsula is best known for its extraordinary sea stacks, most notably the Moai, Cape Raoul and the Totem Pole. Topping out on any one of these thrilling summits is an achievement in itself. For many, these are the main reason to visit the peninsula.

The Moai is a fun day out (tip-toeing past Tiger snakes being the exception) and a great introduction to summit bagging and all the jiggery and pokery that goes with it.

It's no surprise that the routes on the Pillars of Hercules at the far tip of Cape Raoul were only recently established. It's an arduous, committing and somewhat serious adventure but the payoff is exceptional. After a solid two-hour hike, you abseil, scramble, climb, climb, scramble, abseil, scramble and abseil again — just to reach the base of the pillar. *Pole Dancer* (22) is undoubtedly the best route of its grade that I have ever climbed anywhere, period. The climbing is a perfect compilation of balancey moves up the airy arête of an uncanny twisted tower. Add the giddying gyroscopic exposure and encouragement from the barking seals below, and it was an acid trip for the senses which left its mark in my memory.

And then of course the most famous tower of them all, the Totem Pole. This 65-metre natural phenomenon is a piece of climbing perfection, as extraordinary and unlikely as it comes. Years ago I saw a photograph of Simon Mentz and Steve Monks making the first free ascent of "The Tote", and I was in awe. I thought those guys are absolutely raving mad; I never imagined having either the inclination or the guts to climb it. But a seed had been planted deep in my subconscious and I never forgot the image. Over the years the mental barriers subsided and then one day, there I was. I climbed without inhibition, just appreciating the exquisite moves that engaged my every muscle, and focused my mind with a clarity rarely present.

Over the years, this seed had grown and empowered me. It made me realise that I'd placed unnecessary constraints on myself. Was it a lack of confidence in my ability, fear of getting hurt or fear of failure? I'm not sure. But one thing I've learnt is to believe in yourself and follow your dreams. As I reflect on all the areas that I've visited in this book, I know that I am blessed to have experienced this physical — and mental — journey.

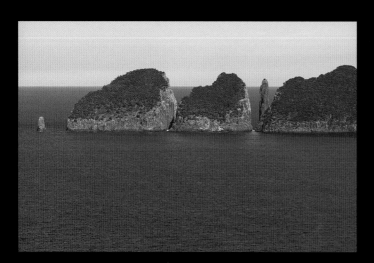

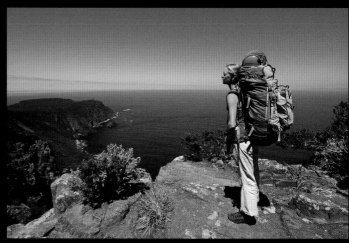

⬆ A view across Fortescue Bay. The Candlestick is the obvious tower (and the Totem Pole is just hidden from view to right).

↗ Monique Forestier surveying the remaining slog to Cape Raoul (the peninsula in the background).

➡ Monique Forestier stepping up to the *Free Route* (25) on the Totem Pole at Cape Hauy.

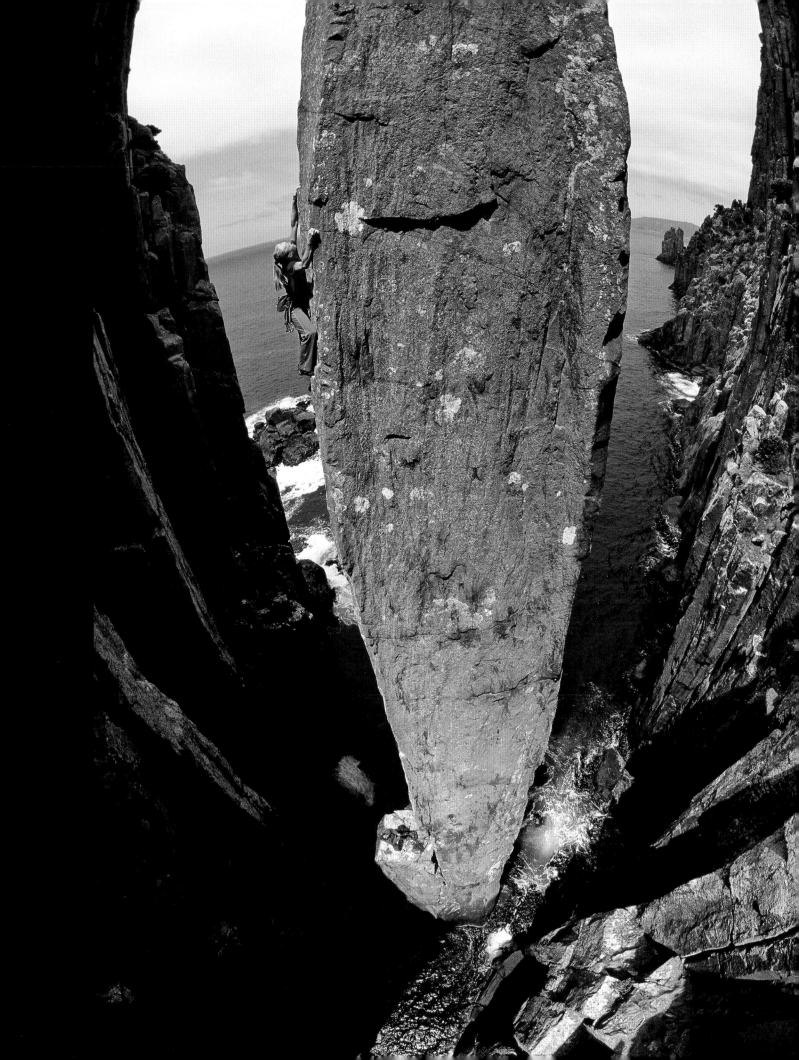

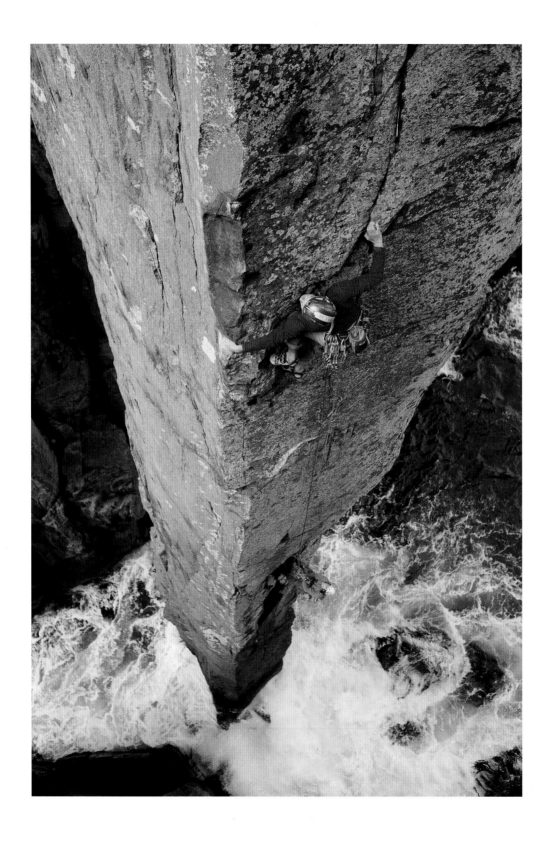

↑→ Doug McConnell and Dean Rollins on *The Ewbank Route* (the original 1968 aid route, now
aka *The Freed Route*), on the Totem Pole, which they freed in 2009 at grade 27. A sandbag?

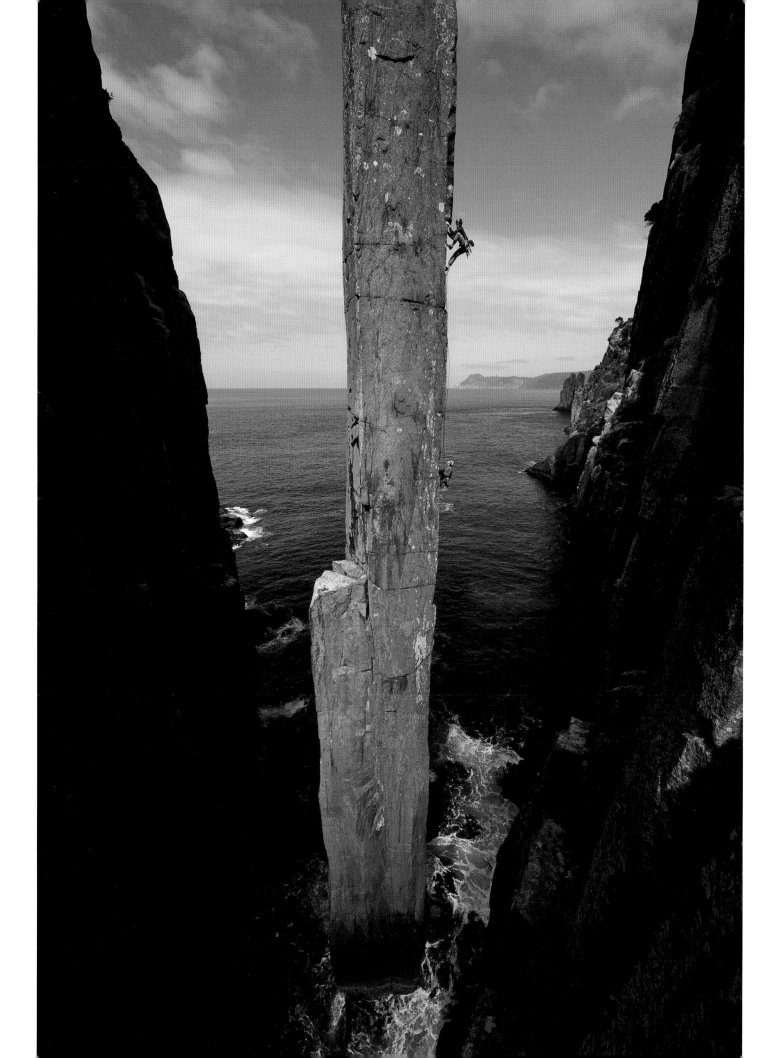

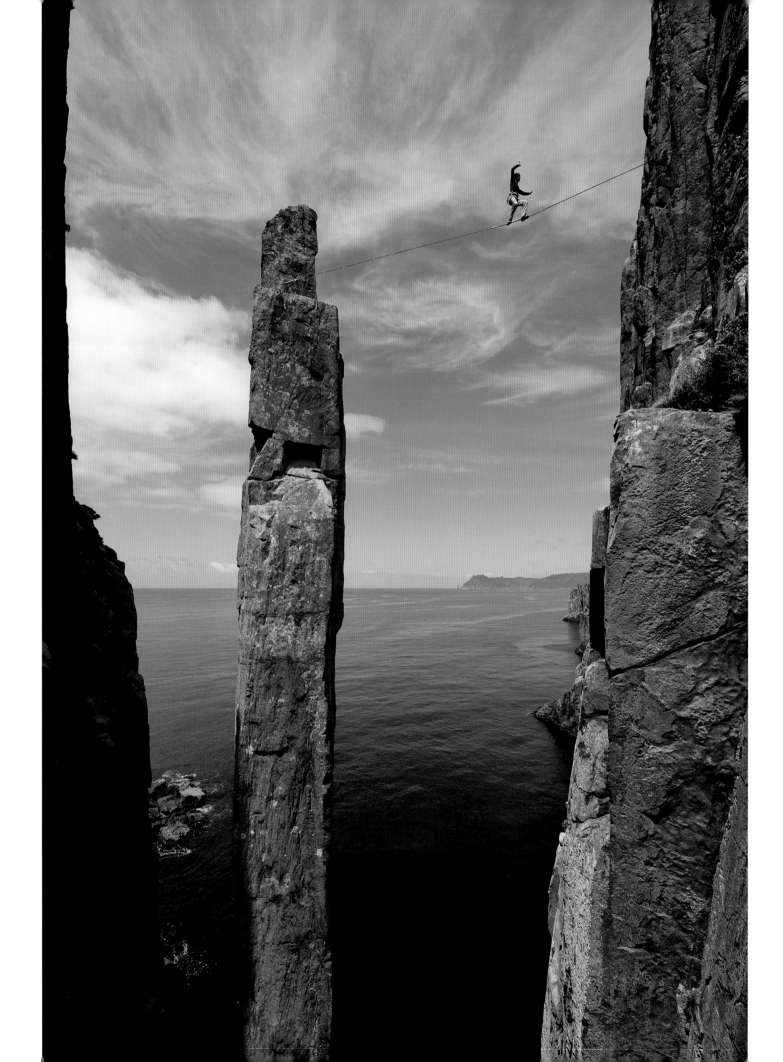

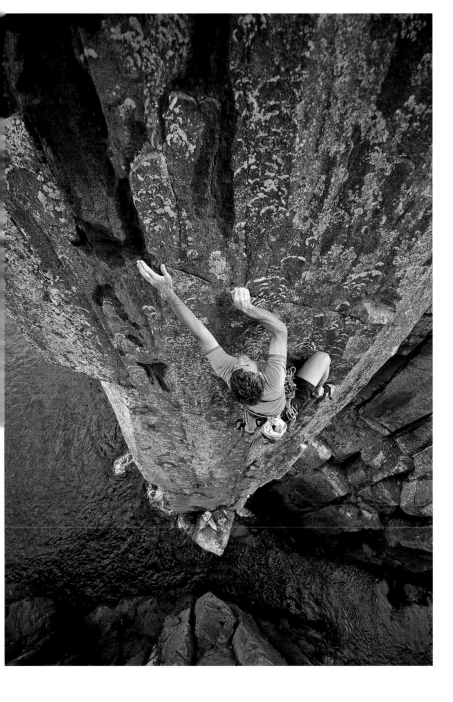

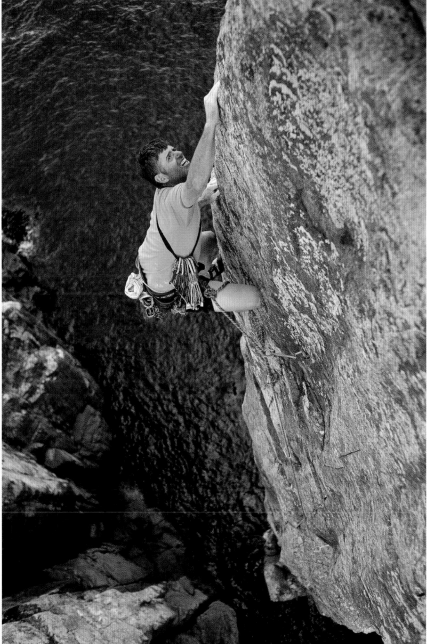

It seems for some the Tyrolean Traverse is just not enough.
Hans Hornberger slacklining between the Tote and the mainland.

Steve ˝Moss˝ Moon ticking The Tote. Pitch two of the *Free Route* (25).

⬆ Summit bagger Sam Edwards sending **Sacred Site** (18) with Garn Cooper,
on the Moai (the Candlestick is in the background across Fortescue Bay).

➡ Steve Monks on the second pitch of **The Golden Pillar of Fortescue** (25, 25, 24 and16)
during the first ascent with Steve Findlay, on the cliffs near the Moai.

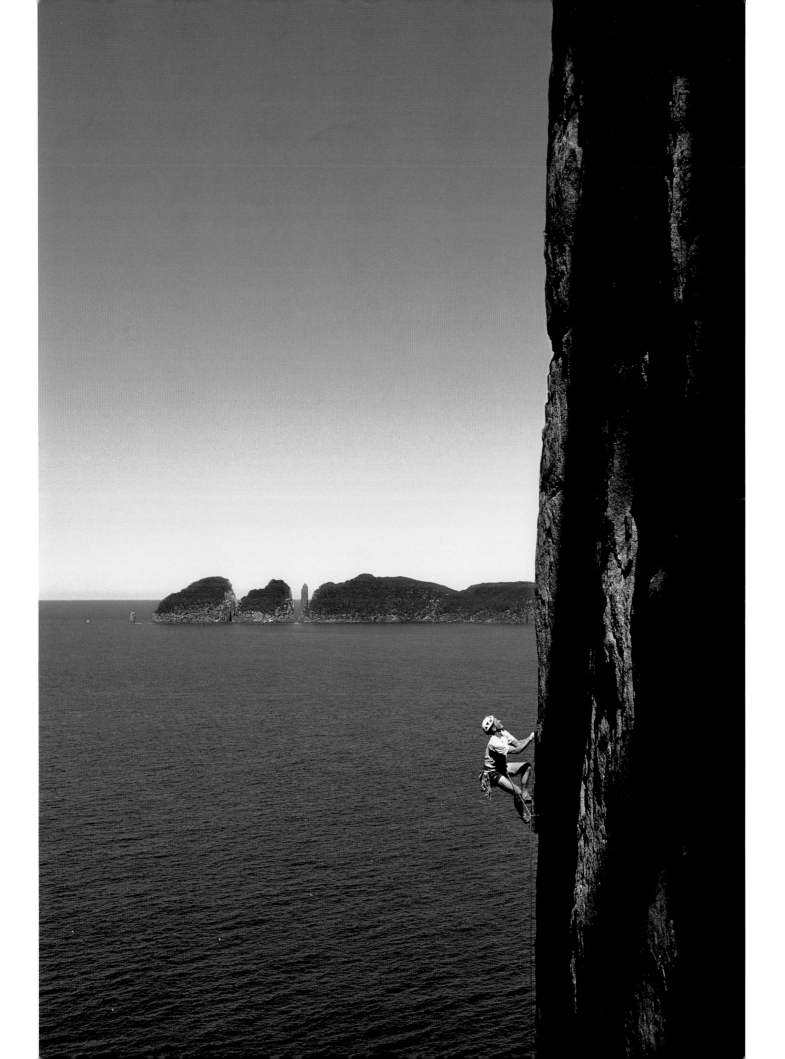

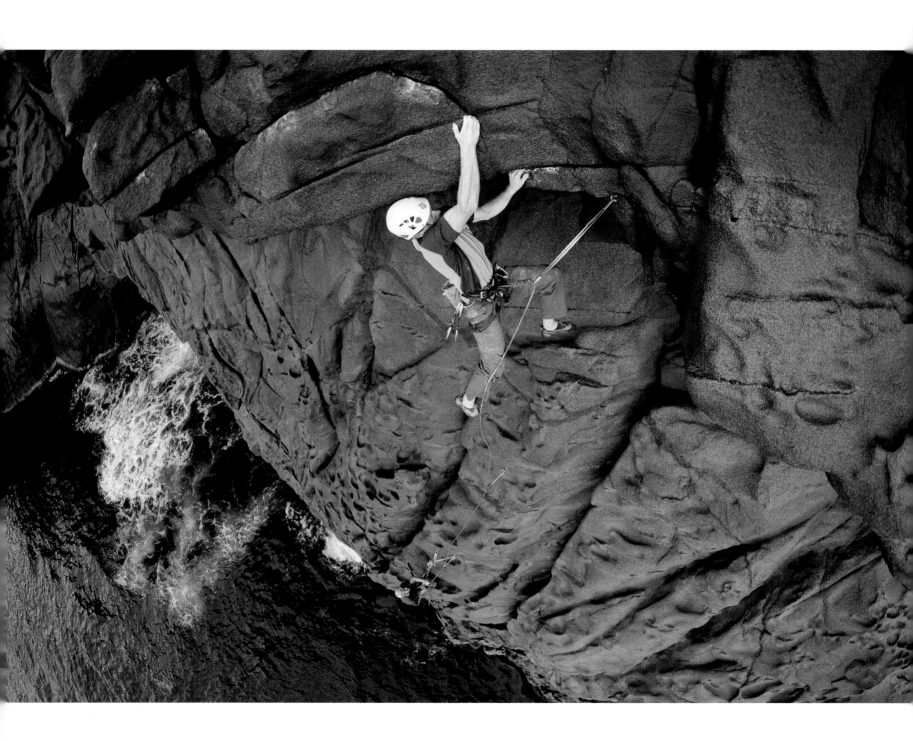

⬆ Garry Phillips with no time for idle gossip on pitch two of **Talk is Cheap** (24), 210 metres (10 pitches), Mount Brown.

↗ Jake Bresnehan walking the walk on pitch three of **Talk is Cheap**.

➡ Mount Brown. **Talk is Cheap** blasts up the centre of the main face. The obvious big roof low down is where Garry is pictured above.

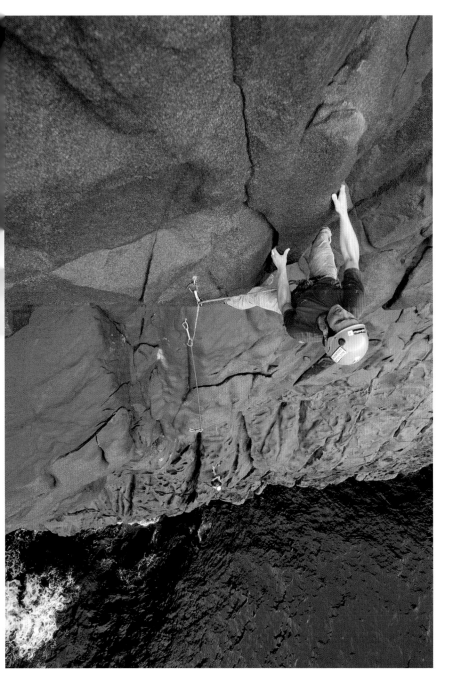

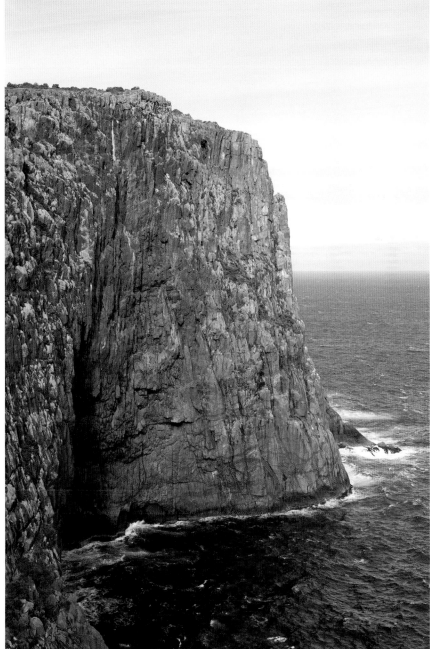

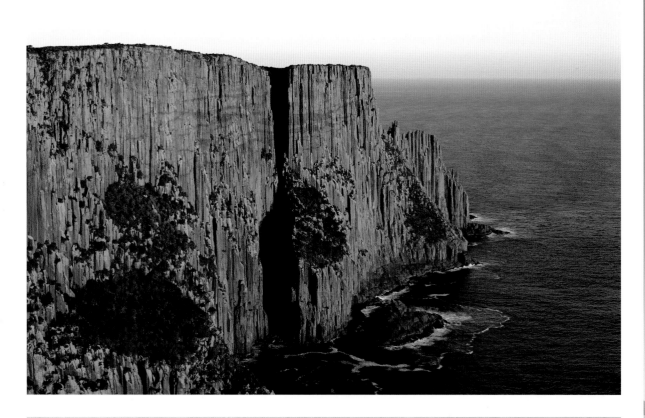

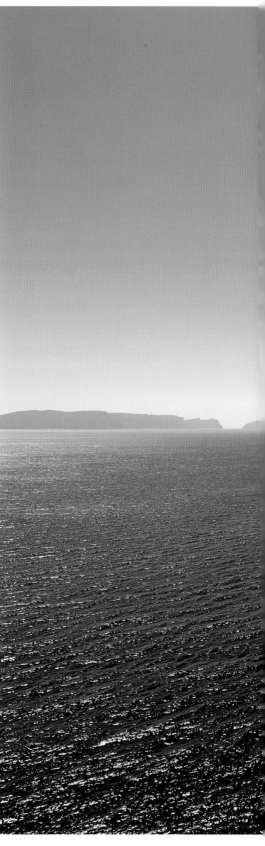

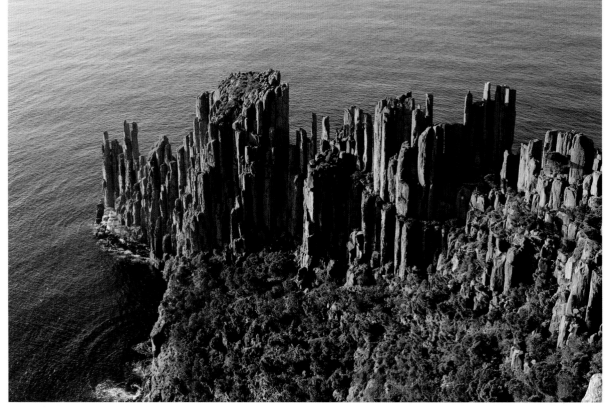

⌃ Cape Raoul, as seen from the west, with the Pillars of Hercules just visible at the far end.

⌃ Cape Raoul, as seen from the east, with the Pillars of Hercules (and the *Pole Dancer* pillar) more visible at the end.

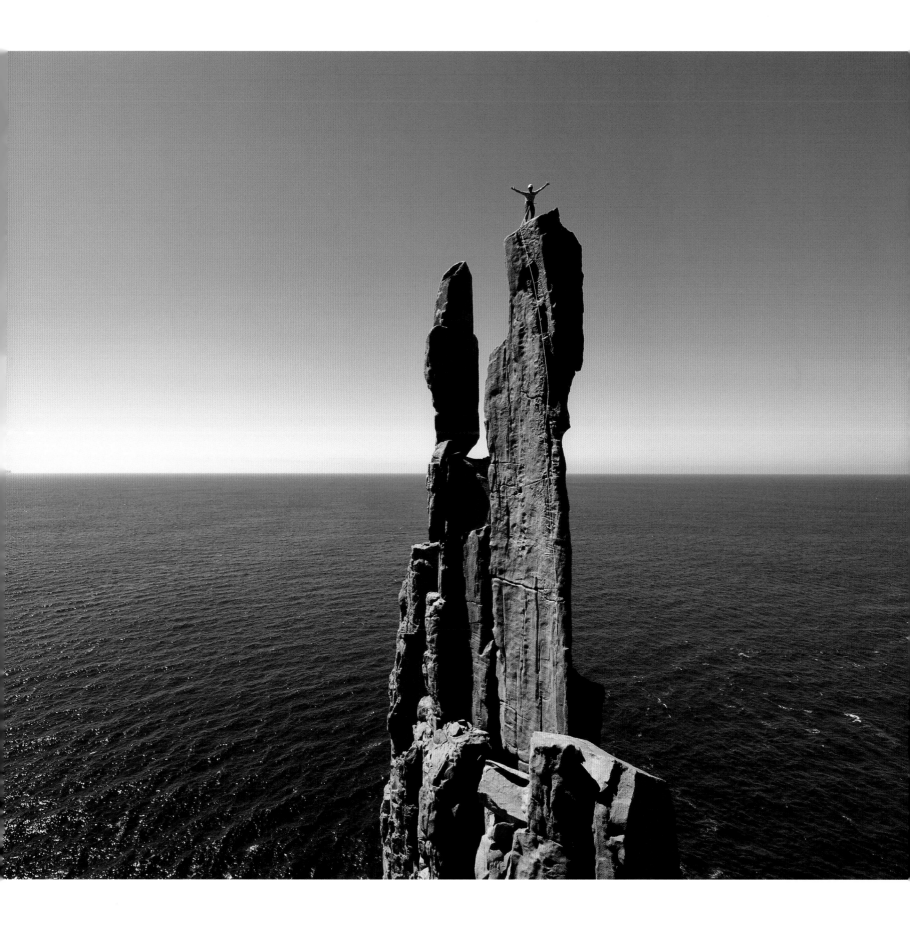

Steve "Moss" Moon doing his **Pole Dancer** (22) summit jig.

PHOTOGRAPHIC NOTES

Since I wrote the Photo Notes for *World Climbing: Images from the Edge* six years ago there have been several significant changes in the equipment and techniques that I employ in my photography, but the issue of safety remains unchanged.

Safety

The warning and disclaimer on page 8 applies to photographers too. If you photograph climbing then take responsibility for your own actions. Mixing photography with climbing means there is simply more to go wrong. Scrambling unroped around cliff-tops and across ledges, especially with equipment, is dangerous. There are many mistakes and misjudgements that you can make. Complacency, bravado and rushing can exacerbate potential problems.

Becoming a better climber will make you safer and more productive. I don't mean you need to climb harder. Instead, improve your rope work, rigging skills and increase your understanding of what's going on. These are not skills learned in a gym, but ones that require time and practice on rock in a range of situations.

No photo is worth dying for — either as a photographer or a climber. And as a photographer you are morally responsible about what you ask a climber to do.

Climbing Kit

My kit for photography differs from my normal climbing kit in a few ways. When fixing a rope I much prefer to use a static rather than a dynamic rope; they stretch less making it easier to use ascenders and have better resistance to cutting. Even with a static, I use rope protectors and re-belay (tie off) my rope below sharp sections. Ascenders are essential for freeing my hands to use the camera and for sprinting to a new position higher up the rope.

In addition to my normal climbing harness, I find a chest harness essential for my photography. A chest harness makes hanging on a rope more comfortable and enables me to lean way out for a better perspective on the climb. Being comfortable enables me to concentrate on operating the camera,

precisely frame the shot and hold that position for a long time. As well as allowing a better perspective, a chest harness is lighter, more versatile and is faster to work with than, say, a Bosun's chair.

Photography Kit

Oh my, how times and technology have changed! Until a few years ago I'd normally carry a range of lenses, a Nikon F100 body and dozens of rolls of Fuji Velvia film. I was a die-hard film-only fanatic and I held out as long as I could, but a few years back some advantages of digital became too compelling to ignore (especially the resolution). A digital camera eventually found a permanent place in my bag in 2008; currently it's the Nikon D3s.

Some of the areas in this book were shot entirely on film (Nosy Hara Archipelago, Tsaranoro and Yangshou), and others entirely on digital (Montsant & Siurana, Kalymnos, Dolomites, Hong Kong and Ha Long Bay). The other areas were a mixture of the two, but bear in mind comparing completely different images will only tell so much. I shoot in Raw file format then make any necessary tonal adjustments to the images in Adobe Lightroom. Digital photography takes the guesswork (or perhaps art?) out of trying to perfectly expose film. One definite advantage of digital is when working in low light — shooting action in the shade has never been easier. A great example of a digital's low light capabilities is the image of *Arête de Marseille* in Les Calanques (pages 52/53) which was taken before dawn: it gives good shadow detail (perhaps otherwise completely black) without extreme grain.

Technological advances have also recently impacted on the design and construction of lenses, generally making them sharper and better than ever. In the past I would use an array of fixed focal length 'prime' lenses despite the inconvenience of changing lenses, because they were brighter and sharper than zoom lenses. More recently, several zoom lenses have been released which are actually sharper than some of their fixed focal length counterparts. So these days my standard quiver of lenses comprises the

Nikkor 16mm f2.8, 14-24mm f2.8, 35mm f2, 50mm f1.4 and 70-200mm f2.8 VR-II, all housed in a Think Tank Speed Racer camera bag.

Methods

My methods depend on the situation, what I have envisaged for the shot, and how familiar I am with the area. I might spend days getting to know a new place, perhaps climb some routes, look around for interesting climbs, see what the light is doing at different times of day, abseil down in different places and see what angles I can find. I believe it's important to have a strong concept for a shot and to be prepared, but also to be spontaneous and seize an opportunity should it arise.

Getting a good angle on the climb is everything in climbing photography: it has the greatest effect but can also present the biggest problems. However, some of my best shots were taken from the ground, a ledge or the cliff top — so getting into position doesn't always have to be epic. But certainly "working the angles", or considering all options, is often wise. A bit of creative rigging can open up new possibilities; sometimes I'll rig the rope (or a second rope) between two cliffs so that I can tension out between the two positions. My photo of Monique on the Totem Pole on page 161 is a good example, to get that angle I abseiled 15 metres down from the top of the "Tote" then tensioned out away from the pole on a second rope anchored to the cliff line 30 metres behind me. Of course anchors must be 'bomber' since the loads can be extreme.

Most of the time though, the creative use of abseil ropes won't help at all; there is simply nothing out there to attach a second rope to. Then how do you get further out from the cliff to get a better perspective and see more of the climb? Renowned American photographer Greg Epperson used stilts as a solution to this. Years ago I built an aluminium A-frame which positioned me five metres out from the cliff. But it was cumbersome, took ages to set up and was fixed in one position, so I didn't use it much.

Over the last few years I've been playing with a new approach, a "photo pole", which has yielded very good results. Basically the

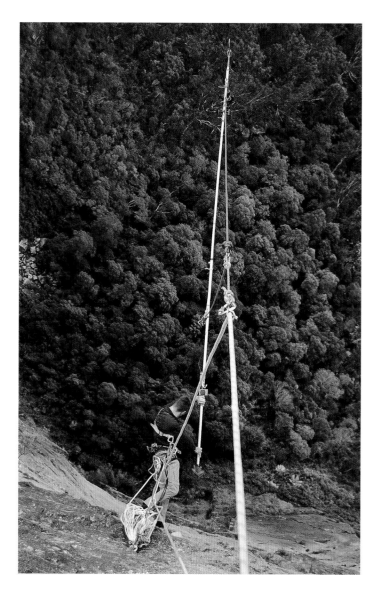 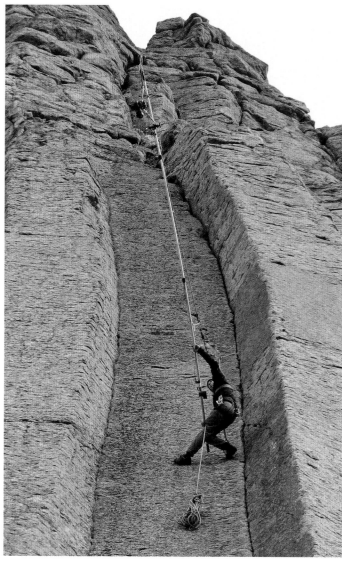

camera is rigged to hang off the end of a long painter's pole (that's right, a low-tech painter's pole available from hardware stores). The camera can be positioned seven metres or more out from the cliff and this has opened some perspectives that would otherwise be practically impossible to achieve. The weight of the pole and camera is taken by guy ropes from above. The camera is attached to a monopod which hangs from the pole to achieve a perspective looking back in at the cliff. I can switch between vertical and horizontal framing. A video feed from the camera lets me see the composition on a small monitor, and I use a remote trigger to fire the shutter. This is a versatile, adjustable and lightweight solution that I can easily travel with. Some images taken with this apparatus in this book are Monique on *Zona 0* at Siurana (page 40 top), Brittany on *Mr Clean* and Crystal on *El Matador* at Devils Tower (p129 and p132 respectively), Bentley on *Hakuna Matata* at Red River Gorge (p143) and Lee Cossey on *Choy Sum* at Point Perpendicular (p154).

With my photography I've used action, angle, composition, timing and natural light as my main tools. I've not used "gimmickry", nor have I "doctored" or "digitally manipulated" my images. I've made a conscious decision to take a fairly "straight" approach so as to allow nature's art to speak for itself.

Simon Carter

⬆ A view from above. Shooting with the photo pole in the Blue Mountains, Australia. Photo: Helen Day.
⬈ A view from below. Taking a test shot with the pole at Devils Tower, USA. Photo: Tom Grundy.

GLOSSARY

ABSEIL aka **RAPPEL** Method for descending a rope.

AID CLIMBING Mechanically assisted climbing. Body weight is supported by protection, or other equipment, and used to directly 'aid' upwards progress.

ALPINE CLIMBING Climbing higher altitude peaks or mountains, commonly involving climbing snow and ice.

ASCENDERS Mechanical devices used for ascending a rope.

BELAY The system using a rope to arrest a climber's fall. Includes the anchors and stance that the belayer uses, and involves using a friction (belay) device to lock-off the rope.

BELAYER The person using the rope to provide safety to someone who is climbing.

BIG WALL A big cliff face offering particularly long routes, possibly requiring numerous days to climb.

BOLT A construction bolt fixed into a pre-drilled hole, used as a permanent anchor or protection point.

BOMBER A particularly dependable gear placement.

BOULDERING Aka pebble wrestling. Unroped climbing, close to the ground.

CHIPPING The deliberate action of modifying the rock to create holds where they do not naturally exist. This is considered unethical in most areas of the world.

CRACK A fracture or split in the rock.

CRAG A smaller cliff or set of cliffs.

CRANK To pull hard on a hand hold.

CRIMP A small hand hold, allowing finger tips only.

CRUX The most difficult section of the climb.

DEEP WATER SOLOING (DWS) Climbing without a rope or protection above deep water, usually the ocean.

EDGES Small handholds. In England it is also the name given to some small outcrops of rock.

ETHICS Widely accepted standards of conduct at an area, particularly relating to actions which may damage the rock.

EXPOSED, EXPOSURE In mountaineering: being susceptible to the elements (heat, cold, wind or rain). In climbing: being a long way above the ground, often resulting in an enhanced feeling of nervousness.

FACE A steep open section of cliff.

FLASH To lead climb a route on the very first attempt but where the climber has some prior knowledge of the difficulties or sequence of moves.

FREE CLIMBING Using hands and feet (and any other body part) to climb the rock's natural features. The rope and protection are there but not weighted or used to directly 'aid' the ascent.

GEAR See protection

GRADE A subjective rating of the difficulty of a climb. There are different grading systems for aid climbs, free climbs and boulder problems.

GROUND-UP To climb from ground level without previous inspection or preparation from above (such as from abseil). As opposed to top-down.

HANG-DOG To attempt/practice the moves of a climb many times in the one session.

JAM, JAMMING OR JAMBING A climbing technique where a hand, foot or other body part is squeezed inside a crack to provide a hold.

JUG A very large hold.

JUMAR A brand of a rope-ascending device. Jumaring is a generic term for the technique of ascending fixed ropes using ascenders.

LEAD The first person of a party climbing a route. The 'leader' clips the rope into protection points along the way whilst belayed from below.

MULTI-PITCH A longer route which has more than a single pitch of climbing.

OFFWIDTH A wide crack, awkward to climb.

ONSIGHT To lead climb a route making a successful ascent on the first attempt. The climber has no prior knowledge of the specific difficulties of the route. This is widely considered the best lead climbing style.

OVERHANG An extra steep (overhanging) section of rock.

PITCH The section of climbing between two belays, not longer than the length of the rope.

POCKET Holes in the rock face, used for hand or foot holds.

PROJECT A climb which has been attempted but not yet properly free-climbed.

PROTECTION, PRO Various types of equipment placed in rock features to stop a falling climber. Natural or traditional protection is removable (non-permanent). Fixed protection is anchor points permanently fixed in the rock (includes bolts or pitons).

PUMPY Strenuous climbing.

RACK A selection of traditional protection carried on a climb.

RAP BOLT To place bolts on a climb from an abseil rope (from above, as opposed to ground-up).

REDPOINT A style of climbing, widely regarded as the minimum standard for claiming a 'free' ascent. The route must be led without a fall or any assistance from the rope or protection.

ROOF A horizontal, or near horizontal, overhanging section of rock.

RUN-OUT The distance the lead climber is above their last piece of protection. A run-out climb has big fall potential.

SECOND The climber who ascends a route or pitch after the lead climber. They are belayed from above.

SLAB A large off-vertical span of rock: seemingly featureless, it is often climbed with balance and friction techniques.

SLACKLINING Similar to tight rope walking but instead of a taut rope, stretchy nylon webbing is strung between two anchor points.

SLOPER A rounded smooth hold which climbers grip with an open hand.

SOLO To climb alone. In free climbing this means without a rope (free solo). In aid climbing a rope is used (aid solo).

SPORT CLIMBING Where permanent fixed protection (commonly bolts) is utilised thereby allowing for an emphasis on gymnastic movement.

TOP-DOWN Using abseil or a top-rope to access, inspect, practice or prepare the route before attempting to climb.

TOP-ROPE To climb with the rope belayed or anchored from above.

TRADITIONAL CLIMBING aka **TRAD** Climbing characterised by the placing of removable protection (slings, nuts, camming devices).

TRAVERSE To climb sideways, horizontally.

TUFA A fin-like rock formation found in limestone.

TYROLEAN TRAVERSE To slide along a rope fixed between two formations which are elevated and separated by a void.

UNDERCLING A hand hold which faces downwards.

WIRED To practice moves until they are engrained.

Mayan Smith-Gobat getting up, very close and personal with *Colossus* (33), Little Babylon, The Darrans, New Zealand.

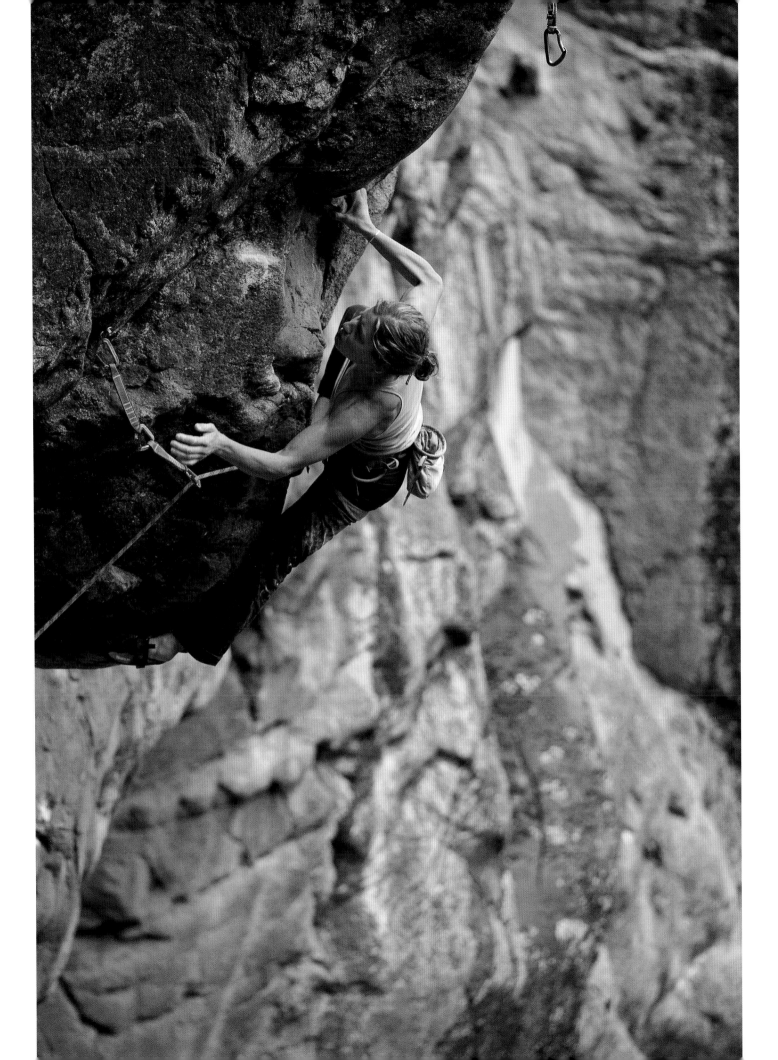

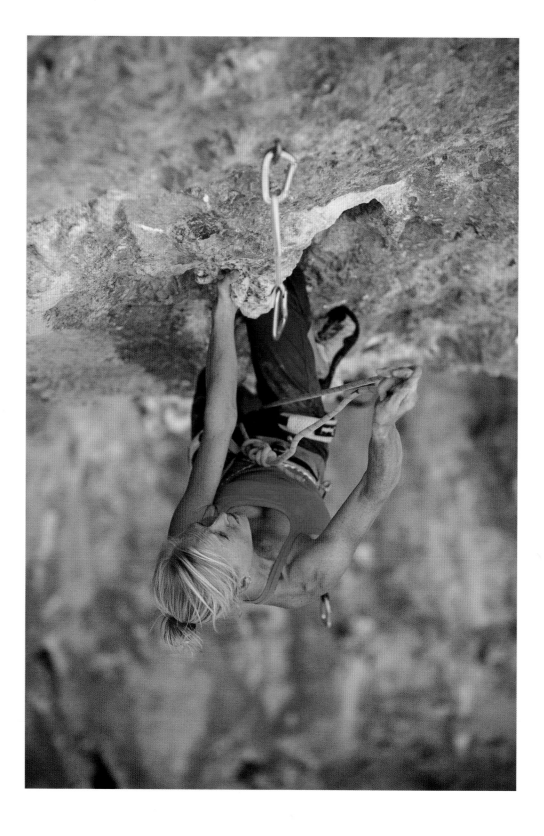

⬆ Monique Forestier gets the jugs on **Daniboy** (8a), Spartacus, Kalymnos, Greece.

GRADING TABLE

AUSTRALIA	FRANCE	US	UK	UK TECH
14	4	5.7	VS	4b
15	5a	5.8	VS	4b
16	5b		VS	4c
17	5c	5.9	HVS	4c
18	6a		HVS	4c
19	6a+	5.10a	E1	5a
20	6b	5.10b	E1	5b
21	6b+	5.10c / 5.10d	E2	5b
22	6c	5.11a	E3	5c
23	6c+	5.11b	E3	5c
24	7a	5.11c	E4	5c
	7a+	5.11d	E4	6a
25	7b	5.12a	E5	6a
26	7b+	5.12b	E5	6b
		5.12c	E5	6b
27	7c	5.12d	E6	6b
28	7c+	5.13a	E6	6b
29	8a	5.13b	E7	6c
30	8a+	5.13c	E7	6c
31	8b	5.13d	E8	7a
32	8b+	5.14a	E8	7a
33	8c	5.14b	E9	7a
34	8c+	5.14c	E9	7b
	9a	5.14d	E10	7b
	9a+	5.15a	E10	7b

ACKNOWLEDGEMENTS

Many people have been tremendously helpful over the years, giving freely of their time and often considerable effort. I am truly grateful for everyone's generosity.

My deepest gratitude goes to Monique Forestier for being incredibly supportive in so many ways and for sharing and enriching life's journey. Cathy McBey, who's invaluable assistance has kept the business running. And my family: Keith and Rosemary Carter, Jon Richardson, Andrew Carter and Austin Bell who have always supported my work and much else besides.

I would like to extend my warmest thanks to those who have been incredibly supportive: Dan Johnston (graphics design whiz), Lizzie Durnan and Michael Law (who gave valuable editorial help) and Brendan Junge (computer guru). Also, Chris Archer, Onslo "Slo" Carrington (Slo Pony Adventures, Vietnam), Lee Cujes (Upskill Climbing), Christian de Laroche (Camp Catta, Madagascar), Mathieu Delacroix (New Sea Roc, Madagascar), Brittany Griffith, Cindy Lefkoff, Kyle Lefkoff, Robert Lindsay, Mariona Marti, Nadine Rousselot, Frank Sanders (Devils Tower Lodge), Sarah Spaulding and Jenny Zhuang. I would also like to especially thank Duane Raleigh (Rock & Ice Magazine) for writing the foreword and for his support of my work over the years.

My great appreciation and thanks go to all whom I have photographed, the belayers, and everyone else who has been generous with their time, energy and kind hospitality, in particular: Doug Acorn, Steven Ahern, Brian Alder, Toni Arbonés, Dan Arkle, Marguerite Arpin, Ilja Bangma, Guillaume Barthelemi, Linda Black (Lago Linda Hideaway, Red River Gorge), Danelle Boka, Whitney Boland, Beate Bongartz, Bentley Brackett, Jake Bresnehan, Duncan Brown, Kester Brown, Celine Calmel, Miriam Caravaca, Sebastien Carel, Blake Cash, Ben Cassel, Amandine Castan, Jasmin Caton, Greg Child, Ron Chow, Robyn Cleland, Pete Cocker, Garn Cooper, Ben Cossey, Lee Cossey, Sam Cujes, Virgile Daubie, Crystal Davis-Robbins, Seth Dee, Eftihia Dikarou, Katerina Dikarou, Sonja Djuricin, Traian Dogaru, Bruce Dowrick, Mike Doyle, Diana Durr, John Durr, Nicky Dyal, Sam Edwards, Sam Elias, Matt Evrard, Steve Findlay, Sarah Fontaine, Felix Frieder, Xavier "Harri" García, Mathieu Geoffray, David Gliddon, Lisa Gnade, Ryan Gormly, Ryan Graney, Tom Grundy, Nick Hancock, Glen Henderson, Roman Hofmann, Hans Hornberger, Olivia Hsu, Matthew Hughes, David Hume, Luisa Jovane, Klemen Kejžar, Philipp Kessler, Christian Kirov, Katerina Klonari, Alex Kobes, Toni Lamprecht, Anders Lantz, Evan Lawton, Heather Lawton, Greg Loniewski, Nicole Lowres, Maria Magdalena, Nicholas Mahmood, Bon Man, Heinz Mariacher, Rich Marshall, Doug McConnell, Steve McDonell, Sue McDonell, Olivier Michellod, Rico Miledi, Grace Millis, Stuart Millis, Chloé Minoret, Taki Miyamoto, Fred Moix, Eric Mongou, Steve Monks, Simon Montmory, Steve "Moss" Moon, Greg Moore, Daniel Murbach, Sean Nelb, Michiel Nieuwenhuijsen, Timmy O'Neill, Adam Ondra, Christine Ondra, Tui Orr, Ryan Pall, Nikolas Papanikolas (Hotel Philoxenia, Kalymnos), François Petit, Garry Phillips, Ekaterina Plotnikova, Stephen Powers, Mario Prinoth, Donna Qwok, Hermann Rauch, Jean-François Reffet, Christine Remy, Claude Remy, Simon Remy, Dean Rollins, Acacia Rose, Georgios Roussos (Mayor of Kalymnos), Katie Roussou, Dave Russell, Kate Rutherford, Muriel Sarkany, Tony Sartin, Kathrin Schön, Michael Schön, Jon Sedon, Tamara Sepetauc, Bob Siegrist, Jonathan Siegrist, Mayan Smith-Gobat, Audrey Sniezek, Gina Sorensen, Julie Sprooten, David Stallard, Swenja Stellfeld, Evan Stevens, Anje Stremfelj, Matt Tackett, Juan Tarditti, Derek Thatcher, Aris Theodoropoulos, Jim Thornburg, Phil Tifo, Niels van Duyn, Fred Vanden Bergh, Kyle Vassilopoulos, Dario Ventura, Silvia Vidal, Maja Vidmar, Benno Wagner, Benedikt Walser, Abby Watkins, Sandra Wieblinowski, Simon Wilson, Kevin Wotherspoon, Liu "Abond" Yongbang and Dario Zanon.

My sincere apologies to anyone I may have inadvertently omitted.

In addition to the many businesses that are particularly supportive and a pleasure to work with, I would like to especially thank Nikon Australia for their assistance and thank you to Five Ten and Sterling Rope for years of support with equipment that I prefer and depend on.

Monique would also like to thank her sponsors: Aussie Bodies, Black Diamond, Outdoor Agencies, Sea To Summit, Scarpa and Sterling Rope.

Monique Forestier, belayed by Fred Moix, attempting *Les Naufragés du Rhum* (8b), on Nosy Andantsara, Nosy Hara Archipelago, Madagascar.

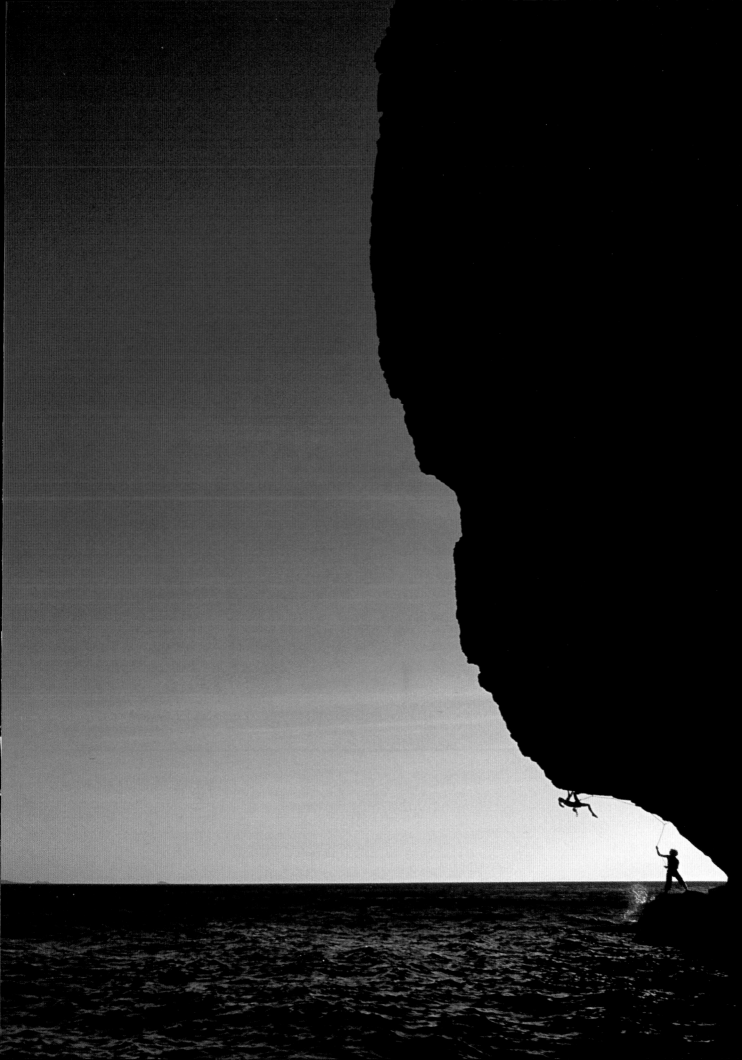

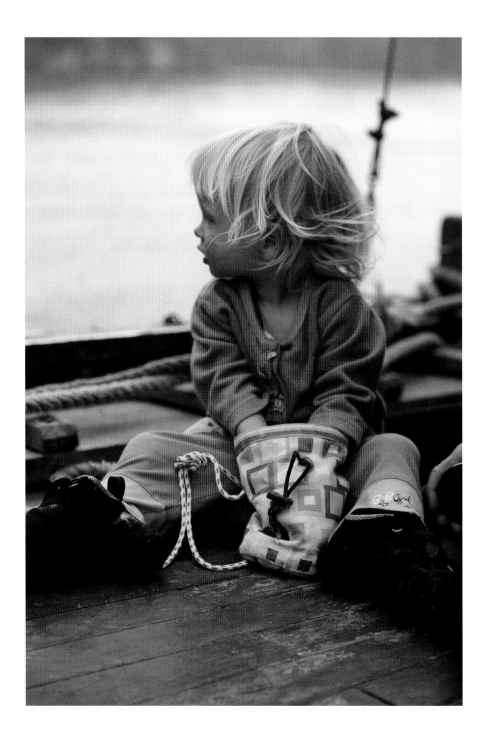

⬆ Coco Rose Carter getting psyched for some deep-water
   soloing on Hawaii 5-0 Wall, Ha Long Bay, Vietnam.

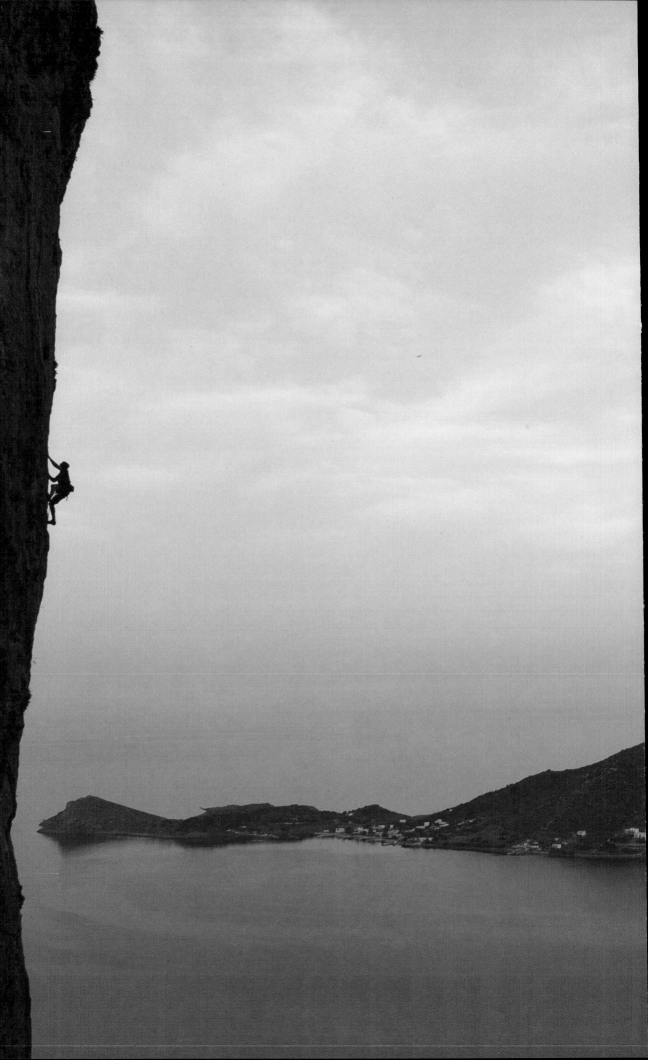